THE GOVERNMENT NEXT DOOR

Neighborhood Politics in Urban China

LUIGI TOMBA

CORNELL UNIVERSITY PRESS
ITHACA AND LONDON

Cornell University Press gratefully acknowledges receipt of a
Subsidy for Publication grant from the Chiang Ching-kuo
Foundation for International Scholarly Exchange (USA), which
generously assisted in the publication of this book.

First published 2014 by Cornell University Press
First printing, Cornell Paperbacks, 2014

Printed in the United States of America

Library of Congress Cataloging-in-Publication Data

Tomba, Luigi, author.
   The government next door : neighborhood politics in urban China /
Luigi Tomba.
      pages cm
   Includes bibliographical references and index.
   ISBN 978-0-8014-5282-6 (cloth : alk. paper)
   ISBN 978-0-8014-7935-9 (pbk. : alk. paper)
  1. City and town life—China. 2. Urban policy—China.
3. China—Social conditions—2000– I. Title.
   HT147.C48T66   2014
   307.760951—dc23   2014004766

Cornell University Press strives to use environmentally responsible
suppliers and materials to the fullest extent possible in the publishing of
its books. Such materials include vegetable-based, low-VOC inks and
acid-free papers that are recycled, totally chlorine-free, or partly composed
of nonwood fibers. For further information, visit our website at
www.cornellpress.cornell.edu.

Cloth printing   10 9 8 7 6 5 4 3 2 1
Paperback printing   10 9 8 7 6 5 4 3 2 1

THE GOVERNMENT NEXT DOOR

Contents

ACKNOWLEDGMENTS

I went to China for the first time twenty-six years ago. It took time and the wisdom of many kind people to learn about that country and its people, to learn what to look for, to shape some questions—the right questions, I hope. My first acknowledgment should be for the ride and for all the fellow travelers—way too many to fit in here. Some of them are teachers, some are family, some, by an accident of age more than knowledge, were students, some were friends, and some were all of the above.

Research for this book took almost a decade, and the Australian National University was my intellectual home during this time. Here I found my main sources of support, stimulation, and engagement with colleagues, mentors, and friends. The characters below are listed in order of appearance. All of them played, consciously or unconsciously, a role in the making of this book.

In the kitchen of the Contemporary China Centre, Jon Unger first engaged me in a conversation about China's middle class. For their mentoring and friendship, as well as many other conversations in that kitchen and elsewhere, many dinners and dry jokes, I owe Jon and Anita Chan a debt of gratitude.

At the Contemporary China Centre I met other important colleagues. With Andy Kipnis I have shared a decade of editorship of *The China Journal* and the intellectual discoveries that came with it. Ben Hillman has, much to my frustration, a heavy forehand on the tennis court, which he counterbalances with weighted suggestions on my work. Now he and Lee-Anne have two beautiful girls who are part of my family as well. Other residents of the center who have generously offered their comments at various times include Graeme Smith, Bob Miller, Peter Van Ness, and Tom Cliff.

I am also indebted to the expertise, mentoring, and kindness of my colleagues and students in the Department of Political and Social Change, where I worked until 2010, during which time the bulk of this book was shaped: Ben Kerkvliet, whose homegrown veggies are sorely missed now that he has moved back to Hawaii with Melinda; Paul Hutchcroft; Sally Sargeson; Tamara Jacka; Ed Aspinall; Greg Fealy; and all other colleagues and graduate students that regularly commented at my seminars and endured my stories of Chinese neighborhoods.

From 2010 I found a new home in the Australian Centre on China in the World (CIW). The support of the center and of its director, Geremie R. Barmé, during the last three years made it possible to complete the task. Geremie's generosity with his comments and time—from the first time he cast his eye on a rather tentative grant application almost ten years ago—as well as the continuous challenge he provides to our way of thinking about China have been an invaluable source of inspiration.

My CIW colleagues Ben Penny and Jane Golley, Gloria Davies and Sue Trevaskes and a community of doctoral students and post-doctoral fellows also provided a stimulating intellectual environment during the final stages of this work. Carolyn Cartier has been the partner of many engaging conversations on "the urban" in China. CIW's administrative staff as well as Cathryn Husdell, Merrilyn Fitzpatrick, Nancy Chiu, Jasmine Lin, and Tanya Fan put up with my anxieties with professionalism and indefatigable smiles. Markuz Wernli rescued some of my old photos that found their way into the book.

An almost endless list of other colleagues have offered precious comments and incisive criticisms of my work at different stages, and their work has acted as a constant motivation: David Goodman, Deborah Davis, Vivienne Shue, Kevin O'Brien, Li Zhang, Martin K. Whyte, Tony Saich,

Dorothy Solinger, Lisa Hoffman, Kathy Morton, Michael Dutton, and Børge Bakken. I have also learned a lot from those who have written about this topic, including Ben Read, David Bray, Thomas Heberer, Christian Goebel, Cho Mun-young, and Friederike Fleischer. Finally, I benefited greatly from the generous comments of the two anonymous readers, who helped me refine my arguments and challenged me to push my argument further.

To conduct the research that lead to this book, I have relied on a great many people. First and foremost are community workers, activists, residents and cadres, whom I will not mention by name but whose stories and ideas are the core of the book.

Yu Xianyang from Renmin University was an outstanding academic host and collaborator. He came along on my Shenyang visits, shared much of the pain and joy of those days, and was instrumental to my access to these communities. His wisdom and sociological work on communities was the foundation of my understanding of these institutions. Beibei Tang put up with my way of traveling and my obsession for debriefing at the end of field days and offered sustained support and brilliant ideas that I hope have found their way into this book. Ivan Franceschini was tireless and enthusiastic in searching for information and in offering one bright new idea per day, at least.

Janelle Caiger, who worked with me and Andy Kipnis as the assistant editor of *The China Journal* for more than a decade, also provided research assistance and hammered my messy text and endnotes into shape. Lindy Allen patiently created the index.

Librarians at the ANU's Menzies Library (Darrell Dorrington and his colleagues) and at the National Library of Australia (Di Ouyang and her colleagues) helped me mine new material, material I often did not even know existed.

Besides the institutional and financial support of the ANU, my work has been supported by four different grants, two from the Australian Research Council (DP0662894 and DP0984510) and two from the German Research Foundation (TO 638 1-2 and TO638 2-1), for which I am grateful. I am also grateful to the Research Office of the College of Asia and the Pacific, Yasuko Kobayashi and Judith Pabian in particular, for its help with my grant applications.

This book includes excerpts from the author's following articles, reprinted with permission: "Creating an Urban Middle Class: Social Engineering in Beijing," *China Journal,* no. 51 (January 2004): 1–26; "Of

Quality, Harmony, and Community: Civilization and the Middle Class in Urban China," *Positions: East Asia Cultures Critique* 17, no. 3 (2009): 591–616; "Residential Space and Collective Interest Formation in Beijing's Housing Disputes." *China Quarterly,* no. 184 (2005): 934–35; "Making Neighborhoods: The Government of Social Change in China's Cities," *China Perspectives* no. 4 (2008): 48–61.

Roger Haydon at Cornell University Press has believed in the project from our first email contact and supported me through the whole process. I am indebted to his guidance. Karen Laun and Martin Schneider have patiently gone through the manuscript and made sure things made sense.

My first quarter-century of engagement with China has also been a family affair.

My parents watched me first leave small-town Italy bound for Shanghai and come back underweight, with an unkempt beard, long hair, two guitars, and mild depression after the 1989 events of Tiananmen Square, which somehow cemented my passion for the China puzzle.

Some of the people I met there became fellow travelers and longtime friends. One, Lina, later became my wife, and she experienced my obsessions firsthand. Tonight, when I am done with this, she'll take me out for a glass of champagne to celebrate. She deserves it.

THE GOVERNMENT NEXT DOOR

Introduction

The Neighborhood Consensus

The first interview I did in Beijing in 2002 for this book was with a young couple. Both husband and wife worked as cooks in a restaurant, making a just-decent 2,000 yuan (US$240) per month. They were sitting in a restaurant at lunchtime, enjoying traditional Beijing noodles in one of the courtyards of their relatively fancy new neighborhood. I had hoped that by just sitting there and being a foreigner who could order his food in Chinese, I could attract the attention of the customers and start a conversation. And it happened. At that time, the neighborhood I was visiting was still one that people on Beijing streets strongly associated with the superior, private, and somewhat "autonomous" lifestyle of the up-and-coming middle class. That the first residents I managed to talk to were a pair of not particularly well-educated chefs was unexpected, but I tried not to draw conclusions based on such a small sample. After all, that single residential community alone was home to over six thousand families. It turned out that the couple owned more than one apartment in the compound and that she was the offspring of a family of mid-level cadres. Her parents were now living with them, and the second apartment they owned had just been rented out (a pity, as I was looking for accommodation), and so was the family home, originally acquired by her parents through their work unit. This and many later encounters prompted me to investigate whether that unexpected path of social mobility (driven by property rather than income, and indirectly dependent on the family's original position as public employees) was the rule or an exception to it.

Among the first lessons I learned was that new homeowners are very active in the manipulation of housing policies. To get those two apartments at subsidized prices, this couple had taken advantage of access to cheap rental housing from their parents' socialist work unit and, later, had successfully purchased a subsidized apartment in a newly built area. Policies for the subsidization of homeownership were, in theory, aimed at people with "special characteristics" (an urban registration, no previous property, and a below-average income), but the reality they described to me was one in which those who had better connections and availability of cash or assets could easily get around those restrictions.

When I mentioned my search for a temporary accommodation in the neighborhood, the husband offered to intercede with his good friends at the management company to get me a fair price on the rent of a small unit. "I know how to deal with them," he said. "Many things here only work if you know the right people." In this way I was able to rent a small unit with a view over a parking lot and to begin a study of Chinese urban neighborhoods, the people who inhabit them, and the way they are governed.

In my initial observation of these residential areas, two things struck me. First, the search for a Beijing middle class (the original goal of my interest) in the new "gated" communities that make up most of the newly built urban residential space appeared elusive. Most of the young people I was talking to in these settings did not fit the image of the wealthy entrepreneurs that dominate the mainstream portrait of a glamorous Chinese middle class often presented by the international media. Rather, they seemed to be, in large part, professionals and public employees whose housing careers often owed much to their position "within the system" (*tizhi nei*) of public employment. This, in turn, drove me to ask the question of what role housing privatization and subsidization policies have played in determining upward social mobility and, as a consequence, to investigate the active role of the state in the production of wealth and status.

The second observation came after more engaging conversations I had with my neighbors and the unexpected narratives that these individuals and groups used to frame not only their many grievances but also their newfound status. Morality, nation building, patriotism, human quality (*suzhi*), and contribution to modernization seemed more significant "frames" for their grievances than the search for societal autonomy generally associated with the emergence of a civil society. This focus and the language used to express it were also strikingly consistent with the government's rhetoric of building "harmonious neighborhoods" (*hexie shequ*), an expression used profusely in public media and narratives to describe a dreamlike world of neighborly efficiency. This moral view of the neighborhood dominated my neighbors' stories in spite of an endless stream of not-in-my-backyard conflicts that characterized almost all communities in the first decade of this century.

I later turned my attention to other parts of the country and to communities of disgruntled workers in the northeastern rust belt. I found that framing arguments changed substantially here, highlighting the moral responsibility of the socialist state toward its once privileged and now ailing working class. These workers' arguments, however, also remained compatible with the dominant political discourses produced by the local government and media in urban areas where the state was still portraying itself more as a welfare provider and a keeper of social order than as a market booster. Communities from different social and economic backgrounds, in different parts of the country and with different life experiences, seemed to agree that espousing the arguments promoted by the dominant political discourses was a productive, sometimes inescapable and unavoidable, way of framing grievances. And grievances they indeed had.

In this book, I am interested in everyday practices of power in the neighborhood. I find Chinese neighborhoods in the early twenty-first century to be a significant arena for the simultaneous analysis of a multiplicity of social and political relations. I do not intend to fall in the trap of elevating neighborhoods to a metaphor of state-society relations or to portray them as a miniature version of China's political reality. While they are not a microcosm of Chinese society, the social and spatial landscapes of residential areas contain and reproduce specific power relations, define discrete spatial patterns crucial to the classification of society, determine and recast identities, produce networks, define the limits of new economic interests, and foster or contain conflicts. As such, they are an incubator of political processes that have significant implications for our understanding of Chinese politics, both local and national.

Neighborhoods, as social, spatial, administrative, and political formations, also express a historical continuity of governmental purpose, based on the preeminence of social order (*zhixu*). They are spaces often designed to define distinct social landscapes and, as such, they perform a crucial governmental function.[1] The increasing segregation of urban spaces over the last two decades concretizes the government's need to classify spaces and places, albeit today no longer through the cellular structure of the work units but through a hierarchy of private spaces. The goal is to make an increasingly complex population more legible and thus facilitate the use of a flexible set of governmental practices. As David Bray argues, the liberalization of housing markets has resulted, somewhat counterintuitively, in an increase of government intervention in urban planning and the design of residential neighborhoods and in the use of residential space as a tool to facilitate a wide range of governmental interventions.[2]

At the same time, residential areas also reveal the many ways in which the increasingly complex interests of individuals, families, and groups interact with the goals of the state. This produces not only conflicts but also forms of loyalty, strategic alliances and behaviors, and possibilities for new social identities.

Since my investigation here will focus on the practices of such interaction, neighborhoods will be not so much the objects of this book as the practical environment of a study of Chinese politics. This focus might appear too neat to have an overall explanatory power: after all, neighborhoods are not all that there is; they are not the only places where people, today, experience government; they are different from one another and are not easily categorized. Even the very use of the English word *neighborhood* to describe Chinese residential areas is controversial. The Chinese expressions *xiaoqu* (literally, "small area," generally associated with a residential compound, either private or run by a company) and *shequ* (literally, "social area," often translated as "community" and generally describing the territory and people under the administration of a resident or community committee) both contain shades of meaning that do not really correspond to those of the English word *neighborhood*. Despite these problems of definition, because of the variety of interactions between government and society that take place in functionally and administratively defined residential spaces, they provide a window on the flexibility and variations that characterize governmental practices in present-day China.

Another caveat on the topic of this book is that it deals with neighborhoods as places, not as institutions. These places are administered and governed but also imagined and experienced. They are never perfectly self-contained objects of observation but reveal much about what goes on around them, even far away from them. In the Chinese neighborhood, the institutional setting provided by grassroots organizations is an important level of analysis. As Ben Read observes, not only are neighborhood organizations subject to significant variations, but their nature is also hard to classify. They "fall between the poles of the oppressive Leninist mass organization on the one hand and the wholly self-initiated and independent citizens' group acting in civil society on the other."[3] Also, the practices of power that neighborhood residents experience are only partly dependent on the state-funded organizations that govern them. In this book I shall ask questions that go beyond the institutional setting and the direct interactions between citizens and institutions but are part of the activity of governing. I will investigate, for example, the social and economic processes that produced these places as they are today (the reform of housing provision, urban deindustrialization, the social engineering of a middle class) but also the different experiences of the state that neighborhoods promote as well as the role they play in maintaining social stability while creating new dependencies and loyalties to the state. This investigation is local by definition, but its success depends on understanding the broader changes in social structure, policy focus, ideology, and political practices.

Important and excellent new work in English has appeared in the last few years, and a couple of shelves' worth of Chinese-language literature have been published about the evolution of the traditional forms of neighborhood governance (the resident committees) and their struggle to adapt to the changing necessities and needs produced by economic and social transformation. While resident committees and other grassroots organizations will feature in the narrative of this book, my intention is to evaluate the broader political consequences of the reorganization of urban society connected with residential practices. I will thus bring into the discussion such issues as housing privatization, hegemonic cultural projects connected to the emergence of a new form of residential segregation, marketing practices, economic and social engineering, social conflicts, and the ideology of urban modernity to reveal the connection between changes in residential practices and China's overall modernization project. I identify five different rationalities connected with this level of governance, namely social clustering, micro-governing, social engineering, contained contention, and exemplarism, which I will describe in more detail in the final section of this introduction and in the chapters to come.

In the next sections of this introduction I will first provide a short explanation of what I mean by "neighborhood." As anticipated, this is less straightforward than one might imagine. I will then discuss the expression "neighborhood consensus," which provides the title to this Introduction and frames my argument.

Chinese Neighborhoods: A User's Guide

Chinese residential communities are traditionally places of intense social interaction and government activity.[4] Not only has China had a long tradition of communitarian political projects and of bounded spaces in its cities, but subsidized residence in factory compounds has also been a central feature of the socialist urban lifestyle.[5]

The elimination of the *baojia* system—a traditional institution of hierarchical and mutual neighborhood policing revived and radicalized during the years of the Japanese occupation to control urban social order—was one of the undertakings of the communist reformers immediately after taking control of Chinese cities in 1948 and 1949.[6] In the early 1950s Chinese residential areas were placed under the control of "resident committees" (*jumin weiyuanhui* or *juweihui*), formally "mass" organizations that were meant both as structures of social control and as catalysts of political and social mobilization whenever residents were asked to participate in government-organized campaigns (*yundong*).[7] In the radical years of the Great Leap Forward, cities were also organized in "urban people's communes" (*chengshi renmin gongshe*) that were supposed to integrate the traditional residential functions of neighborhoods further with production activities, autarkic food production, and security and military mobilization functions in cellular territorial structures within the city.[8] The industrial strategies of the late 1950s, aimed at the creation of "cities of production," resulted in the dominant territorial and functional role of publicly owned "work units" (*gongzuo danwei* or *danwei*). At the same time, a draconian control of rural-urban migration characterized the period between the end of the Great Leap Forward in the late 1950s and Mao Zedong's death in 1976. With a lack of alternative employment opportunities and mobility under control, urban residential spaces became characterized by the individual and family dependence on the work unit.[9] Without a real estate market and with work units monopolizing the construction and provision of housing to their members, urban neighborhoods also became increasingly tied to employers and became largely homogeneous in their composition. Since economic activities in the cities between the late 1950s and the late 1970s were concentrated in the hands of state-owned industrial enterprises, *danwei*-run neighborhoods also became hubs of the redistributive network of the socialist urban economy.

As a consequence of this situation, over the first three decades of China's socialist experience, collective and state-sponsored life in industrial Chinese cities contributed greatly to setting urban dwellers apart from the daily struggles of rural life and producing a sense of collective superiority among employees in the public sector and state-owned enterprises. In the absence of markets for either labor or resources and products, the work unit became the center of the urban redistributive system, and the neighborhood became the specific arena where that redistribution took place.

The hardened boundaries between city and countryside established to favor the extraction of agricultural surplus to fund urban industrialization were never uncontested, but in the cities they led to increased dependence of residents on the state-controlled system of redistribution.[10] With the dependence created by this redistributive regime, access to public housing through membership in a state-owned *danwei* was also crucial to the definition of the status of individual urban residents and their families. In a system of redistribution that was, at least in principle, fiercely egalitarian, prestige and social standing (as much as access to resources) were determined more by the status of one's employer (with centrally owned state enterprises on top of the hierarchy and local collective enterprises at the bottom) and by the size of the company than by the type of employment.[11] The quality of housing and the access of residents to other resources as education, health, and regimented consumption had a lot to do with where their employers were situated in this hierarchy.

Despite the sweeping changes introduced starting in 1978, residential situations and housing in the traditional industrial and administrative centers of the country changed very slowly. The role of the *danwei*s as organizers of the urban resident population did not change substantially until the beginning of the 1990s, when the reform of life-tenure employment (started in 1986) began to modify labor relations within the public enterprise, and the restructuring of state-owned businesses became a priority of the economic reform.[12] A real estate market in the cities emerged progressively in the 1990s after *danwei* began to sell their housing stocks to employees at very low prices. Since 1998, when employers were eventually prohibited from allocating housing to their employees, the development of a private real estate market (accompanied by a booming mortgage market) took on a whole new dimension, with large residential developments, mainly in the form of gated communities, radically changing the landscape of the cities and the lifestyles of urban Chinese.

Not even a formal prohibition, however, prevented work units, employers, and local governments from subsidizing (often substantially) the housing needs of their employees and residents.[13] The distortion created by this situation brought about the upward mobility of certain groups over others, and its effects continue to be felt to this day (see especially chapter 3). Despite the dominance of private housing and the 1998 edict ending the allocation of free housing, employers (especially large state-owned enterprises and administrative and government work units) still devise policies to subsidize housing, taking advantage in particular of their historical control of significant portions of urban land.[14]

With work units no longer directly administering the population and regulating their consumption, this new situation also required an evolution of neighborhood governance. In almost all large cities, the weak and volunteer-based resident committees were reorganized into more professional service providers, in some cases named *shequ* (the official translation of the English word *community* or the German word *Gemeinschaft*). Functions and practices of *shequ* committees and their grassroots cadres vary greatly, depending on the social and economic conditions of the neighborhood. Heberer and Göbel describe the emergence of these committees, which have the dual function of maintaining social control and providing services to the resident population as a form of "authoritarian communitarianism," meaning that the state is moving away from traditional forms of paternalist and "direct" techniques of government but imposing the ideas of community and self-governing over a territory and a social organization where the population remains skeptical about direct participation in community affairs.[15] *Shequs*, therefore, become administrative structures that provide security and services where needed but hardly achieve a transition from direct "government" to more participatory "governance." They also fail to penetrate the upper echelon of Chinese society, as they are concentrated mostly in poorer and dilapidated neighborhoods, while many wealthier urban dwellers today rely on management companies for the provision of services in their privately managed compounds.

Beginning in the second half of the 1990s, private housing compounds were also allowed to establish self-governing and self-elected bodies (homeowner committees, or *yezhu weiyuanhui*) to administer the residents' relationship with the private management companies and to organize homeowners' interests inside the neighborhoods. As we will see, such organizations have very limited capacity to represent broad societal interests but have been seen by some as a sign of an incipient democratic inclination among new homeowners.[16]

One characteristic of China's urban built environment in the twenty-first century is that Chinese planners, real estate tycoons, and citizens alike appear to share a passion for gated residential spaces. I will discuss the significance and reasons for this domination of gated spaces in more detail later in this book, but for the purpose of defining neighborhoods, the permanence and dominance of gates should be seen as the reproduction, in urban planning practices, of an element of order to facilitate the social and political legibility of new and socially complex residential areas. Large developments dominate the real estate industry, and lifestyles are prepackaged by developers and property managers to fit different niches of the housing market. In the old *danwei* compounds in many cities, traditional neighborhood life has almost disappeared. Traces still remain in some residential compounds; they are more intense in traditional industrial cities, where, nonetheless, the forceful uprooting of workers and the redevelopment of traditional worker areas into up-market gated communities is proceeding unabated.[17]

There is therefore a great variation among Chinese neighborhoods, over and above the common fact that areas of the urban territory are devoted mainly to residential purposes and are thus subject to significant planning and intense administration. In this book I am focusing on how citizens and residents become members of certain communities and administrative units, take part in the redistribution of essential services, and, at times, become customers of private service providers and real estate managers. At least two important dimensions will be central to my analysis. The first includes the factors that determine the production of identities, interests, networks, and (potentially) community ties inside the neighborhood. These factors result from political and social change at the national level as well as from the planning of the central and local state.

The second dimension is the variegated daily experience of government that is produced in these spatially and administratively delimited areas, an aspect that goes beyond the role of resident committees. Neighborhood-level political activities reveal that the functions of government are today performed by a mix of actors, including both private and public organizations, state-controlled agents, individuals, and groups with different levels of autonomy. Infrastructure, lifestyles, governance arrangements, and social landscapes differ markedly, according to the social and economic situations of the neighborhoods' residents. High-class gated community residents appear to enjoy a much greater "distance" from the government than those of dilapidated working-class areas awaiting "re-construction" (see chapter 2).

Governing Practices: A Focus

When I began this research I expected that studying urban communities would expose deep cracks in the regime's ability to govern society. The popular image of the modern Chinese cities slowly being taken over by private owners in new residential settings (producing, in the process, a more marked segregation of social groups, lives, and lifestyles) points to a societal structure radically different from that of the 1970s and 1980s. Increasingly stratified and complex societal interests are becoming harder to control or "harmonize," as the pet expression of former President Hu Jintao went (harmonious society, *hexie shehui*).

The narratives on how such social change should affect the process of democratization are becoming part of the mainstream discourse about China, with commentators and the media often concentrating on what are

seen as unmistakable signs of weakening authoritarianism and of coming democracy.[18] For example, as their numbers increase and their political
attitudes mature, China's burgeoning middle class is expected to become
more vocal and to seek more participation in the decision-making process. It is also thought to be inevitable that, when pushed to the edge of
personal bankruptcy, the disenfranchised peasants-turned-migrants and
disgruntled workers in the deindustrializing cities will create havoc for
the Chinese Communist Party and its legitimacy to rule. As a consequence
of either or both of these factors, the argument goes, the ability of the ruling elites to control social entropy will sooner or later reach a breaking
point. Democratization looms large in our imagination about the future of
China's political transition. However, this book is not interested in providing yet another answer to the question of whether, when, and how China
will democratize but rather in investigating how grassroots governance
practices are affecting the regime's legitimacy and ability to rule.

Among the central paradoxes is the apparently growing, diffused support for the regime in the face of growing conflicts. In her book *Accepting
Authoritarianism*, Teresa Wright explains it by reference to the structures
of incentives to support and disincentives to oppose the regime to which
each social group has been collectively exposed.[19] This interpretation of the
"acceptance" of authoritarian rule, as much as the popular thesis that associates government legitimacy with its ability to produce economic growth
and improvement in the quality of life of its citizens, tends to focus on
the active production and reproduction, by the government, of a reward
structure that boosts legitimacy. Wright and others suggest a structure of
interests that binds social groups to the destiny of the regime. In the process
of the reform and restructuring of China's economy and the changes in its
social makeup, different groups have clearly been the target of political
projects aimed at maintaining their loyalties to the state.

I want to suggest a different approach to this question. I support the
argument that incentives and the institutionalization of social stability are
indeed central features of a strategy to govern society. At the same time I also
suggest the need to focus not simply on interests but also on the way that
the daily interactions between citizens and whatever is perceived as the
authority produces legitimacy in the practices of government. I call "practices" the daily manifestations of the rationalities of governmental action.
At the neighborhood level, these include the ways in which, for example,

such social principles as segregation, social distinction, community building, and *suzhi* ("quality") are elaborated and accepted as well as how such moral and political ideas as the national interest or patriotism are internalized and reproduced. Chinese neighborhoods are places of intense governing, even at a time when a greater variety of players, both private and public, are involved in the exercise of governmental action. Here, legitimacy appears less as the result of an elaborated understanding of the good and bad of a certain regime and more as the consequence of one's assessment of the acceptability of everyday governing practices and of the moral discourses that justify such practices under a variety of material conditions. I suggest that the concrete reward structures that Wright and others focus on are not a zero-sum game and are instead continuously elaborated in the daily experiences of the community, eventually becoming part of the strategies and framing processes of common citizens.

To become legitimate and accepted, the practices (as much as the enforcers) of government need to be internalized and recognized. Their legitimacy is thus the result of continuous negotiation in which the understanding of acceptable practices is shared by all involved.

Framing Neighborhood Conflicts and Lives

Thanks to the separation of residence and employment that characterized the late reform period (especially starting in the 1990s), interests and identities in many neighborhoods are not as homogeneous as they used to be when the *danwei* was in charge of residential arrangements. When moving into new residential areas (a common experience for many urban dwellers over the last two decades), solidarities often need to be reestablished around shared economic interests and newly defined values of coexistence (see chapter 4). For many in urban China, however, homeownership and community participation are new possibilities and experiences. As a homeowner activist in Beijing once said, "The Chinese already know how to get along with their leaders, how to get along with friends and relatives; what they don't know is how to mix with strangers, and this is the reason that we haven't had communities yet." Life (and conflicts) in the new residential communities often require access to a familiar repertoire of framing arguments to apply to each situation. This process of acquiring, internalizing, and finally performing such a repertoire in neighborhood life is affected by three main factors: the long-term lived experiences of the residents; the governmental discourses on social order percolating through the system, from the center to the remotest periphery; and the bounded societal autonomy (or the appearance of autonomy) allowed or denied by the physical, mental, and administrative boundaries of the neighborhoods.

These factors can be seen as the constituents of a place-specific habitus ("a system of durable and transposable dispositions," in Bourdieu's words) that informs the perception of government practices.[20] For Bourdieu, "the dispositions durably inculcated by the possibilities and impossibilities, freedoms and necessities, opportunities and prohibitions inscribed in the objective conditions . . . generate dispositions objectively compatible with these conditions, and in a sense pre-adapted to their demands."[21] In Chinese neighborhoods, these dispositions are the result both of the experience of a specific place and of the conditions of an authoritarian system, through a structure of material incentives and a new social space.

William Hurst suggests framing processes as a useful way to interpret one aspect of these dispositions in the context of the social conflicts of the Chinese working class.[22] He finds that these frames, or "mass frames," as he calls them, are different under diverse circumstances (in his cases, the deindustrializing rust belt of northeastern China and the wealthier areas near Shanghai) but are invariably the result of structural factors, such as the nature of the local political economy. He finds that, while a "market hegemony" frame (individualism and opportunism) characterizes workers (and officials) in the advanced regions of the country, a "Maoist moral economy" frame (assistance and welfare as part of the social contract between the government and the masses) still dominates the way workers in the rust belt frame their grievances.[23]

Similarly, Ching-Kwan Lee's research on worker strategies in the Sunbelt and Rustbelt registers different attitudes, strategies, and frames in the two areas.[24] Disgruntled members of the former worker elite in the rustbelt "draw on political discourses of class, Maoism, legality and citizenship" and take to the street to protest, while workers in Shenzhen complain mainly about discrimination and are more inclined to take legal action.[25] Lee, however, attributes this diversity to the different nature of the workers' employment and relationship to the state (social contract and traditional reliance on political bargaining and work unit dependence in the rust belt; legal contract and lack of a similar support structure in the city for migrant workers in Shenzhen) and maintains that such frames are "strategically" mobilized rather than the result of structural factors.

If, following Hurst, we understand frames under the conditions of an authoritarian political system as more than strategic discursive devices mobilized on the occasion of a conflict, and instead as long lasting arguments produced by the structural features of a locality, its political economy, or the long-lived experiences of individuals and groups, then the attitudes and discourses they generate can reveal much about the relationship between state and society. In other words, these frames are not simply the result of a strategic choice that allows the participants in a collective conflict to justify their grievances toward the state but rather a structural feature of state-society relations.

Further, if frames are structural, then the convergence of framing arguments (those of the local elites and those of the grieving workers, for example) becomes reminiscent of what Antonio Gramsci would have called cultural hegemony or (in this case) a "multiple" cultural hegemony, constructed differently and imposed by local political elites on subaltern groups rather than by the national political leadership.[26] In this respect, grievances and conflicts, by adopting the language and frames set out in these hegemonic discourses, would result in the reproduction and strengthening of the legitimacy of the elite while empowering subaltern groups to act in defense of their interests.

In addition to clarifying the realm of conflicts and grievances, a structural interpretation of frames in a hegemonic context can also contribute to understanding the underlying logic of state-society relations and thus of the legitimacy of governing practices. While workers use existing, entrenched ideas to frame contention, other social groups adopt dominant discourses shaped by their deeply structural "dispositions" to define themselves as legitimate subjects within the existing system of power relations rather than producing alternative or revolutionary worldviews. When limited conflicts erupt, circumscribed by material, specific, and local interests and within a frame of the overall legitimacy of the state, their effect might well be to reinforce the overall legitimacy of the regime rather than to undermine it. Peter Lorentzen and Xi Chen, among others, have argued that the state gains political advantage and legitimacy from social conflicts and popular contention.[27] Xi Chen calls such a situation "contentious authoritarianism" and suggests that, paradoxically, the "routinization of social protests is mainly due to the facilitation of such activities by the Party State."[28]

My idea of a consensus suggests that, not only at times of conflict but also in daily interactions, even complex and different social identities internalize public and local discourses and practices that define the boundaries of an arena of interaction. In these arenas, the penetration of the state discourse about social stability is palpable, while the boundaries between state and nonstate actors become increasingly blurred.

As it turns out, neighborhood life in China is often characterized as much by acquiescence in the official rhetoric of social order as it is by conflicts: Community activists use the language of patriotism to justify their grievances against real estate developers; disgruntled ex-workers invoke the socialist spirit of central policies to frame their dissatisfaction with the local leaders who abandoned them to a life of misery; middle-class homeowners claim that harmonious communities are the cornerstone of a modern, stronger China; private management companies and state-controlled neighborhood organizations act together to implement social campaigns; the same discourses of "harmony," "quality," and "security" are equally used by the state to justify intrusive policing activities inside the neighborhood and by real estate developers to sell prestigious properties to status-hungry families; laid-off workers are co-opted in the social security system to become the organizers of a new community-level welfare system; and professionals advance their career aspirations and social role by resorting to patriotism.[29]

Such occurrences might, indeed, be interpreted as "strategic" framing, in the sense that the historical opportunity for action is provided to independent social actors by the ubiquitous presence of public discourses (harmony, quality, patriotism, and the strengthening of the nation) that, if embraced, shield limited social action from repression.[30] Nonetheless, by permeating the content of state-society interaction, the consistent reappearance of "hegemonic" frames (which result from the broad-based adoption of elite-produced discourses) is also producing legitimacy for daily practices of government. Such frames do not only appear at a time of crisis or conflict; they also pervade community activism, marketing strategies, media content, personal interactions, and even self-produced rules of coexistence, all the way down to residents' patrolling of social behavior inside the neighborhoods.

These frames, in turn, influence institutions and governmental practices, and grassroots institutions and practices contribute to disseminate meanings and values even further. Social life in contemporary neighborhoods is therefore not simply a modern reassertion of state domination; it also suggests the potential for agency. By framing social relationships in the neighborhood through the (locally) accepted rhetoric of the Chinese Communist Party, groups in society are calling upon the Party to live by its own rules and transform empty rhetoric into concrete behavioral standards. Doing so allows them to apply pressure on local cadres to be accountable and efficient in resolving daily conflicts and problems.[31]

Governing Communities and Their Spaces

Another argument I make is that the segregated nature of residential areas contributes to classification of the population and to the deployment of a variety of flexible strategies of government, each tailored to the different social groups of China's urban population. Far from being simply the result of the liberalization of housing markets and of the globalization of residential forms, residential communities contribute to the spatial legibility of urban society and facilitate the government's "social management" (*shehui guanli*). Residential spaces are markers of different social groups that are seen as distinct "objects" of government. On one end of the spectrum are those who can govern themselves (presenting limited risks for social order, like the professionals and the "high-*suzhi*" upper middle class); at the other end are those who need governing because of their lack of social capital or deficient social situation, such as migrants and downwardly mobile ex-workers. Governance practices change accordingly.

In the contemporary neighborhood, disciplinary strategies and liberal techniques of governing coexist. Formal grassroots institutions as well as private companies and market operators, informal groups and individuals, become involved in forms of governance that resemble those familiar to citizens of liberal democracies. The work of Nikolas Rose, among others, has alerted us to the fact that "governing" in liberal democracies happens "through" such ideas as "freedom" and "community."[32] In China, despite the disciplinary nature of the authoritarian system, "self-government" (*zizhi*) has become part of the political repertoire of governing agencies, assuming that citizens are to become responsible for the government of their communities. David Bray has usefully applied the Foucauldian idea of a disciplinary space (the Panopticon) to suggest that contemporary Chinese communities' design promotes shared values of self-government in apparently autonomous private spaces.[33] While the official use of the term *zizhi* refers to the narrow functions of neighborhood and homeowner committees, it also highlights the expectation that individuals and groups are progressively driven to "govern themselves" and that their access to resources and rights is increasingly bound to their ability to do so.

Other authors have already highlighted that governmental control over people and territories produces a variety of governing techniques and that people are governed flexibly, depending on their position in society. The logic behind these variations in the practices of government has been explained through the need to control skills, imposed by the demands of global capital under local conditions. Aihwa Ong, for example, wrote about a "graduated sovereignty" where states are no longer administrators of national matters but are rather "regulators of diverse spaces and populations that link with the global markets."[34] I suggest that such regulatory techniques of government are also a consequence of an authoritarian political system adapting to the new conditions of its own economic liberalization.

In this respect, the first question to be asked is whether liberal technologies of government can coexist with an authoritarian system. For Michel Foucault, domination on one side and individual freedom and subjectivity on the other cannot be treated as a simple matter of opposition. As he famously put it:

> If power were ever anything but repressive, if it never did anything but to say no, do you really think one would be brought to obey it? What makes power hold good, what makes it accepted is the fact that it not only weighs on us as a force that says no; it also traverses and produces things, it induces pleasure, forms knowledge, produces discourses. It needs to be considered as a productive network that runs through the whole social body much more than as a negative instance whose function is repression.[35]

Even in a liberal system, in Mitchell Dean's words, "liberal rationalities and authoritarian measures are far from incompatible. Governing liberally, or governing in a free 'political culture,' is quite compatible with the demand for a form of government of the state that places the question of order—whether personal or social—as its primary objective, and the reiteration of authoritative direction as its primary means."[36] Research on China's evolving civil society has long focused on the search for forces in society that could somehow "limit" the awesome power of the state. I suggest the need to research not only the conflict areas where society is engaging and possibly limiting the power of the state but also the ways in which citizens elaborate, internalize, and ultimately accept governing practices, developing their agency in the process.

The second question concerns the relationship between governmental techniques and the making of citizens. The importance of subjectivities in the study of governmental practices has attracted increasing attention to processes through which the Chinese state "makes" citizens that fit its governing rationalities better. Some observers have insisted that China is increasingly governed "from a distance" and that the technologies employed in today's China are increasingly "neo-liberal."[37] To cite Ong again with regard to what she calls the "disarticulation of citizenship," rights and benefits flow to the "bearers of marketable talents and [are] denied to those who are judged to lack such capacity and potential." Those who are considered "too complacent or lacking in neoliberal potential may be treated as less worthy subjects."[38]

My contention is that such overarching rationalities are indeed at work and can be clearly observed in the daily expressions of power relations in the Chinese urban neighborhoods. I am, however, reluctant to attribute them to the effect of global capital flows alone, as this explanation would lead us to assume that the Chinese state is only an agent (albeit a very conscious one) of global capitalism.[39] While economic competition is a source of legitimacy for the Chinese government (both domestically and internationally), it is not the only reason that it needs to classify its population, standardize the spaces where they live, control their reproduction, manage their well-being, educate them to patriotism and order, or divide them up into different groups according to their contribution to production or their ability to govern themselves. Such techniques indeed imply, although only for some, a more distant, possibly less disciplinary (but not weaker) state than the one that Chinese citizens have experienced in the first half-century of their socialist experience. They also require, however, increasing state visibility in numerous areas of state-society interaction in order to manage the destabilizing effects of economic, social, and cultural change. As Mun Young Cho notices in her study of the poverty-stricken community of former state workers in Harbin, in some occasions the state, far from shrinking, has become "bigger," because it has progressively coopted former workers into the role of community cadres (see chapter 2).[40] Legitimacy, for the Chinese ruling elite, still depends on its ability to renew, adapt, and indigenize the reasons for its authority, rather than simply on its capacity to serve the needs of global capital. The expectation that a neoliberal rationale is the only way to see China's social and political change is challenged by the contradictions of its governing practices.

While discourses of globalization can be at work to define the way that individuals cope with the economic and social transition of the recent decades, other ideas that are both locally produced and useful to the preservation of an authoritarian system of government are extensively at work as well. In other words, if power is seen as "a productive network that runs through the whole social body," its effects on the Chinese population are most visible in the daily practices of government. They aim as much at social stability, order, and legitimacy as they do at economic efficiency and competitiveness. Therefore, they are flexible and shaped both by global trends and by the concrete structures of the local political economies. Neighborhood social interactions reveal how practices of government are often inspired by discourses that seem to go against globalizing trends (such as that of a "socialist moral economy" or "patriotism").

Consensus

With a focus on the locally produced practices of government and their rationalities, this book researches the engineering of political consensus. It does so by investigating one of the social and physical spaces where this is produced, negotiated, experienced, mobilized, and governed. I use the term *consensus* to suggest that the legitimacy of social and political practices is not the result of authoritarian coercion alone. For the practices of government to become legitimate, the values that justify them need to be broadly accepted.

Thus, the consensus I am suggesting does not require an acknowledgment of the legitimacy of the government but rather the acceptance of the legitimacy of its daily social practices and discourses. In this constructed and contested middle ground, social order is placed at the center. As we will see, the neighborhoods are highly contentious spaces; consensus about a system of values and practices—centered on social order, the need for a hierarchical social organization, and evolutionary ideas of social development aimed at producing "better" and "modern" citizens and communities—contributes to containing the systemic impact of social conflicts and social diversification on the legitimacy of the regime.

In discussing a neighborhood consensus, I do not mean to argue that the legitimacy of the government relies on the submissive attitudes of a silenced populace or to deny the important role of popular contention in producing social change. I wish instead to highlight the role played by the daily practices of power in the production of an idea of legitimacy that might, in turn, result in concrete dividends for the authoritarian rulers. I do not refer to the legitimacy of the government itself or of its officials but rather to that of some of its more ingrained social practices. I am not interested in what people like (little) or dislike (much) about their institutions and their leaders but rather in whether and why individuals, groups, and communities subscribe to such social projects, ideas, and practices as "residential segregation," "community building," "quality," "civilization," and "modernity," all of which make up a consistent part of their daily perception of politics, power, and government. When this aspect of the state-society nexus is considered, questions of legitimacy take a very different form.

At this point it would be wise to establish some important caveats about what I do and do not mean by consensus. First of all, consensus is not political support; it entails only the setting of the boundaries of a "consensual arena" of interaction between state and society, the hardest boundary being the ultimate political survival of the regime. It does not mean unconditional support, a moral and political blank check for the governing elite. Political support in electoral democracies is often understood as a matter of intensity (somewhere between "I strongly support the government" and "I hate the government") that guides voting behavior. Opinion polls in China, however, often suggest that overall systemic satisfaction does not extend to appreciation for cadres (generally perceived as corrupt, inefficient, or unfairly privileged).[41] Local cadres also attract a significantly lower level of satisfaction than the central government. One nationwide survey, for example, suggests that the oft-cited widespread dissatisfaction of the Chinese population with rising inequality is in fact mitigated by the acceptance of the meritocratic principle permeating the reform spirit and that, while corruption attracts anger, inequality is generally seen as the result of talent and abilities, thus reducing the potential for the explosion of China's "social volcano."[42] In other words, while unequal distribution is understood as a negative outcome of market reform, the processes through which it has come into being and the discourses that justify it are still considered legitimate.

Social order constitutes another hard boundary that constrains both the actions of the enforcers of governmental rationalities and those of activists engaged in conflicts and organization in the neighborhoods. The same could be said of other discourses that justify the supremacy of social order: the need to strengthen the nation, the inadequate level of *suzhi* in the population, a moral and social hierarchy based on values and self-discipline rather than rights.

Second, consensus is not "naturally" or culturally determined but rather engineered. As I will show in this book, it is achieved through a variety of governmental techniques, including the monopoly over ideology, the active promotion of the interests of certain social groups, the reproduction of chronic dependence on state welfare among the new poor, limited forms of autonomy, the specter of social control and repression, or a mix of social and administrative institutions. Consensus is thus constructed and not the outcome of good governing, but it allows space for bargaining and contestation. In fact, the neighborhoods I will be investigating are beset by large numbers of conflicts. As mentioned, however, it is in the framing processes of these conflicts that a consensus is manifested.

Consensus expresses itself, for example, in the convergence between state-produced discourses of morality and social order, on the one hand, and discourses reproduced and elaborated by community activists, both in their daily experience of organization and socialization and during conflicts, on the other. Appeals to morality, quality, nation building, or the protection of collective interests or social entitlements often feature among the framing arguments for social conflicts. To be sure, a discursive consensus does not inoculate the leadership against systemic criticism, but it contributes to containing destabilizing political effects to a familiar rhetorical ground such that it can be addressed by acting within the system (for example by removing a corrupt, incompetent, or insensitive cadre) rather than by revolutionizing the political landscape. Consensus, in other words, envisions the ability of societal actors to speak the language of the government to achieve political gains and to reduce the risks implicit in social action. While this appears to strengthen the interest and position of the rulers and to produce a more governable society, it also provides autonomous actors with avenues to protect and represent their interests, even in an authoritarian environment.

Third, consensus is divided and selective whenever the state produces diverse and often conflicting governmental rationalities that involve the role of different social groups. Unemployed ex-workers in the northeast of the country, for example, subscribe to the pastoral view promoted by the government that they are entitled to welfare and support for their long-term contribution to nation building.[43] Middle-class homeowners in Beijing, on the other side, rely on the rhetoric of consumer rights as fundamental to China's smooth modernization as a way of framing their arguments against predatory developers or greedy property managers. Without representative institutions but nonetheless with the need to please public opinion in order to be legitimate, different and even opposite and contradictory governmental logics can be applied at the same time (moral economy versus self-entrepreneurship is the classic example). Individuals and families in their neighborhoods, similarly, mobilize different discourses and resources.

Finally, I want to warn readers about the risk of interpreting consensus as a normative category or of taking my choice of words for a way to subscribe to the inevitability of authoritarianism in China. It would be preposterous (and certainly not my intention) to think of China as a consensus society, where the adherence of some part of the citizenry to the civilizing project of China's reform (produced and imposed by an authoritarian government) ultimately replaces the need for political participation, due process in the resolution of conflicts, or a more participatory decision-making tradition. I do not use the term *consensus* to justify or indulge authoritarian rule but rather to understand practices of daily government as an expression of higher rationalities of government. I will refrain from saying "how much" consensus I found, of what "quality" or "intensity" it was. As I said above, consensus also signals a changing polity, where citizens are actively elaborating very pragmatic discursive strategies that do indeed have the potential to affect the long-term structure of power relations. Consensus, in this respect, is not simply an attitude but a practice, which is always contested and becomes a bargaining chip in the relationship between citizens and the state, different levels of government, institutions, and communities.

The Rationalities of Consensus: A Précis of the Book

Communities are places where the presence, rhetoric, and activity of the government meet individual and collective interests, where collective interests are more or less homogeneous. The government has mobilized different rationalities that are translated into the practices of the neighborhood. As mentioned earlier, they are not only related to the specifics of state-society interaction but rather are also the basis for certain practices that influence governance at the neighborhood level. Each chapter focuses on a different rationality and on the way they become social and governing practices, namely: social clustering, micro-governing, social engineering, contained contention, and exemplarism.

In chapter 1, the book addresses the social clustering and classification that accompanied the recent housing privatization, which resulted in significant flexibility in the governing strategies. The chapter compares different types of neighborhood and how their residents are differently exposed to techniques of government. It finds that, in gentrified residential areas inhabited by "high *suzhi*" citizens, residents enjoy a significant (albeit spatially limited) autonomy to govern themselves and successfully avoid the direct control of public neighborhood organizations. In socially troubled neighborhoods, however, the presence and visibility of the state has often increased after the reform and rapid urbanization of the last decade. I call the practices described by this phenomenon "social clustering," and I argue that the deployment of such a specific form of government is made possible by a spatial and social classification of social groups to which both public and private actors have contributed.

I then focus (chapter 2) on the formal structures of administration and government (the resident committees and community committees, *shequ weiyuanhui*) in the city of Shenyang, where industrial decline (and the slow demise of the traditional work-unit system) required an overhaul of neighborhood governance to deliver essential services to a large number of unemployed people through grassroots organization. The chapter looks at both the working practices of these offices and at the role of community cadres. One of the by-products of the devolution of social functions to the *shequs* is, in fact, a new generation of low-level cadres who are often forced to engage with the social distress produced by the recent transition. Chapter 2 investigates the careers, experiences, perceptions, and strategies of these cadres (often themselves the victims of economic restructuring) directly involved in the reproduction of Party rhetoric but also exposed to the struggles of the disenfranchised. If the collapse of a structure of socialist entitlements has produced disenchantment in one "lost" generation of former workers, how is the Party redefining its role and its language? How are such traditional (as much as socialist) values as "responsibility," "quality," "harmony," and "participation"—recently redeployed as pillars of the political culture of the Chinese Communist Party—being rewritten and concretized in what is arguably a hostile environment? I suggest that, while the burden of governing in middle-class neighborhoods is becoming "lighter," the government of social distress is attracting more resources, "heavier" governing practices, and new challenges at the grassroots level, according to a strategy that I call micro-governing. This trend signals the continuity of paternalistic practices of socialist governance.

Chapter 3 introduces the social and cultural engineering behind the two-decades-long project of housing privatization and its wide-ranging impact on the redefinition of urban social distinction through extreme forms of residential segregation. It argues that the increase in residential segregation is greatly influenced by the state's strategy of selective incentives. Such strategy has favored groups "within the system" over others. Individual housing careers and access to material resources therefore still remain affected by one's position with respect to the system of public employment. Residential settings reflect the structure of access to homeownership created by subsidization policies and is consistent with other policies to "make" a high-consuming cluster of society. This chapter challenges the normative assumptions generally made about the role that the middle class could play in pushing China toward democratization and reveals how the growth of a property-owning middle class is the result of a process of social engineering.

Chapter 4 investigates the nature of the growing number of social conflicts taking place in the new neighborhoods and the articulation of collective interests around property rights issues in middle-class residential communities. Through an analysis of their framing mechanisms, I find that they do not carry the potential for societal autonomy that other authors have suggested. I also find that this potential is effectively contained by the physical form that these residential compounds have taken (gated and walled compounds, often managed by private companies). The walls provide a concrete marker of how broadly certain interests are allowed to coalesce without triggering a reaction by the authoritarian state. This contained contention also reduces the potential for systemic unrest and the risks for the overall stability of the regime.

In chapter 5, I investigate the practical and material consequences of the dominant discourse of a "civilized" middle class on China's urban governance and address the significance of the newly emerging neighborhood-based stratification for the overall project of governing Chinese cities. I find that the discourse and practices it produces are functional to the creation of "value." Urban renewal and the rebranding of traditional urban centers as postindustrial and global metropolises rely heavily on the promotion of "middle-class" exemplarism. The "values" produced through this process are both monetary and political. By targeting the middle class as a potential buyer, the state increases the value of use rights, thus making it more attractive for local governments to redevelop traditional, dilapidated, and industrial areas in the city center to rebrand them as "middle-class paradises." Also, the educated and affluent groups inhabiting the new compounds become exemplars of a self-responsible, well-behaved, and "high-*suzhi*" citizenry that embodies the values of the civilizing project China embarked on.

A Note on the Method

This book is the result of a number of different research practices applied over the years during long periods of fieldwork in China. If I had to call this book anything I would say it is a collection (as it deals with different localities) of political ethnographies. Over the years I have compiled over two hundred interviews with different stakeholders. I have participated in and observed all sorts of activities, including demonstrations, elections, cultural festivals, and meetings; collected printed material and internet postings; given lectures to local community members on issues I knew very little about but that gave me a way into their lives and interests; dressed up in a significantly undersized Eighth Army uniform to sing "red" songs with a community choir; taken many photos and had innumerable private conversations with individuals and groups; surveyed the community directors of an entire district; and have occasionally been checked out by the local law enforcers.

I conducted a total of about one year of fieldwork over the years, beginning in 2002 when I first visited the sites of what in this book I call Hopetown. I spent four months in Chengdu over three different trips starting in 2005 and about five months in Shenyang starting in 2006. Several times between 2010 and 2013, I went back to each of these places for shorter visits. I was last in Hopetown just a few weeks before writing these words. I also visited and conducted interviews in neighborhoods in cities that were not the main site of this research, including Shanghai and Guangzhou, and visited "street offices" and neighborhood committees that did not end up being incorporated into the narratives of this book.

Different social settings and cities called for different types of observation and for different approaches to recruitment of informants. The different methods I had to use to crack the codes of individual neighborhoods was also a sign of the variety of political environments I encountered during my fieldwork; this is one of the main findings of the book. Poorer neighborhoods needed a much more formal approach to avoid making the local authorities nervous, but the access I was granted as a result of that approach and the information I was able to obtain were often deeper and more significant. "Guided access" to some of the neighborhoods in Shenyang, for example, was necessary at the beginning of my investigation, but the control of the authorities often subsided after a few days, allowing for easier and more direct access to neighbors. It also allowed me to observe interactions between state officials and residents in a more formalized context and, in some cases, to have access to significant samples of officials to survey, as in chapter 2.

On the other hand, much to my surprise, it was often harder to organize interviews in middle-class areas, despite the relatively low visibility of state control. Owners in these neighborhoods have developed a much greater sense of their privacy, and management companies sometimes enforce a stricter brand of public security. In some cases I chose to become a resident myself and to experience the community in all its different daily manifestations. This allowed me also to collect stories of housing practices I would have otherwise missed and to be immersed in the conflicts that engulfed these neighborhoods.

I first began my research in Beijing, but I later realized that what I was looking at was inherently local and thus guaranteed a "yes, but" reaction among readers. To provide a slightly more representative picture of neighborhood politics, I therefore decided to include both other locations and other types of neighborhood. Shenyang's industrial decline and dire social situation and its emergence as a model city for the community-building campaign were the factors that brought me there, and I was lucky enough to obtain access to communities thanks to the offices of my local academic host. Chengdu suggested itself as a further possibility for comparison, a city that was less central to the strategies and concerns of the central government than Beijing and Shenyang but has a strong local culture and a long urban tradition.

In each city I adopted a mixed strategy to recruiting informants, sometimes accessing neighborhoods by participating in their activities, sometimes relying on the introduction of either local officials or local residents. Interviews took place in all kind of venues, including the residences of my neighbors, a local teahouse, an office of the resident committee, a bench in the neighborhood garden, or an elderly activity center.

My original goal was to investigate the everyday life and politics of the emerging middle class. What I soon realized when I started my research in 2002 was that neighborhoods were an ideal "place" to study this developing identity, even if they were not enough to reveal the reasons for certain behaviors, conflicts, and power relations, which needed to be explained by looking at broader trends of social change and cultural transformation in China. My observation therefore extended to other residential areas and to the residents' interactions with different sources of power and authority as well as with different stakeholders. I realized that security guards, property managers, and the various levels of the state combine in an ever-changing constellation of power relations that also needs to be considered and that tells something deeper about the changing political rationalities of the Chinese state. I also realized that the middle class does not exist in a vacuum and that, for all the fetishism that attaches to the growth of the global market in China, the middle class emerges in urban areas that are contested. I therefore decided to direct my research toward other neighborhoods and to try to connect the dots. Much of what I say here has to do with the lines drawn in that exercise.

1

SOCIAL CLUSTERING

Neighborhoods and the Governing of Social Distinction

In 1997, discussing the American obsession with gated communities, Edward Blakely and Mary Gail Snyder wrote: "The setting of boundaries is always a political act. Boundaries determine membership: someone must be inside and someone outside. Boundaries also delineate space to facilitate the activities and purposes of political, economic, and social life."[1] As mentioned in the introduction, the political and social use of such boundary-making exercises is nothing new in China, as clustering of social groups has been central to the classification of society as well as the organization and administration of the territory, the rationalization of consumption, and the policing of individual lives. What is new, however, is that such state-sponsored social clustering continues deep into a period characterized by an explosion in private homeownership and by a reduction in the dependence of urban Chinese on the state-owned enterprise.

With economic reform, marketization of housing policies, and real estate market happening rapidly and concurrently, urban spaces in China have taken on some of the characteristics seen in metropolitan areas in

other parts of the world, in particular extreme residential and social segregation. Some of the discourses of class distinction and security that have
underpinned such phenomena are found in China as well, including a
widespread discourse of violence and social risk such as that which Teresa
Caldeira, for example, has identified as the source of Brazil's increasing
physical separation of social groups through walls and security technologies.[2] In China's case, however, the local state has played a major role both
in the physical production of such spaces and in the spreading of the hegemonic discourse that justifies the rise of residential segregation. Public
control over land and the ability to mobilize resources and capital for the
first wave of the real estate boom in the 1990s have placed the state and its
agents at the center of China's spatial revolution.

The discourse of violence derived from social degradation and urban
sprawl is thus replaced here by the slogans of social stability (*shehui wending*), an overarching idea that goes beyond fear and individual security to
provide a benchmark for lifestyles, social organization, and indeed the classification and segregation of different clusters of the population into distinct spaces. The rational organization of the population in visible spaces
remains central to China's strategies of urban governance, and neighborhoods reveal how this strategy is inscribed in spatial patterns and results in
diverse experiences of government in residential communities.

To begin explaining social clustering, let me start by juxtaposing two
different neighborhoods: every day, in a public housing residential community in the former heartland of China's socialist industry, the city of
Shenyang in Liaoning province, a group of thirty-one old ladies and one
old man patrols the two gates of an old residential compound inhabited by
large numbers of laid-off workers and their families. Their main concerns
are the incursions of "low-*suzhi*" rural migrants into the compound to sell
their goods and services in competition with the informal "courtyard economy" of shoemakers, bicycle fixers, and fruit stalls that the local government allows the laid-off to run tax-free inside the residential compounds.

In a different city, Beijing, at the same time, in a gated middle-class
neighborhood, a group of homeowners are giving the final touches to a
newly built garden. It is, in fact, not just a garden but also a self-funded
memorial to the four years of struggle necessary to force the real estate
developer to complete the park that was originally included in the plans
for the community. At the center of the small area, engraved on a large

Figure 1. The stone at the entrance of a neighborhood garden in Beijing engraved with the Chinese characters *shouwang jiayuan*, meaning "the garden of vigilance"

Figure 2. Residential buildings in Tiexi's "workers' village" before the renovation

Figure 3. Residential buildings in Tiexi's "workers' village" after the renovation

white stone, are the characters *shouwang huayuan*, signifying "the garden of vigilance."

The two communities watch over spaces that are socially, economically, and politically different. The grannies in Shenyang have mobilized to protect the entitlement to what is left of the once-generous welfare benefits reserved to China's industrial working class from new competitors in a residual economy. The Beijing homeowners, for their part, watch over their right to see a contract honored and their aspiration to a better and more autonomous lifestyle fulfilled, at least in their backyard. Each group is acting in the limited, shared interests of its respective community and contains its grievances within the gates of its respective compound. The framing arguments they use, however, are radically different: on the one hand, the modern political rhetoric of consumer rights produced by the state and its media outlets in the attempt to guarantee consumers and increase overall consumption rates; on the other, the traditional arguments of entitlements on which the socialist state has based its moral legitimacy for decades.

The two strategies and framing discourses materialize inside specific spaces that are themselves the result of a radical transformation of China's cities. Rather than being solely an outcome of the commercialization of urban spaces, the spatial distinction within the city is the result not of deregulation but of planning and the overhaul of governance strategies.

In this chapter, I introduce two main objectives of this book, which will frequently recur in subsequent chapters: first, I argue that, beyond the imperatives of economic liberalization, there remains a direct functional relationship between the Chinese state's goals of maintaining social stability and containing social conflicts, on one side, and the privatization, reorganization, and apparent deregulation of urban residential spaces, on the other. The same "hair-splitting" marketing strategies, through which developers offer different lifestyles and levels of services to different niches of housing consumers, apply to tailored styles of governance, implemented differently with regard to social groups with defined social status.[3] The goal of urban governance is now shaped more by the need to service and police a complex population than by the need for ideological mobilization and campaigning. Different communities, defined by the space they live in, have become objects of different strategies of government within a broad range of options ranging from direct intervention and dependency-inducing social welfare to a laissez-faire attitude and the privatization of governance functions.

Second, such spatial segregation of social groups also produces a convergence between private and public discourses of social stability as a crucial element of the neighborhood consensus. This chapter will reveal the role that residential spaces and their new governance arrangements play in producing loyalties toward the state. The distinction between different residential clusters, created through status-defining spaces, contributes to the state's ability to address the demands of different social groups. I will focus on the demands for limited societal autonomy and the protection of consumer rights expressed by the middle class living in self-managed gated communities and on the claims to support and basic welfare, inspired by the socialist moral economy of discontented workers still anchored to the traditional neighborhoods by their dependence on state subsidies. I will use examples from Beijing, Shenyang, and Chengdu.

The Logic of Segregated Social Spaces

The recent pace of social change and the need to adapt to the pressures of global capital have produced new challenges to the late socialist Chinese state. In response to these challenges, however, rather than evolving into a more pluralistic system of interest representation, the Chinese state has adapted and maintained control over governing processes. Its governmental techniques today serve both the interests of capitalist development and the need of social stability and political legitimacy. At their core is the reclassification of the population through social structures, new social institutions, and the language of stratification.[4] Ann Anagnost has chronicled how, in the study of Chinese social patterns, a class analysis of the social structure was replaced in the 1990s by an analysis of "social strata" (*jieceng*), which, by claiming a scientific approach to a political problem, "references social inequality in a way that does not assume social antagonism."[5] This change in language and the increasing rhetoric of a party that aims to represent different social groups was mirrored in spatial and governmental practices that contributed to map social differences on the ground.

The traditional cellular structure of the socialist city allowed the government to classify and administer the urban population through the organization of urban families into all-encompassing "work units" and on the basis of their role and contribution to China's industry-first developmental model. While work units have today lost many of their traditional spatial, operational, and administrative functions, public employers still provide privileged employment conditions. They are also among the urban "land masters" that control large chunks of prime urban real estate.[6] Cities also maintain a network of grassroots political organizations and a clear spatial subdivision into administrative units that survived recent urban construction and the privatization of housing stocks.

Social clustering and spatial privatization have accelerated (rather than declining) since the completion of the housing reform in 1998, resulting in higher levels of residential segregation and the rise of gating residential spaces. Local governments have facilitated the emergence of this new form of segregation, for example by encouraging communities to build gates around their compounds and to hire private security guards. According to the Ministry of Public Security, at the end of 2010, 2,966 private security companies were operating in China, employing an estimated 4.2 million guards.[7] A 2006 survey published by the journal *Community* revealed that as little as a third of all residential neighborhoods in urban areas were allowing free passage to nonresidents, while about two-thirds were requiring registration for guests and employing private security guards.[8]

This obsession with security and spatial segregation can be interpreted as resulting as much from the converging interests of developers, managers, and the governing bureaucracies as from the free choice of homeowners. A number of economic and political reasons account for the success of gates in China's urban built environment. The first follows from the structural need for the rapid provision of large-scale housing estates to curb the chronic urban housing shortages of the 1980s, as a result of increased population pressure in urban centers and a dilapidated stock of public housing. This meant that large, new, concentrated, and privately managed projects attracted more interest than renovations or small, dispersed developments and seemed to serve better the public need for a great deal of new residential space as quickly as possible. Despite a significant increase in population, the per capita living space in urban China has quadrupled in the last thirty years (387 square feet in 2011, or 1,252 square feet per average household), and the floor space built in the same period is twelve times the amount Communist China had built in the previous three decades.[9]

Under the work-unit system, housing had remained a component of the welfare benefits attached to life-tenure employment. A real estate market did not develop fully until the second half of the 1990s, when work units started to reduce housing distribution and were eventually prevented by law (1998) from allocating free housing. At the same time, the sale of large quantities of housing stock at highly subsidized prices was accompanied by policies favoring access to homeownership for public employees and urban professionals, and financial institutions have entered the equation by issuing housing loans.[10] With a growing demand for higher standards of housing, new developments have increasingly been planned in the newly reclaimed land in the suburbs. They have also become enormous. According to Miao, in the early 2000s these new residential communities averaged between 12 and 20 hectares and housed roughly 2,500 families, thus requiring some form of private governance, usually in the form of a management company.[11] In most Chinese cities, the single-function "sealed neighborhood" (*fengbi shi xiaoqu*) has become an architectural standard. Alternative ways of designing residential neighborhoods have been almost entirely abandoned. While a theoretical discussion has indeed developed on the advantages and disadvantages offered by "sealed" (*fengbi*) as opposed to "open" (*kaifang*) neighborhoods, planning practices and design standards are still privileging large gated developments over small, open neighborhoods. Furthermore, the mingling interests of developers, local bureaucracies, financial institutions, and large enterprises (what are often called urban China's "pro-growth coalitions") also favor large, high-quality, privately managed projects over scattered and small residential developments.[12]

In some cities, most prominently in Beijing, the local government has explicitly supported large developments. New projects during the 1990s typically included both commercial housing sold at market prices and housing built on subsidized rental land ("economy housing," *jingji shiyong fang*) to be assigned to middle-income families at a substantial discount. The gated version of the residential compound was attractive for developers, who also saw large communities of several thousand families as opportunities for long-term and stable flows of management fees. The overwhelming majority of the over twenty thousand property managers (about 70 percent in 2007) are fully owned subsidiaries of the developers or the commercial appendages of such public agencies as the *fangguansuo* (the Housing Maintenance Bureau) taking advantage of privatization to establish profitable operations.[13] Management companies in large compounds are able to yield profits of hundreds of thousands of yuan a year. Some of this inevitably trickles into the hands of local bureaucrats, both in the form of land use fees and as bribes and kickbacks, which are often connected to the issuance of construction licenses and land leases.[14]

State agencies and public enterprises entitled to use rights on prime urban land also privilege large centralized housing projects. A major university in Chengdu, for example, managed to profit from the availability of its unused land in the center of the city. Its deal with a local developer included the construction of residential housing that the university was able to sell to its employees at a considerable discount, while the developer was allocated use rights over a portion of the same land for a private commercial development.[15]

Similarly, city and district governments exploited the fact of growing prices to increase the value of their land holdings. The marketing of certain dilapidated areas of the city as "new middle-class paradises" produced an artificial increase in the value of the land and contributed to an excessive supply of unaffordable housing.[16]

The dominance of the gated micro-district (*xiaoqu*) formation and of large projects requiring significant investment and a considerable amount of land over small projects and renovations produced an imbalance in the housing market in favor of high-quality building and contributed to a rise in housing prices.[17] Expensive compounds in a better and more profitable market thus outnumbered more affordable housing projects. In several cases I encountered during my fieldwork, developers obtained subsidized land but were left with a great deal of freedom on how to allocate apartments to entitled families. They often hijacked subsidized projects by building apartments of a much higher quality, size, and price than expected in order to satisfy the growing demand of those who could afford to invest in real estate.[18] As a consequence and often with the collusion of complacent local authorities, low-income families were left out of the buying frenzy in which professional and middle-income public employees engaged. Also, due to a "double" land market (one for the land assigned by the state and one for that auctioned at market prices), a black market rapidly developed around land use rights in the cities, pushing the prices of land developments even higher.[19]

The third and possibly the most important reason behind the success of gating is its association with the preservation of security and social order. Official discourse directly associates gating with the need to protect citizens from the "dangers" of urbanization, the imperative of social stability, and the goal of "harmonious communities." The "forting-up" of Chinese cities is driven by the convergent concerns of home buyers and local governments with security. Demand for secure spaces ranks highest among home buyers' priorities, while local bureaucracies are trying to ensure that as much urban land as possible is enclosed behind walls and patrolled by private security guards.[20] The Public Security Bureau; the Bureau of Land, Resources and Housing; and the Civil Affairs Bureau of Beijing municipality, for example, issued a joint document in November 2001 explicitly requiring that residential communities be "sealed."[21] Those communities that could "satisfy conditions for closed management" but had not established a patrol system were encouraged to take formal steps to hire a private security company (article 7), while those without a wall were encouraged to "raise capital from the owners to seal off [*fengbi*] their housing estate" (article 8). The authorities' concerns about how to manage a very large population in case of an environmental or health crisis have also contributed to strengthening the rationale for enclosures. During the SARS pandemic in 2003, communities quickly enforced very strict segregation, with unmistakable success in preventing the spread of the virus.

Despite awareness of the risk that "stratification of communities" (*shequ jiecenghua*) can result in further segregation among the already highly unequal groups of China's urban society, spatial differentiation among the population is seen by Chinese commentators as an advantage for "administrative efficiency" (*xingzheng xiaolü*) and a way to enhance the "level of governance" (*zhili shuiping*). Spatial distinctions between social groups are seen as helping not only the government in targeting services more efficiently to different groups with different needs but also the residents' "sense of community" (*shequ qinggan*) as well as participation in the self governance institutions of the community. Stratified communities could ensure that people live alongside compatible neighbors with similar economic, social, and cultural characteristics.[22]

Gating residential spaces has also been forcibly extended to villages at the urban fringe. In Beijing's Daxing district, where the "floating" (*liudong*) population greatly outnumbers locals, sixteen villages affected by a "population imbalance" (*renkou daogua*) have become "segregated villages" (*fengcun*). Gates and fences have been erected around the areas of the natural villages, with security guards patrolling and screening access at the gates. Villages at such urban fringes are mostly where migrants who cannot afford rents in more central districts choose to live. The measure was suggested by the local police chief after an increase in violent crime he described in an interview as the result of the low quality and limited education of migrant workers. "The majority of them have limited work skills, and 90 percent have lower middle school or less education. Many commit crimes of passion. How do you stop them? . . . When they have money they are all right, but if they have no money their spirits are unsettled."[23] The result of enclosing the villages and placing over three hundred new cameras in a single township was, indeed, a reduction of criminal activities. It also resulted, however, in increased rents, which in a tight housing market migrants were required to pay, and in complaints of discrimination from the outsiders who also provide many of the commercial and other essential services inside these suburban villages.

Such practices not only result in discrimination against certain groups and between groups but also become markers of the urban territory, as they define who has control over the territory and how control should be experienced. The gating of villages is a way to assimilate these formally rural areas into governance forms typical of urban communities (in fact, it is called "community-style village governance"). The spatial enclosure marks a formal transformation of villages into urban neighborhoods, recognizing the inclusion of their territory and their residents in the city. At the same time, the renting migrants remain excluded from it. Paradoxically, what for migrants is a conscious act of exclusion becomes for villagers, themselves "urban fringe peasants," a step forward in their march to integration into the dream of urban modernity. Authorities see the city as more "civilized" at its core than at its periphery. As the district police chief reminded us, "Such a security situation would never be tolerated inside the third ring road."[24]

Local governments also often encourage a functional planning of the city, targeting certain areas of the city for "gentrification," favoring residential developments in the inner city and moving productive activities toward the peripheries. An efficient use of urban land has been central to the project to modernize China's postindustrial cities, which are dependent on the income generated by land redevelopment.[25]

This gentrification not only refills the local authorities' empty coffers but also serves an important double function of government: It creates spaces where certain social groups (the professional middle class as well as traditional bureaucratic elites) can enjoy, exclusively, the advantages of economic transformation, and it contributes to isolating and containing the resentment of the losers in the process of reform, the traditional holders of socialist entitlements who are now relegated to the remaining old socialist communities or have been relocated to new, anonymous suburbs.

As Aihwa Ong observed regarding the "zoning technologies" that led to the Special Economic Zones in the initial years of reform, a reclassification of spaces is "often coordinated with diverse modes of government, that administer the population in terms of their relevance to global capital."[26] Arguments that focus on the impact of globalization to explain flexibility in governing practices provide a plausible reason for how urban spaces have been reorganized after the *danwei* era and why governing strategies are different between spaces and between places. However, while neoliberal practices explain global capital's need for graduated forms of citizenship, they can account only for differences between localities and treat individual cases as the result of local-global interaction. In order to explain the patterns within those differences, it is also necessary to discuss the rationalities of local and national governments, cultural constraints, and forms of everyday adaptation and resistance.[27]

I believe, for example, that the conscious enclosure of social spaces evident in China's cities contributes not only to a neoliberal economic rationale but also to the perpetuation of the legitimacy of the state and helps to extend the reach of its order-fostering authority. In the same guise, while new neighborhoods produce a variety of different lifestyles, they also facilitate a graduation of government interventions. As we shall see at different stages in this book, disciplinary and pastoral forms of government combine in different residential areas to produce varying degrees of societal autonomy and state intervention: for example, laid-off workers in old public housing compounds are subject to more intense social control, indoctrination, and policing in exchange for access to residual welfare and assistance, while professionals in gated communities enjoy autonomy from state interference in exchange for more "responsible" behavior and the privatization of governance functions.

Governing Heterogeneous Cities

Modern Chinese cities have a reputation for being large, crowded, jammed, and polluted. After years of controlled urbanization during the 1960s and 1970s during which migration from the countryside was kept in check by draconian limitations on geographic mobility through the household registration system, the economic transformation of the last three decades has boosted a dramatic growth in urbanization. According to the 2010 national census, 49.7 percent of the population (about 665 million people) lives in urban areas, up from 17 percent in 1975.[28] As in most other urban areas of the developing world, urban social groups in the population resulting from this rapid growth are kept apart in China not only by their economic and social conditions, cultural affinities, ethnicity, and race but also by each group's specific relationship with and ability to benefit from state policies. In the Maoist period, being a registered urban resident was enough to provide substantial privileges within a largely egalitarian system, especially in times of scarcity. Today, different social groups share and compete in the Chinese city. Residents include traditionally state-protected urbanites who were employed in state factories and are today suffering from the dismantlement of state-owned industry; public employees and administrators who still enjoy state patronage; professionals and educated youngsters who moved to the cities in search of new employment opportunities offered by foreign and local investments; and those who obtained urban residence for being "assigned" to an urban work unit through the official channels in place until the end of the 1980s. Other groups of "unregistered" outsiders also populate the city—newly arrived urban dwellers, many of them rural migrant workers who might be either temporarily or permanently attracted to the city by a deregulated labor market and by the demand for household services. These groups' chances to achieve social security and a decent level of livelihood depend greatly on their employment situation or on social networks, as they have very limited access to public welfare or to those subsidies granted by large enterprises or public employers to their own workers.

This mix of people, of differing status and relationship to the state, is a recipe for social conflicts regarding space and resources and a nightmare for stability-hungry local institutions. Its emergence has posed new challenges to local and national administrations and has required a substantial overhaul of socialist cities' traditional planning culture and of their practices of urban governance.[29]

The rationale for the new governance structure was, therefore, to balance two apparently contradictory goals: (1) stimulating urban consumption and turning the better-off citizens into "autonomous" and "responsible" consumers while (2) maintaining a direct patronage over the worse-off and those potentially more dangerous to social stability. Under the old socialist system, the population was managed by the work unit to which individuals belonged.[30] Employers provided all essential services, produced economic and political dependency, and were the main point of contact between urban residents and the state.[31] Social stratification and processes of status attainment depended largely on where one worked (a centrally managed state-owned enterprise would guarantee better status than a locally owned collective enterprise), rather than on what job one had (a manager would have enjoyed only marginally better status than a worker within the same enterprise).[32] Also, status, consumption, and access to resources were almost invariably channeled through the work unit, and membership in the work unit community often stretched over more than one generation. The sense of entitlement among privileged urban employees and residents became entrenched through generations of urban workers and remains deeply rooted today, despite the demise of the work-unit system. A person's position within the system when reform started also determined his or her ability to profit from the reform. Employees in high-status enterprises with better housing, for example, obtained more than others from the subsidized sale of work unit–owned and public housing stock that began in the mid-1980s and could also use their housing as collateral to obtain finance in the booming real estate market of the 1990s. Laid-off workers or those in work units with a poor housing stock were unable to profit from the same situation. Stable employment and access to the privatization of public goods such as housing have therefore been important factors contributing to social polarization and to shifts in the strategies of urban governance (see chapter 3).[33]

Urban areas also experienced a rapid and substantial privatization of residential spaces. Large "new cities" for several hundred thousand people now house a new generation of homeowners that today amounts to a large percentage of the resident urban population, whose property dream has often been funded by public subsidies and, increasingly, bank mortgages. The privatization of housing has produced a variety of different residential settings with regard to housing quality, management forms, and services as well as lifestyles. Chinese urban residential areas today include commercial developments alongside publicly subsidized residential communities, employer-subsidized areas, and public housing. Based on their management forms, communities can experience more (or less) self-organization, more (or less) social control, and more (or less) exposure to political mobilization. Thanks to this variety and the interaction of public and private actors, Chinese cities also foster a great variety of lifestyles that are often embedded in different residential settings: from the remaining work unit–built compounds where residents share the same history of employment and unemployment, to middle-class areas offering a high standard of services and facilitating consumption, to villa compounds for the elites producing exclusive and atomized existences. Besides their ability to express physical separation of classes or status groups, these spaces also often give visibility to the difference in "quality" between different groups.[34]

While typologies of residential settings could contribute to a simplification of a new urban landscape of this kind, they would inevitably have limited explanatory power.[35] My interest here is to highlight that (1) there is a social hierarchy among communities that is concretized by spatial arrangements and that is rationally supported by local governments, and (2) this hierarchy leads to different governmental outcomes. To do so, I will now focus on two largely different types of space that reveal how different urban residents' experiences of government can be.

These two types of physical and social space (the struggling working class neighborhood and the private gated community), while differing substantially in quality, management style, and forms of socialization, share two characteristics: both are enclosed within walls and behind gates, and both require exclusive membership, in the form either of administrative registration or property rights or both. They are enclosed territorial and administrative units, which, despite the privatization of urban life, facilitate the classification and control of the population and are used to this end by local administrations. Because of the pervasive involvement of public actors in controlling the form and organization of residential spaces, where one lives determines the type of governance one experiences, and ultimately, affects one's level of autonomy from or dependency on the state.

Struggling Working-Class Neighborhoods: Managing Industrial Decline

Chinese cities today generally evoke an image of rapid economic growth, bustling construction, and rampant consumerism. This impressionistic portrayal of urban life in China often eclipses the impact of the progressive collapse of the state-owned industrial system in the second half of the 1990s, which has left many traditionally state-sponsored urbanites struggling with declining life chances.[36] Some urban administrations were faced not only with previously unknown rates of unemployment and the related risks of social instability, but also with the disappearance of the work unit, the institution that had administered the population, overseen welfare provision, and governed social control for more than three decades.[37] Urban governments were thus forced to shift the locus of grassroots governance away from the workplace to the residential area, where families of what remained of the worker elites generally maintained their residence. This required beefing up the languishing remains of the traditional "resident committees" (jumin weiyuanhui).[38] When I asked residents about these socialist agents of political mobilization, I often heard that the cadres of the old neighborhood committees were nothing but "old ladies with a red armband." These old ladies often served mainly as neighborhood watchdogs and political organizers, and their effectiveness in managing the community depended largely on their individual ability and their connections with higher-level officials. Thus, to respond to the changing residential situation, the privatization of housing, and the unemployment crisis, public funds starting in 1999 were pumped by municipal administrations into grassroots governance. New "community committees" (shequ weiyuanhui, as they were called in some cities), generally with one elected director and two vice directors, were established to oversee residential areas in every city.[39] In Shenyang, these territorial units administer between 1,500 and

6,000 families and employ between six and twenty people (almost all of them women). The number of employees depends less on the population than on the type of community and the number of resident families in dire social or economic situations. Inside the compound of a major tertiary institution in Beijing, for example, where almost all the academic staff have relocated to private, purpose-built housing complexes, the committee, with only six members, is relegated to a cramped room between the bookshop and a photocopy stall. In Shenyang's poorer neighborhoods, I often found that even small communities housing unemployed state workers typically had as many as twenty employees.

Directors and vice directors are generally elected every three years. The election is not very competitive, and candidates are preemptively examined at the district level (*qu*) and approved by the "street" level of government (the *jiedao banshichu*, or street office) before facing the residents' ballot.[40] Nonetheless, the elections provide the residents with some sense of "ownership," and I found that, under the daily supervision of their residents/customers, elected directors generally enjoy a good reputation. The low income and hard work of these cadres often earn them the respect of local residents and Party members. In a resource-starved environment, such public figures also become important marketing tools for communities and channels in lobbying the municipal or provincial authorities for more investment or funding for their own activities.[41]

Salaries for community employees (categorized in many cities as "subsidies"—*butie*—to ensure that they are not confused with the guaranteed "salaries" of civil servants) vary substantially from city to city. Despite a steep increase, in Shenyang the monthly salary of a director was still only 1,500 yuan (US$222) in January 2010, while vice directors are paid 1,400 yuan (US$207) and employees 1,300 yuan (US$192).[42] This is comparable to the average monthly income in the city but is substantially lower than the salaries received by employees in public administration. In Beijing, where professionalization and the adoption of computer technologies for community services were accelerated in the run-up to the Olympics, in 2009 the average annual income of a community worker was 34,000 yuan (US$4,964), or 2,833 yuan (US$413) per month.[43]

As well as the regular employees, these structures also give work to a number of "volunteers" (*gongyixing gangwei*), who are generally unemployed persons "working for the dole" in exchange for the subsidies funded by the municipal labor bureau. It is not uncommon to find that they out-number regular community employees. They are utilized in such services as security, assistance to the elderly, street cleaning, and other casual duties. Communities in such areas are therefore a form of direct intervention in the social issues that affect these areas of industrial decline, as they are at the same time an institution to manage the social crisis and a source of marginal but greatly needed employment opportunities.

Beyond organizing social activities, arranging Communist Party festivals, and promoting cultural, physical, and educational activities in the neighborhood, *shequs* have taken over most of the administrative functions previously performed by either the work units or the higher levels of urban government. These include health and security, household registration, the distribution of unemployment subsidies, minimum-income subsidies, retraining and reemployment services, and family planning, as well as the monitoring of "dangerous elements" such as falungong practitioners.[44] Every member of the committee is assigned the supervision of a variable number of families (in Shenyang, generally around two hundred), and the first task at the beginning of each workday is a field visit to their assigned area within the community to check for developments or new problems. The "Minimum Living Standard" scheme (*zuidi shenghuo baozhang*, or *dibao*) is paid for by both local and central funds (the share of central funding in Liaoning grew to over 38 percent in 2003 at the height of the crisis) and is distributed and monitored through the communities.[45] Families under the threshold (*dibao xian*, set by the Ministry of Civil Affairs for the different localities) are entitled to a small subsidy to help them attain the minimum level and to exemptions from utility, education, rent, and health care fees where applicable. In 2006, 22.4 million people were entitled to the urban *dibao* nationwide, with almost 80 percent of these classified as unemployed.[46] In 2010, *dibao* recipients in the cities had increased only slightly to 23.5 million, while rural recipients had climbed to over double that figure (52.1 million), revealing increased attention on rural poverty. Liaoning urban residents entitled to such support in 2010 received 190 yuan, or US$28, less than half the average amount distributed to other areas like Beijing.[47]

Despite a startling array of functions, for which the communities receive funding from the relevant municipal departments or are supported by the local police office, the committee is not a level of "government" (*zhengfu*) but one of "administration" (*guanli*), although salaries and activities (propaganda, social initiatives, or campaigns) are generally funded by the municipal Civil Affairs Bureau (*minzhengju*). Regardless of how much official discourses emphasize the self-administration (*ziwo guanli*) nature of these institutions (that is, the responsibility and rights of residents in selecting officials and governing their communities), in my interviews with residents in Shenyang I often found that the committees are indeed perceived as government (*zhengfu*) agencies and elected cadres as government officials.[48] Whenever I tried to explain the difference between government and self-administration to the residents, I obtained responses such as: "The community [office] does much more than the government, so I think it is the government," or "Of course they are the government, they do anything the government does," or "If the community isn't the government, then who is?" For those who remain dependent on state support (the unemployed, low-income families, the disabled) these cadres remain, as the work unit used to be, the most likely point of contact with the state and its policies. Visits to the higher-level "street office"—generally just a couple of blocks away and also often featuring storefront offices—have become almost unnecessary, unless conflicts emerge.

A double line of authority (Communist Party and civil administration) exists formally within the community as in all other Chinese institutions, although in most places the community directors often double as the secretary of the local Party office. Where this is not the case, the director also becomes the deputy secretary, and the secretary also becomes the deputy director. Although it remains important for directors to be Party members, not even the majority of community employees in Shenyang have joined the Party. Generally, communities do not seem to be an efficient recruitment tool for the Party, as average membership within even the poorest communities did not reach 5 percent of the resident population.

Volunteers helping to run community affairs or taking up positions in the different subcommittees are elderly, have had a past as cadres, and have a higher-than-average education.[49] They are generally respected as leaders for their reputation and knowledge of the system, contribute generously in both time and money to social activities and community education (as in the *shequ daxue*, or "community universities," for the elderly), and play an important role in crucial moments of communal life such as major political festivals or the rituals of community election day. When asked to indicate the person in the community whom they consider to be "of the highest *suzhi*," residents and cadres alike generally thought of these sorts of people, who are active, relatively educated and longtime members of the Communist Party.

In Shenyang, where the restructuring of the industrial system has produced a generation of laid-off workers, the need for localized and careful management has been felt more in the residential districts where this disenfranchised working class is living than in booming cities like Beijing.[50] Administrative areas here have been consolidated and merged (some now include up to ten micro-districts, *xiaoqu*) but have remained relatively small compared to Beijing. To serve the needs of poor residents better, the municipal Civil Affairs Bureau is making an effort to expand the size and visibility of the community offices, to the point that regulations now require every community to have at least 400 square meters of public offices. Their advancement toward a "harmonious community" (*hexie shequ*) is constantly monitored, and communities are required to reach predefined standards and targets in such categories as organization, service provision, and Party-building. Depending on their ability to attract funding from higher levels of government, communities feature activity rooms, sporting facilities, public libraries, and conference rooms. In one particularly well-funded community, the activity area and the offices occupied over 2,000 square meters. Another element of state visibility in these communities is the increasing use of CCTV security systems. Staffed 24/7 by guards on "voluntary" posts, these very expensive and sophisticated systems, installed with funds from the Civil Affairs Bureau, monitor the street intersections within the walls of the compound, even in dilapidated areas where there is not much of value to steal. The whole strategy works more as a deterrent (in one community, footage of the arrest of a bicycle thief was the only recorded criminal activity over two years), but residents are generally satisfied that it improves the feeling of security. In particular, this type of control seems to establish a clearer boundary between the safe and protected territory and population of the community and the unregulated open spaces of the city.

The spaces inside poor communities also provide an environment for the unemployed to start small trading or service activities that are shielded from the competition of the migrant stall-owners outside the community. To cope with a deteriorating economic situation, communities often support a *yuanli jingji* (courtyard economy) to take advantage of the tax exemption that residents enjoy for family-run economic activities within the gates of the community, including courtyard kitchens, guarded bicycle parking, small repair shops, or fruit stalls.

This exemption from taxes and more flexible enforcement of regulations in the communities often also turns into opportunities for informal businesses. In one Shenyang community close to the long-distance coach station, residents have reorganized their dwellings to offer budget accommodation to recently arrived migrants or students. These activities, generally unregistered, mostly ignore safety and hygiene regulations but are largely tolerated by both the community officials and the police.

In such struggling communities, committees perform a number of social, policing, economic, and political functions and contribute to recreating community solidarities and marginal economic opportunities, which had disappeared for many with the collapse of almost all of the large factories. Their pastoral government of the population is largely justified by the traditional socialist discourse of solidarity, state intervention, and welfare entitlements and, in these residual residential areas, is specifically aimed at the weakest groups in society.

Gated Communities: Serving Middle-Class Desires

While neighborhoods that are perceived as potentially troublesome attract significant public resources and lead to the perception of more government and more visible local authorities, residential areas rich in private resources tend to succeed in escaping intrusive government interference. The *shequ* committees' work almost entirely ignores wealthier and privately managed compounds within their jurisdiction. As a director said to me dismissively, "They don't need us. They pay management companies to take care of their problems." In cities like Beijing, with a large home-owning class living in gated communities, the amount of territory that the state and its traditional agents are unable (and, arguably, unwilling) to monitor actively has grown considerably in recent years.

In the last decade, large numbers of urban residents who could afford to purchase an apartment have moved from a work-unit district to a new gated compound. Many areas of the city have changed shape, and a large number of new residential blocks have been built. This transformation has largely transferred traditional functions of urban governance to private "agents." Riding the ongoing housing boom, a high percentage of the urban population has purchased apartments, and many of them depend more on private providers than on the state for their daily services. Many have only sporadic and insignificant contacts with neighborhood officials and often do not even know what or where the "committee" is. Community committees set up by the government, of the type described earlier, do exist—at least on paper—in all areas, rich or poor, newly built or old, but wherever a management company runs the show, the community officials have difficulty even entering the compound, let alone performing the same pastoral work as in the poorer communities. Here, gated spaces have therefore also produced the privatization of some governance functions (security, hygiene, education, sometimes even family planning).

The practices of such private governance resonate with the state's discourse of community self-government. Managers often present the aims of their service as a tool to foster responsible and harmonious coexistence, while homeowners reproduce to their advantage the rhetoric of consumer rights and ethical behavior that now dominates media reporting on community life.

These spaces are regulated privately. State regulations on the management of private estates require that management companies sign a contract with a democratically elected "homeowner committee." In different compounds these committees act more or less autonomously, depending on the situation. In Beijing, for example, the number of disputes between homeowners and managers has been very high in recent years; it is common for homeowner committees to act openly and autonomously to protect owner rights and, with other spontaneous and more radical associations, engage in protracted conflicts with the developer or the management company. Where disputes are not very common, though, spontaneous organization is less likely, and management companies generally succeed in neutralizing owner committees by controlling their formation, election, and composition and by funding their activities.

In all cases, however, the gated environment leads to a privatization of governance functions. In some residential compounds, this is taken to an extreme. ZX, a medium-sized Chengdu developer, built and marketed three different compounds specifically targeted at upper-income, middle-income, and lower-middle-income customers. Like those of many other elite developers, ZX homes are sold with a "lifestyle" attached. ZX brands its estates as entirely different living experiences, where not only do owners become part of a specifically designed and organized quasi–self-sufficient environment but the management company also takes an active role in facilitating social interactions, cultural and social activities, and security. The brand "ZX lifestyle" (*shenghuo fangshi*) includes all aspects of social life and, at the time of my research, the company was in the process of applying for a "lifestyle trademark." With a strategy reminiscent of a consumption-oriented version of the socialist grassroots mobilization, each resident is encouraged to join activity groups, created based on surveys of residents' interests (a chess group, a soccer group, dance, music, art, travel, the environment, and so on). The management company claims proudly that owners are kept busy and always have something to choose from. ZX calls its management philosophy *shede* (loosely, "giving back" to the community) and prizes the idea that "if society is like a big family, our company is only a member of that family." (I was struck by the similarity of this to a government slogan often associated with community work: *shequ shi wo de jia*, or "the community is my family.") In this case, the management company has entirely replaced the official community committee as the organizer of social activities. One of the principal goals of this form of management remains, to be sure, the manipulation and control of the consumption of goods and services by directing residents' consumer choices toward specific forms of consumption and specific providers. For example, among the marketing strategies of the ZX lifestyle is free membership in a car-owner club, which grants ZX residents significant discounts and financial assistance for the purchase of brand-new imported cars from a car dealer that, unsurprisingly, is owned by ZX. In the same way, family vacations and classes for children and adults are marketed through the "ZX lifestyle office" and redirected to friendly providers, turning ZX's owners into quite unconscious members of a comprehensive consumption scheme offered to them as a consequence of their new status as homeowners.

This style of management, which is replicated to different degrees in many different neighborhoods, prevents traditional government organizations from intervening in the shaping of lifestyles and community affairs and makes policies favoring social integration harder to implement, if not outright irrelevant.

In some of Shenyang's gated compounds, the collaboration between private and public actors has taken the shape of a merger between management companies and government-run community committees. The director of a management company is often also elected as the director of the community committee, and the two organizations share facilities, funding, and personnel. One such multifunctional director explained it to me as follows:

> We call it the "three-in-one" system: management company, developer, and community, all under the supervision of the Party. . . . We do not even need a homeowner committee. The homeowner committee's function is to oversee the management company, but if the management company and the community were merged, the controller and the controlled would be also the same. The efficiency of the oversight is not very clear; it is not convincing. For this reason, we do have to win the approval and support of the homeowners.

To increase this sense of devolution of powers to privately run gated communities, the State Council passed on September 1, 2003 the national "Regulations on Property Management" (*Wuye guangli tiaoli*) making it possible for the state-sponsored community committees to delegate some traditional government functions to private managers. In practice, this generally takes the form of a contract spelling out the responsibilities of the management companies. Apart from direct management, maintenance, service delivery, and security functions, managers' responsibilities include reporting on and implementing family planning policies. However, cases of *chaosheng*, or unplanned birth, are said to be common inside gated communities, because the residential areas are "sealed off" and private operators often have little knowledge of the policies. A Xinhua report in 2003 blew the whistle on gated residential areas becoming "safe havens of illegal births" (*chaosheng bifeng gang*) and denounced the phenomenon of "unplanned birth guerrillas" (*chaosheng youji*) or resistance to the one-child policy, despite the fines imposed on births outside the plan.[51] Officials in charge of the family planning campaign are often not allowed in and must rely on the liaison person at the management company. Because family planning is not a priority for the private operators, the person in charge of it is likely to be unskilled (one company admitted that their family planning manager was an unemployed ex-driver) and not very motivated.

The difficulty in implementing family planning on private, gated ground is an indication of the effect governance reform can have in spaces that are enclosed and governed privately as well as of the state's willingness to govern such areas through reliable agents, rather than directly. The ability of traditional organizations to penetrate and influence lifestyles is drastically reduced within the spaces of the proprietary community, while private organizations such as the management companies are increasingly determining consumption patterns and rules of cohabitation that are, nonetheless, based on the dominant hegemonic discourses of the state.

The result is not a dilution of the power of the state but rather the ubiquitous reproduction of its rhetoric through unexpected agents. Rather than simply allowing private agents to run certain kinds of spaces, however, as would be expected in a purely neoliberal arrangement, the government maintains a regulatory influence through the control and supervision over the operation of such agents, requiring specifically that functions of government are performed according to the agenda of the state and requesting coordination between private and public bodies. The emergence of privately governed spaces is largely the result of the convergence of the interests of local governments and real estate developers: With the dominant policy focus of social stability now central to local decisions, local officials see a conservative and value-producing middle class as preferable to hardworking but troublemaking migrants or disenfranchised workers. Developers seek to maximize their returns by reaping long-term profits from managing the homeowners' existence. To do so, they are eager to replicate functions that are the realm of the political for the Chinese government. They also willingly buy into the moral discourses promoted by the government about ethics, quality, and moral probity. One of the most successful and profitable private developers in China, for example, describes its business as "building a boundless life" based on "humanism" where "morality and ethics are more important than commercial profit." The company claims to "persist in its moral value principles and refuse the temptation of profits" and highlights in its creative new neighborhoods the principle of "civility" (*wenming*).[52]

Assistance and Autonomy: Communities
and the Legitimization of Dominant Discourses

As mentioned earlier, these two forms of enclosed neighborhoods (the traditional public housing enclave governed by a community committee and the gated community organized by a management company) are certainly not the only ones that can be found in a Chinese city. I have concentrated on these examples because they are also the places popularly associated with the two most contentious and rebellious social groups in late socialist urban China: disenfranchised and unemployed workers, and the educated, socially active new rich keenly intent on expanding their claim on civil rights, especially of expression.

The laissez-faire practices and highly moral discourses that permeate the governance of the middle-class communities serve the desire for quality of life and bounded autonomy that drove these affluent professionals to buy apartments in these neighborhoods. On the other hand, the economic dependence and socialist moral economy that drives the work of community cadres among the struggling unemployed produce different frames of reference inside poorer communities. Both groups are vocal about their own condition, while at the same time express support for the principles that drive the social, spatial, and political engineering explicit in the community-building project.

Shenyang's middle-aged unemployed workers largely see their communities as the only visible incarnation of the state and, as such, the only remaining institution protecting their entitlements to welfare as former public employees. Orphans of their work unit, they are likely to have lost their extended social networks as well. After experiencing a "series of opportunity-depriving events" in the course of their life (from missing out on education and occupational opportunities during the Cultural Revolution to becoming the sacrificial lambs in the restructuring of industrial enterprises in the 1990s), the current generation of 40- to 50-year-olds sees public assistance as the only remaining vestige of lives spent as "masters" (*zhurenweng*) of the socialist economy.[53] While Shenyang is the source of a large flow of young out-migrants, I noticed among the unemployed of this generation interviewed in Shenyang a remarkable resistance to "leaving" the community and moving to a different city or even to a different part of town. Residence in the community allows families to maintain at least a marginal form of membership "in the system" and to claim the residual support that comes with the rhetoric of "saving the working class." Also, when material conditions are very harsh, the availability of housing (often sold by the former work unit at extremely discounted prices) is the single best reason to remain in the community. In cities with weak labor markets and low salaries, children often remain dependent on their parents for longer periods and thus stay in the small family apartment, eating up resources rather than contributing to the household's economy.

That many housing compounds today are not a reflection of the same "community" of co-workers with whom these people used to share grievances also makes residential areas less likely to become arenas of collective, class-based protest. Collective grievances are much more common in factories than in communities. The relationship between the state and the unemployed at the level of the community seems to be based on the mutual acceptance of the rhetoric of assistance. Off the job, former state employees often still regard the state as a provider. As one interviewee who has been on subsidies for a while said,

> What job do I want? I would be happy with one that pays 800 to 900 yuan a month [US$125], but that is about the same my family makes in subsidies. Now it's impossible anyway. Nobody wants someone like me with only a basic education. Enterprises now want you only for a few months, no security, and they don't pay your health insurance. So I am better off staying at home. My parents were small cadres and have pensions, so they can help us, and my daughter is going to school. When she is finished she will get a job and help her family.

Another interviewee, age 38, who gets a 350-yuan-a-month (US$50) unemployment subsidy to work as a security guard, said, "I'm not really looking for anything else. This is enough to survive on, and the situation in the labor market is not good—I wouldn't be able to make more money. This is clean and secure, and the state will take care of me if something happens."

This is largely also a consequence of the depression that often occurs in the face of a collective destiny. As I was constantly reminded during interviews, unemployment has affected almost every Shenyang family I have been in touch with, across a number of educational, professional, and status groups. For those who have not found alternatives, dependence on community welfare is felt more as a right than as a choice.

This attitude is echoed in the words of cadres at different levels in the city. One municipal official said, "These people have been working for the state and the revolution all their lives, and we have a duty to support them, whatever the cost." Another took me to a small exhibition of old photos in an old workers' neighborhood, and the narrative of *chiku* (eating bitterness) was a constant presence. He said, "The workers built the city, but look at how they used to live, and what the district looks like today." The role of the state is constantly presented as being to give them back their dignity and to produce a better future (and better neighborhoods) for them.

In the first years of this century, the government made efforts to favor the reemployment of laid-off workers (with tax breaks for companies who hire them, and subsidization of the fixed costs of hiring), but in the absence of economic growth the efforts did not seem to be paying off. A survey among "minimum income support" recipients in Liaoning province in 2004 revealed that only 30 percent of the recipients made use of community-based reemployment services, while the overall satisfaction with the minimum income subsidy scheme reached 70 percent, a sign that the community was perceived more as a provider of subsidies than as an actor in the local labor market.[54] In short, the visibility of community governance, the preservation of a roof, subsidies, and a highly propagandized but inefficient reemployment system fits the image of these workers' expectations, and their dependence keeps them docile, despite the obvious deterioration of their living conditions.

In the view of local cadres, the community's role is also to contain discontent through direct engagement and continuous monitoring of social conditions. The state's intervention through the community committee is visible but at best palliative, and there is a widespread perception of a competitive labor environment in which laid-off workers are at a disadvantage. This helps to perpetuate dependency and produce loyalty to the provider-state, even though living conditions have fallen off in a way that seems likely to affect two or three generations. It also turns the problem into an endemic but slow-burning issue, rather than an explosive one, and that is useful for the Chinese state.

At the other end of the spectrum, among homeowners in middle-class areas, I found a different way of producing loyalty, based as well on a convergence of state discourses and individual expectations that limits the potential for conflicts to leap beyond the walls of the community. Groups of angry homeowners often justify their collective actions against greedy developers, management companies, and even local officials by their collective desire to contribute to building the nation and strengthening China. This claim finds support in the dominant rhetoric of the middle class being a "high-*suzhi*" and responsible vanguard of modernization and nation building (which I will further discuss in chapter 5). Greedy developers, inefficient management companies, and even uncooperative neighbors became the embodiment of a drag on China's modernization, whereas "harmonious communities" acting collectively remained a fundamental force in the advancement of the nation.

Lisa Hoffman has written about the "patriotic" attitudes of young professionals in Dalian, who appropriate public discourses on responsibility toward the nation in the definition of their new professional subjectivity.[55] During interviews and in community materials, I found a similar attitude among community organizers and homeowners. Socialization in an ethical community is often described as "the best school for building citizens," "the cornerstone of society," or "the foundation on which the nation is built." The narratives justifying actions against greedy managers or developers therefore puts communities on the side of the government's wish for a stable and "harmonious" society. "There are over 100,000 communities in the country," declared a document from a community organizer in Beijing. "If each community succeeded in training its residents to be reliable citizens, consulting each other and participating [in community life], then what would China become if not a harmonious society envied by all?" The emergence of a private discourse of reliable, responsible, self-disciplined, "high-*suzhi*" citizens justifying their grievances through the need to improve the nation and contribute to its advancement and modernization envisages the construction of a new form of subject, disciplined and in tune with the goal of the "community" project, that is, the transition to a form of government that relies on the responsibility of private stakeholders in administering the management of society.

Rather than embodying a societal autonomy that represents a challenge to the authority of the state, new middle-class neighborhoods often project the image of virtuous organizations that will contribute to social stability and nation building, a step forward in the civilization of urban China. They become tools for reinforcing the state rather than for "limiting the state" in the way that liberalism expects autonomous social forces to work.

By arguing in favor of morality, selflessness, and mutual responsibility, one Homeowner Committee chair in Beijing turned his community into a model of cooperation among owners, managers, and local authorities in stark contrast to other surrounding, conflict-ridden neighborhoods. The idea of a community "where 'good people' are bred, self-disciplined, idealistic, understanding, cooperative and tolerant" was an instant hit. I met him for the first time in 2003 when he had not yet assumed his office. When I met him again a year later, we spent an afternoon watching the tapes of all the TV programs he had been invited to. His responsible communitarianism won him recognition from the local and central authorities, and he became an adviser to many newly built compounds struggling with the same types of problems. In my meetings with him and in one of his numerous interviews, he argued that the conflicts in communities are a "question of mentality": "Chinese people became rich too fast, but their spirit is still trapped in simple houses and messy courtyards."

Outlining his grand project for turning neighborhoods into "ideal kingdoms" (*lixiang guo*), he described self-governing communities almost as the culmination of an evolutionary civilization path:

There are three types of human groups:

First, there are the motley crowds: these get together only to protect the petty profits they see in front of their noses. Their moral standards are very low; they have no values, and they can't see their interests in the general context. They are scattered like birds and beasts.

Then there are the subjugated groups: these people, for the sake of their survival, are for historical or practical reasons subordinated to some kind of authority and accept the will of that authority as a condition of their existence.

Finally, there are the "communities of aspiration" [*yiyuan de gongtongti*]: in these communities people have common expectations; everyone expects that collective interests will be safeguarded, that the private interests of some will not hinder the interests of all, that in order to protect some, others will not be bullied and mistreated, that their leaders will not abuse their power . . . and that everyone will protect the fundamental rule of this community: that everyone—individuals and organizations alike—accepts the authority of common regulations and the highest values of law and justice. Our neighborhood is such a community![56]

While autonomy is a central issue for community organizers, its emphasis on social order means that it is not an antagonistic value, producing an alternative worldview. Rather, it is based on the principles of responsibility, order, self-restraint, lawfulness, and morality explicit in the government's idea of self-governing communities.

Members of these communities seem to have developed a sense of their entitlement not only to a higher standard of living that sets them apart from other citizens but also to a driving role in the nation-building process. For a variety of reasons and with a focus on civilized socialization and daily life, residents often appear as concerned as their government with the need to improve the population's *suzhi*. The following, from the head of an Owner Committee, is an example of how the rhetoric of the strong country and autonomy can find common ground in private discourse about community ethos:

> The problem of Chinese people not being aware of or disregarding cultural rules will not be overcome in the "big issues." Their education will instead be nurtured in the small matters of daily life. . . . We have to understand that managing our community according to the law and creating good citizens within our community are the most basic foundations for the stability of our country and are the first steps towards the renaissance of the Chinese nation. . . . If the family and the communities can't produce good citizens, what should the state rely on to create a good society, a good country? . . . The education of the people has to start from the family and the community, especially the community. Communities are a civilized environment, the place where family meets society. They are the cornerstones of a civilized society.[57]

The Logic of Social Clustering

The privatization of residential spaces has facilitated segregation and has not reduced the ability of the state to classify the population and to influence social hierarchies. In China's urban life, the place of residence, the different discourses associated with it, and its meaningful spatial separation are increasingly becoming the concrete expression of distinctions, not only between lifestyles, status, and consumption habits but also between styles and forms of government.

Chinese urban communities are traditionally spaces of intense socialization and intense government activity. New tools and practices are now in place for governing social order, but these practices are still inspired and justified by the two discourses traditionally behind the CCP's legitimization: the rhetoric of "serving the people" and that of "strengthening the country and the nation." Clustering can therefore only be a successful governing practice if such rhetorical appeals to state intervention are not only considered as legitimate but are also promoted among the different social clusters as a legitimization of their collective and individual claims. These two discursive strategies, however, appeal differently to different people; in the cities, governance practices as much as space are being tailored to address the specific needs of a stratified society and to respond to the expectations created among different social groups by China's economic reform.

The Chinese Communist Party has adapted its language and narrative repertoire to the new subjects that it is helping to create (such as the middle class, the unemployed who are still in the system, and other clusters not discussed here) by conflating the ethic of self-government with that of socialist assistance, both in the communities and in society at large. The language of "class struggle" has been replaced by an emphasis on "harmony" (hexie), but the entitlements of some groups to access public support are constantly upheld. Social conflicts are no longer the engine of a revolution; they are a threat to it.

In the cities, tailor-made governance is largely a spatial, locality-based process in which the local state uses its control of the territory to achieve a classification of the population and reshape governing practices accordingly. By defining status and creating segregation, bounded urban residential spaces favor the implementation and delivery of these forms of governance.

In this context, China's long-term processes of privatization and reform have, in fact, worked to reinforce, rather than reduce, the legitimacy of the authoritarian rulers, as the state and its policies are perceived by the weakest groups as the last line of defense against the deregulation of the market and by the middle classes as the guarantors of newly acquired "rights."

Although only one piece in the puzzle of how China is governed, these multiple, stratified interactions between state and society in the communities reveal how, while adapting its strategies, this regime success-fully maintains the ability to shape the territory and govern its people. In some cases, this still happens by expanding and mobilizing its bureaucracy to provide means of social stabilization; in others, by devolving to reliable stakeholders and private agents the task and responsibility of preserving social stability.

The aim of this strategy is not the elimination of social conflicts (in favor of a harmonious future) but rather their containment. This containment is not only the outcome of repressive techniques; rather, it works in three interconnected ways. First, local officials, mass organizations, or manage-ment companies are made directly or indirectly responsible for the places they manage, and the territory is often clearly marked and locally adminis-tered. Pressure on these agents to achieve "harmony" comes not only from the local state but also from the resident stakeholders. Second, claims by different groups in society, while catalyzed by the geographic proximity of the community, are prevented from interacting and spilling out of the gates to produce class-based action or systemic forms of protests. Finally, while in some cases the sense of entitlement to state support, often mobilized by the unemployed, contributes to framing personal identities as dependent on or supplicant to the state, in other cases the sense of involvement of middle-class high-*suzhi* citizens in the project of national strengthening justifies them in advocating rights protection for themselves and order for the nation. This is in line with the public discourse about civilization and harmony, which implies the support and patronage of the weaker social groups and the adding of responsibilities to the wealthier.

The idea and the language of "community" and "self-governing," else-where associated with the potential to produce social and political change from below, have been used by the Chinese regime to propagate new forms of loyalty to its rule. These are sometimes framed using the lingo of socialist solidarity and, when necessary, with the language of autonomy, self gov ernment, and "quality." Both appeal not only to very concrete aspirations and necessities, but also to deeply seated perceptions of the state held by different social groups. Social stability remains the principal objective, one that can, however, no longer be achieved only through the imposition of state-designed norms; it requires the agency of formally autonomous and private agents and the making of new citizens.

2

Micro-Governing the Urban Crisis

What motivates me? If you want me to put it in nice words: I haven't yet
reached my retirement age, so . . . if they ask me to make a contribution,
I make a contribution. In not-so-nice words: I wouldn't be working if it
wasn't for the money.

These were the words of a community worker in Tiexi, a Shenyang district in which what remains of a once-mighty working class have, for the
last two decades, been micromanaged at the level of the residential communities through a huge network of poorly remunerated cadres (mostly
former workers themselves) for whom community work is not a glorious
revolutionary task but another way of accessing much-needed state subsidies or receiving social security for their family.

In discussion of the changes in Chinese cities, new governance strategies
are sometimes linked to the progressive disengagement of the state and
the Party from the pervasive practices of government that characterized
traditional socialist institutions. With the demise of employment-based
administration in the urban centers and with the substantial overhaul of
cities' economic function away from industry and toward services, real estate, and tertiary activities, conventional wisdom suggests a more distant
role for the state. Governing in this new situation requires bending to the
demands of the global market, a process that is informed by historically

produced "regimes of truth," technologies of control and computation, an efficient and professional bureaucracy, and citizens who adhere to the need for self-regulation and self-governing.[1] The question is whether the market and its globally reproduced discourses are the only source of China's contemporary "regimes of truth." I see a need to investigate some potential contradictions in this assumption: first, governing is an exercise that needs to take into consideration the conditions of the governed and the priorities of the locality. At times, these conditions suggest the state's need for a proactive role and a level of visibility that goes beyond the regulatory role of the state in a neoliberal order. Second, the forms of governing and the discursive regimes justifying them can vary for different social groups. While some citizens experience a more and others a less visible state, both continue to be intensely governed. Third, as already mentioned, the apparent retreat of the state and the involvement of numerous other actors do not result in less governing but rather in governing by other means. My research in Tiexi, however, reveals that where and when the state fears a systemic loss of control (as, typically, in the northeast of the country, which has been hit the hardest by economic restructuring in the last two decades), the state's governing strategy shows a remarkable continuity of practices and discourses. Here, visibility, rather than invisibility, remains crucial to the governing strategy. The experiences of these communities reveal the ways in which multiple and at times contradictory "regimes of truth" exist and are largely elaborated in daily interactions and practices, in bureaucratic interactions, and in locally embedded narratives, rather than being simple translations of the global logic of the market.

Increasingly, the territorial micromanagement of social problems requires the involvement of an array of people whose motivation, preparation, willingness, and ability to reproduce the messages of the state is limited at best. Mun Young Cho has already observed that community officials have a double identity as citizens and as cadres, pointing out that their very existence defeats the "distinction between 'the state' and 'the poor.'"[2] Their miserable economic circumstances make disgruntled ex-workers, such as the one quoted at the beginning of this chapter, easily coopted into a system of community cadres that is both a network of social control and a safety net for some of the "weaker groups" (*ruoshi qunti*), persuading them to perform a public service in exchange for subsistence salaries. Community cadres and employees stand at the crucial crossing between assistance and social control, and in many cases they are both the distributors and the recipients of public assistance, left to embody the voice of the state and to be, at the same time, the victims of its contradictory rationalities. They, too, *are* the state and contribute to governing the city. They thus occupy the shared moral space between the depression, nostalgia, and disenchantment of a betrayed generation of laid-off employees and the harmonious and optimistic messages that the government is promoting.

This chapter narrates a discursive and practical continuity in the forms of government experienced by weaker social groups in society. Despite the emergence of a dominant logic of the market and open attempts to create subjectivities that fit the bill of modern, flexible, self-responsible, and consuming citizens, the socialist state has not completely abandoned the forms of pastoral rule that characterized it in the years after 1949. The attention devoted in recent years to the similarities between the Chinese strategy for governing its market transition and the neoliberal ideals of self-responsibilization, self-discipline, and calculability has often blinded us to the fact that such strategies also existed in the high socialist period and earlier. They now stem from an ideology that, while compatible with the demands of the market, also allows for a reproduction of the state and of its interests.

By "micro-government," I refer to traditional practices aiming at containing the risk of social and political instability through administrative means or social control. This management of social problems through a generation of local cadres deeply embedded in Shenyang's history of industrialization and deindustrialization is therefore one of the ways in which loyalties to the system are reproduced among social groups that also include the losers of the reform process. While targeting social order, as discussed in the introduction, does not make a neoliberal order impossible, the continuity of such practices suggests that in describing this order as neoliberal, we might be missing part of the point.

Indeed, the quotidian and pervasive activities of governing used by China's police state are replaced by norm-based regulations, segmentation, dominant discourses of responsibility, and stratification that make subjects more suited to the different roles they play in the economy.[3] Governing happens increasingly through forms of regulation different from formal institutions based on a rationality of government that relies on the ruler's ability to inform and reproduce organic behaviors and opinions.

Here I shall argue, however, that any governing practice is also the result of very local processes of elaboration and contestation. The problem I see with the "governing from a distance" metaphor applied to China is that, while it usefully illuminates the relationship between the goals of governing and the need to regulate the behavior of the subjects, it assumes that the elaboration of governing practices takes place "elsewhere." The practices that result from any rationality of government, however, are also a product of the material conditions in specific communities, of the contestations and resilience of local interests, and of the individual elaboration of one's position in society.

In Shenyang's poor communities, the main goals of the practices of governmental intervention are (1) a formal involvement of the stakeholders (or, as the Chinese official jargon calls it, "self-government," *zizhi*) that leads to community cadres being both the provider and the recipients of assistance; (2) the preemptive management of social risk (more monitoring and auditing than ex post policing); and (3) the reproduction of chronic economic dependence on state support.

The Poorer the Place, the More Numerous the Cadres

In this chapter I focus on the local conditions in which such a strategy develops. Importantly, the legitimacy of such practices in Tiexi's urban communities is also framed by established and shared local frames on which all parts seem willing to agree: the acknowledgement that the traditional working class is "suffering," the rhetoric of state responsibility toward the "weaker social groups," and the need to raise the "quality of the population," but also a diffused consensus on the paramount importance of order and social stability.

Different from the hands-off government of middle-class private areas, in Tiexi, where laid-off workers make up the majority of the population, the state continues to adopt paternalistic, pastoral governing practices and intervenes heavily in the management of daily life, in the definition of social hierarchies, and in the distribution of resources, despite the dramatic changes in the economic environment.

As discussed in the previous chapter, depending on the material conditions, the action of governing can result in a hands-off approach or in the state zooming in on individual lives using mobilization, social control, monitoring of social behavior, and economic dependence. In other words, the best predictor of *how* a community will be exposed to social management, for example, is not so much the shape and direction of a national policy as the material conditions of the local community. The perception of the government's action seems, accordingly, to depend largely on where a citizen sits within the system: the wealthier the community, the less state intervention it might experience. Numerous actors, both public and private, as well as the state's institutions become involved in the activity of governing and, to a large degree, mobilize or implement the state's rationalities; nonetheless, such convergence produces a governmental outcome only once it is elaborated in the local context.

As a retired worker told me: "In China, more people [in a community] mean more cadres. But it also depends on how poor you are. The poorer a place, the more numerous the cadres." In the case of these Shenyang communities, one could also say that the poorer the community, the more likely it will be that residents get involved in its management, both as subjects and as agents of the state. The cadres who populate this chapter are both part of the problem (many are laid-off workers) and part of the solution (they are charged with the zealous implementation of governing practices).

In the next section, I will refer to a survey of 107 out of 126 community directors in the district of Tiexi and about 40 in-depth interviews with community workers and cadres to investigate this junction.[4] The picture that emerges is one of both increased state visibility and regulation on one side and of increased dependency, negotiation, and conflict on the other. This chapter will also reveal that both the material and the discursive bases of the neighborhood consensus in these residential areas are substantially different from those developed in the highly conflictual middle-class compounds that will be the focus of the next chapters of this book.

Unmaking the Working Class

Shenyang's Tiexi district, separated by the railway tracks from the rest of the city, was the chosen site for many of the 156 Soviet-funded large industrial plants established in the 1950s. Still today, if you ask Shenyang's residents what makes up the city's "culture," the most popular answer is "its industrial tradition."

There is, however, little left of that industrial culture in today's Tiexi. The district has almost completely abandoned its industrial vocation to embrace the improbable dream of becoming a postindustrial hub and buying into the commercial and residential craze of other inner city districts. Industrial production has largely been moved to new areas in the farthest periphery, in what is now known as "New Tiexi" with newly developed industrial zones. Almost all of the industrial plants that made up Tiexi's landscape have disappeared, and only sporadically preserved buildings, small museums, and industrial "public art" remain to remind the people of Shenyang of its industrial heritage. This transition has been rapid, painful, destructive, often merciless. Old industrial areas have been swiftly reconverted into prime real estate locations. One could also say, in particular, that Tiexi's reconversion to a postindustrial district has been so rapid that it forgot the workers. In fact, while many of the factories are gone, many of the working-class neighborhoods (some built in the 1950s) are still standing and are inhabited by those who, twenty years ago, still

Figure 4. Elderly people in a workers' village activity center with images of Mao Zedong and the ten revolutionary generals

Figure 5. Public industrial art in the streets of Shenyang

Figure 6. Public industrial art in the streets of Shenyang

Figure 7. Photographic exhibition inspired by Tiexi's industrial tradition

Figure 8. A cast factory that was recently turned into an industrial museum. Most factories in Tiexi have disappeared.

Figure 9. Demolition of a worker neighborhood in Shenyang. The writing on the wall encouraging residents to move out reads, "Do not wait and see: The demolition and relocation policies will not change!"

Figure 10. The official sign for the Community Committees in Shenyang (*shequ*). The Chinese character *jia* (home, family) can be seen on the stylized map of the city.

made up the industrial urban elite but have today come out on the wrong side of history.

The stories of Tiexi's residents appear all very similar. Almost all of the families I contacted during my fieldwork can be said to have experienced *xiagang*, a word Shenyang people do not even feel the need to explain to a foreigner. The *xiagangs* are those who have been laid off by a state-owned enterprise. They are likely to have been entitled to a small pay-off (*maiduan*) or to an early retirement if they were older than 45 or 50. Unemployment rates in Shenyang reached more than 20 percent during the late 1990s, when many of the socialist behemoths with tens of thousands of employees completed their long agony and went broke (*daobi*).[5]

Also, when their jobs went, most families lost their attachment to an administrative unit. When the factory disappeared, it all but eclipsed a social system until then organized around employment and belonging to a work unit that also administered the population, managed the redistribution of goods, and provided services. Without a job and a work unit, the population's only remaining point of contact with the state became the residential communities where they had lived and where they were still entitled to live. Compared to other cases of industrial decline, the members of this portion of the Chinese working class at least kept the "luxury" of a roof over their heads. With it, they also kept alive their deeply seated moral entitlement to being "saved" by the state.

In this deteriorating social situation and threatened with a risk of social instability in the rustbelt, the central government intervened with a substantial infusion of cash that urban administrations in the northeast used to beef up the social security system at the last remaining point of contact, the residential communities. At the beginning of the new century, Shenyang's "community-building" (*shequ jianshe*) became a nationwide model (*moshi*) and a crucial component of the attempt to contain the city's social decay and the risk of instability.

In the initial phase of experimentation, different models (*moshi*) were put forward by different municipal administrations. The first, at the end of the 1990s, was the Shanghai model, which aimed at increased efficiency in the delivery of services and focused on the role of organizations below the level of the sub-district (the *jiedao banshichu*, or street office). Shenyang's model was based on the "two levels of government, one level of administration" concept. It was used in communities that were called on to deliver services on behalf of the government but without being part of the government hierarchy. This situation did not result in greater autonomy or increased capacity to solve the problems of the residents (communities still depended entirely for their funding from government agencies above them) but rather in under-resourced and overburdened offices, with cadres paid less than public servants but often required to perform much more complex tasks.[6] The Shenyang model was more about building a government presence in the neighborhoods than the Shanghai model.

In Tiexi, a little over a million residents are organized in sixteen street offices, which oversee 126 communities. These differ in size: from small (up to 1,700 families) and medium (up to 2,800 families) to large (up to 5,500 families). The rationale for this distinction, as numerous cadres explained it to me, is that newer, affluent, and quiet communities tend to be larger, while the oldest and most problematic tend to be smaller and more abundantly staffed. Each community has roughly twelve employees, generally including a director and two vice directors (all elected) and one Party secretary. The hierarchy between director and secretary can vary, but in Tiexi, where the Party has traditionally been very strong, it is invariably the Party secretary who has the final say (*shuo le suan*). Communities also receive funding from the Labor Bureau and the Civil Affairs Bureau to hire "volunteers" (*gongyi xing gangwei*). These often outnumber the community personnel and perform daily tasks such as monitoring and patrolling the community and managing garbage collection. They also often help with the implementation of household registration regulations, family planning, and the organization of political activities. These jobs pay a monthly subsidy (*butie*), not a salary, but also guarantee health and retirement insurance. There are tens of thousands of these jobs reserved to *xiagang* workers in all areas of public life, and they represent a fundamental safety net for many unemployed. According to interviews with provincial Civil Affairs officials, at the end of 2006 the community system in the whole of Liaoning province employed 330,000 formal employees and an estimated 750,000 volunteers. Including cadres, employees, and the "volunteers," the system of residential communities in Tiexi alone employs an estimated five thousand people. They are the front line of Shenyang's government of industrial decline, but they are also its victims.

Their duties include the distribution of various types of subsidies (including the *dibao*, the all-important minimum income subsidy), certifications, reemployment services, family planning, household registration, authorizations for small community businesses, pet registration, security, monitoring of dangerous elements, maintenance of public areas and gardens, and housing maintenance but also such campaign-like activities as the collection and distribution of clothing to poorer families, recreational activities, the registering and support of local associations, people's education (including the "community universities" and "old age universities"), health and hygiene, the organization of propaganda activities required by the higher levels of government, and the recruitment of volunteers, in particular for "community patrols" (*xuluodui*).[7] Each employee is also assigned a certain number of families on whom they must report. In some communities, employees know everyone and live inside the compounds. In many cases, they share the same run-down accommodation as the residents for whom they are responsible.

Of the directors, 93.5 percent are women, and women make up a similar proportion of employees as well. Labor market conditions are probably responsible for this, as it is harder for women to find employment in higher-paid sectors. During interviews, however, the main explanations given for this dominance were cultural (women are better at dealing with people and are more precise in the work they do) and cultural/economic (men are not willing to take on these jobs, as they are poorly paid and are not enough to sustain a family).

The second observation has to do with age and education. Community committees were established around 2000, when many of Shenyang's factories closed down. Shenyang found itself with unemployed in all age brackets, but with much more difficult prospects for the *siling wuling* (those between 40 and 50 years of age). This might be one of the reasons that 62.5 percent of the directors in Tiexi are between 46 and 60 (no one was below 25, and only five were below 35), and almost all had previously been employed in public enterprises.

For many, adapting to the new environment is not very easy, and communities represent a step backward in their social status.

The research institute I was working for was not doing very well, and it offered early retirement to women at 45, so I took it. I spent a couple of months at home, mostly buying and selling stocks [with the severance payment], then I tried to work for an insurance company, but I was not suitable; I can't really do that kind of work. Then someone said to me: "Why don't you try to work for the neighborhood committee?" At that time the salary was 110 yuan [US$16] per month, and I still had to pay for my own lunch. I ended up losing money. There was an old lady I worked with who used to be a factory director. She helped me and taught me a lot of things about this work. Then slowly the salary increased to 300, then 500, then 700 yuan [US$100]. Until then, I was not even a Party member, but at one point at the [street] office they told me, "You have to be a member. It is not good for you not to be Party member." It should be Party members who hold this office. So I joined the Party, and I have been the director ever since. The first couple of years, I thought I didn't want to do it. The salary was very low, and I was always so tired. In this community there are people of all sorts. Coming from a scientific work unit, I couldn't get used to it. My family said that I was changing, that I was no longer the same person that I was at the institute. Even my voice was getting softer, quieter.

Probably because they often come from public enterprises, community directors also have more education than average. Almost all of them have either a professional tertiary degree (*dazhuan*, 84.1 percent) or a full university degree (15 percent). Again, the collapsing Shenyang economy provides the context for this high incidence of educated women in low-paid jobs and their inability to recycle themselves in a labor market lacking opportunities for women over 40. A look at their earlier professional lives also reveals that 82.2 percent of the respondents were previously employed in state-owned businesses as office clerks (33.6 percent), middle-level administrators (48.6 percent), or managers (10.3 percent).

Most of the interviewees explain their choice of working for the community by their age and lack of alternatives, but they also insist on the comparative status advantages that working for the community can bring. The great majority of respondents (83.7 percent) agreed with the proposition that "being a community director is a good way to realize my value," and 75 percent said that they would "proudly introduce themselves by saying that they work in a community."

For many former state employees, community work represents one of the few remaining chances to gain the job security that they had lost when their work units collapsed. This is true not only of the directors but also of all other employees, and even of the "volunteers," who still see the low-paid community work as a more dignified solution for an urban dweller than selling cheap clothes in a market stall. Another explanation is that, in Shenyang's job environment, community work is still perceived as a "foot in the door" of the public service. For example, regulations introduced in 2007 make it possible for community directors to be promoted to fully fledged public service positions in the higher-level sub-district government offices, under much better employment conditions. At the moment, community employees are considered administrative personnel and do not have access to many of the perks, higher salaries, and low-cost housing available to public servants working in higher levels of government, so the carrot of a potential promotion is very important to the motivation of the directors and to their willingness to accept high workloads in poor conditions. Becoming a public servant is still regarded by most of my interviewees as a good and secure career perspective. "Why did I send my son to study sociology?" asked one of the directors. "Because when he is finished, he can go straight into public service. Being a public servant in China is still the best thing" (*yiliu de*).

Self-Government and Its Discontents

Despite the difficulties, the community cadres I have met are generally motivated and committed and enjoy a good reputation among residents. They provide local residents with their first point of contact with the state, and they know the local community inside and out. All but one of the directors in the survey were elected by the residents for a three-year term in office. As Heberer and Göbel have shown, one should not over-estimate the importance and the level of involvement of the local community in the choice of their directors: This is still very much a multi-stage selection process in which residents are called on mainly to rubber-stamp candidates nominated by the sub-district government.[8] Despite the interest that community elections (and their comparison with the village elections in the countryside) have generated, there is hardly any evidence that, as a grassroots expression of Chinese democracy, community elections are contributing to more democratic urban governance.[9]

In spite of such limited participation, however, being an elected cadre is generally the result of long-term involvement with both the higher level of government and the community itself. Cadres' reputations among residents are built through the perception of hard work and respectability but also through the support of a network of active residents who endorse the political and social work of the officials.

Secretary Song is in charge of a community with a proud worker history in which most of the residents have been left stranded by the industrial restructuring. A laid-off worker himself, he feels squeezed between the grievances he hears every day from his residents and the constant demands from "the office" to fulfill endless tasks and to prevent social disturbances. He struggles to match the language of harmony he is encouraged to propagate with the rough and cynical remarks of his neighbors.

> Three things are most important in my work. First, to provide a safe environment in the community, one that's clean and better to live in. Second, to improve people's quality (*suzhi*), so that they don't fight or make trouble. Third, that there is someone to take care of things when something goes wrong, providing the services people need. . . . The most important thing here is that people are satisfied.

Secretary Song is concerned that the increasing number of tasks imposed on him by his superiors can distract him from the daily duty of keeping the community orderly. Despite significant public investment in infrastructure inside the communities, including increasing office spaces and CCTV monitoring systems to control crime, cadres feel that communities are left to their own devices. In my survey, 59.4 percent of the interviewees said that one of the biggest problems in the communities was that the government expects them to perform too many functions; 49.1 percent indicated the lack of financial resources as their main source of frustration. In Song's words:

> On the one hand, there are the tasks passed down from the "office" [the street office, sub-district government]; on the other, the things that our people need. There are too many meetings and other activities that the office wants me to attend. They take 60 to 70 percent of my time. The office has twenty employees, but every time there is something to do they call the community. "Make the community solve it!" they say. They also continuously come and inspect our work. Up there they write policies; down here we just rubber-stamp them![10]

A no-nonsense, chain-smoking Dongbei man, Song is a loud and respected voice in the community, but he is challenged by the widespread cynicism produced among his residents by a decade of what they perceive as a betrayal of their social contract with the socialist state. The complaints are mostly about losses, about the unfulfilled promises of a lifetime of public employment, low compensation, low pensions, poor living conditions, and the unfair loss of status of the once "privileged" working class. In the words of one of the residents: "China has developed quickly and . . . sure, we can understand that the country has difficulties in these times of change. But why should we be the casualties? I am out of work, but I am too young to get a pension. So the state also wants me to pay tens of thousands of yuan to get a pension in seven years' time." Said another:

> I'm 50, but I'm not entitled to a pension. They say one should not use the word *unemployed* [*shiye*], and if you use the term *out of work* [*xiagang*], they say, "The country has difficulties, society is in bad shape." Our community has the highest number of unemployed in the district, the district the

highest in Shenyang, Shenyang the highest in Liaoning, Liaoning the highest in the country. . . . We are left eating our own fat [*chi lao ben*]. We are all so servile, give us a place to live and a full—or even half-full—tummy and we won't rebel. . . .

Anger often becomes a performance in which the system is both blamed for the betrayal and courted in the quest for welfare. Grassroots cadres, whose own biographies often lead them to be sympathetic to these grievances, rarely become the objects of such complaints, as they have had similar experiences of loss. There remains a gap between the variable and differentiated origins of these residents' poverty and the inflexible nature of the policies aimed at alleviating their situation.[11] Cadres therefore live with the frustration of being unable to respond to the demands. As one of them put it:

> Most of the work we do [in the community] is for the weaker groups, minimum income support recipients, *xiagang*, the unemployed, and the elderly . . . particularly the unemployed. We try our best to find them a job. Sometimes we are helpless, but we do everything we can. They become so angry when we try to explain to them what the policies say and what the regulations are. But we have to stay cool, control our feelings. That's why sometimes I think the community is like a garbage bin. Whatever people say, we have to swallow.

In order to create visibility and reduce social tension, the state relies on some trustworthy cadres like Song but also on a large number of poorly motivated employees who see community work as a second-class public service job, with security as the only advantage. Said one community worker: "I have no aspiration. My only aspiration is to live an orderly life and have a stable job. If you don't have order in your life, you become upset, and it is easy to get sick." Another said: "What do I hope for the future? Before, I was working in a factory, and I think I wouldn't be able to do well in business, because I am not very clever. Also, I have no one helping me, because all my friends are laid-off workers like me. I am a single daughter, my parents are old, I can't rely on them. A stable job and self-sufficiency, that's all I want." One important area of community work, reemployment activities (*zai jiuye*), is often run by volunteers with very low skills and little motivation. The community acts as a potential go-between in the relationship between local companies looking for employees and the local unemployed. While the government regularly claims very high levels of successful reemployment, unemployed people in Tiexi complain that the available jobs are short-term, don't pay well, or do not include the all-important benefits of social security and health insurance. As mentioned, Shenyang has a "40 to 50" program (for people between 40 and 50 years of age) that provides tax breaks to encourage companies to hire laid-off workers in this age bracket. Procedures and certification for such programs are also generally in the hands of the community cadres. Some of these reemployed workers also work directly for the community. One of these volunteers, himself a laid-off worker, worked from eight to five every day for 450 yuan (US$65) a month, acting as a liaison with employers. He said:

> My wife works in a community too, but she makes more money because she is a Party member and is better educated. I spend my time here looking for jobs for other laid-off workers like me. Why don't I look for a job myself? This is a good enough job. I don't mind making little money, as long as I have old-age insurance, health insurance, and unemployment insurance. Most private companies don't give you that.

On the one hand, the communities feed this sense of collective entitlement toward the state. On the other, however, without a factory as the place for collective grievances, they also provide the state with a way to segregate and contain social discontent and to tackle the most dangerous situations, ultimately preventing the escalation of conflicts.

Performing the Working Class

Without a factory and with communities under strict monitoring, grievances sometimes spill out into public spaces. Every afternoon at 2 p.m. in the summer months, one of the largest Tiexi parks was the site of an informal "freedom square" (*ziyou guangchang*), a very animated gathering of retired and unemployed people where "we discuss the big questions of the country" (*guojia da shi*). This "freedom square" has allegedly been the origin of several petitions to the city government. Everyone in Tiexi seemed to be aware of its existence, but authorities were content simply to monitor these activities without intervening. On the "square," in fact, grievances often took the form more of a spectacle than of an active forum for political debates and alternative worldviews. As one participant once told me in a disappointed tone: "Nah, today it was no fun at all. Come back tomorrow when there are those who really abuse the Communist Party [*ma gongchandang*]."

Also performing in the park are the remnants of the popular "industrial culture" that Tiexi has all but lost. In different corners of the park one can find not only musicians, singers, dancers, gamblers, people drinking tea, people playing cards but also the only remaining "yellow" (*huangse*) version of Shenyang's famous *er ren zhuang*, the two-character comedy that is the passion of northeastern China. Theaters in the city only allow the "green" (*lü*) version of it, cleansed of many of the political and sexual references (although not of rough jokes about the "Japanese dogs").

In addition to these spontaneous expressions of workers' anger and of their residual cultural expressions, worker culture is also performed publicly in the neighborhoods in different ways across the district by the government in order to reinforce the narrative of the historical achievements and entitlements of the Tiexi working class. Numerous colorfully repainted pieces of discarded industrial machinery provide the street decorations in Tiexi, while at the entrance of the Model Workers' Park a gigantic bronze bas-relief sculpture portrays the role of China's working class in the revolution. In June 2007, the Tiexi district government inaugurated a permanent exhibition about the residential quarters of the industrial workers who had been living in a neighborhood known as the "workers' village" (*gongren cun*) for the last five decades. The exhibition is located in one of only seven buildings singled out for preservation in this Soviet-style residential area, built in 1952, which originally included 143 large three-story constructions and a total area of over 700,000 square meters. The exhibition features reproductions of the single-room apartments with shared basic facilities and kitchens and displays the evolution of daily life in the neighborhood since the 1950s. Young university graduates wearing wireless microphones tell the curious visitors about the pioneering adventures of China's working class and pay tribute to their struggle to build the glory of the socialist state.

Next door, in a twin building, I encountered another expression of this worker narrative. An art management company was holding the vernissage of a new commercial art space, interested in attracting the cashed-up consumers who have started moving into the renovated buildings. Ironically, it included an exhibition of highly aestheticized photos of the ailing industrial sites of China's rust belt, abandoned and mostly demolished. The remaining five buildings under renovation, I was told by one of the young long-haired art managers, will host cafes, restaurants, and art studios.

These competing performances of working-class culture seek a convergent goal: workers' anger is framed by the terms of the social contract broken by the Party and seeks access to residual welfare provisions. The state, on the other hand, which can only abandon the socialist rhetoric of assistance and entitlements at its own risk, strives to maintain a monopoly over the representation of worker culture both inside and outside the communities, making a museum of the past and focusing on the positive changes brought by the reform. Grassroots cadres, once again, are right at the crosspoint of these two representations and play a relevant part in the bargaining.

The rhetoric of "saving the working class" is thus an important component of the quest for legitimacy and the visibility of local leaders' efforts to improve living standards. Communities are the spatial, political, and moral force behind this effort, the place where individuals who are suffering from the restructuring of Shenyang's economy are supposed to see and experience the presence of the state.

In Tiexi, where municipal leaders and high-level cadres are often the object of popular suspicion of corruption and undeserved privilege, community cadres sometimes become examples of "the way cadres should be," for their apparently endless energy, low income, and dedication. One of these is Mama Zhang, an elderly cadre who has been doing community work for longer than anyone can remember. Her community is today better known by Zhang's own name than by its original toponym, to the extent that local businesses in the area have adopted her name as their brand (such as the "Mama Zhang Grocery"). Residents treat her with great deference and attribute almost everything that the community has achieved in the last decade to her efforts. The district government invests heavily in her model community, and large amounts of money have gone into the expansion and renovation of its premises. Now the community has a 2,000-square-meter activity center, extremely spacious offices, large and well-organized outdoor areas, and a gym, and its facilities are the best in the district. Not surprisingly, it is also the community that central leaders are taken to visit when they come to inspect Shenyang, and the pictures of Zhu Rongji and Hu Jintao's meeting with Mama Zhang are posted prominently at the community entrance. Local district leaders often ride the popularity of Mama Zhang and use the community not only as a model but also as a setting for such events as the monthly "leaders inside the community" (*lingdao jin shequ*) functions in which residents are given public audience with district or municipal level cadres to discuss their grievances and "make suggestions" (*ti yijian*). This "borrowing" of credibility from respected community cadres is very important for the political legitimacy of Shenyang's leaders. While the legitimacy of the central government can rely on the country's steady economic performance, cadres here cannot claim to have achieved great success in a situation where the economy has long been in dire straits. This leaves local leaders exposed to criticism and requires them to resort to different forms of legitimization, including the traditional norms of a moral economy of mutual socialist solidarity and paternalism.

Communities are thus central to the framing of the legitimacy of the Shenyang leadership and result in even more pressure on community cadres. In communities that are home to "weaker social groups" (*ruoshi qunti*), including the unemployed, the impoverished elderly, and the disabled, cadres operate in a difficult environment in which they are often confronted with demands from both above and below. In addition to the many tasks now performed at the community level, cadres are often asked to participate in training courses or to organize an endless succession of new initiatives designed by the district leaders, such as information hotlines for citizens or a web-based community service network.

Auditing Self-Government

The formalized principles of *shequ zizhi* (community self-governance) are "self-administration, self-education, self-service, and self-discipline" (*ziwo guanli, ziwo jiaoyu, ziwo fuwu, ziwo yueshu*). This mantra of the self is often reproduced on large signs that tower over community offices and is emblazoned on banners inside the communities, much like other slogans have done in earlier times. Despite the ubiquitous presence of the discourses

of discipline, responsibility, and self-government within the communities, in reality very little room for decision is left to the cadres, even less
to the citizens. Communities are entirely dependent on the higher levels
of government for the funding of their initiatives. Employment activities
are directed and funded by the labor bureau, security activities by the public security bureau, family planning activities by the family planning bureau, and so on. The community's ability to produce their own version of
self-government is limited to a tiny "activity fund," which in Shenyang in
2007 amounted to around 20,000 yuan (US$3,000) per year, barely enough
to cover the general cost of running the offices.

Communities have therefore very little "self-management," as they
mostly perform functions imposed from above. They are also under relent-
less scrutiny from the district government and other higher-level offices.
Districts produce a yearly evaluation scheme of community performance
through which communities can be awarded or denied the label of "harmonious community." The evaluation consists of a scoring sheet with 100
points that is compiled during inspections by the relevant departments.
"Building of community organizations," for example, amounts to a maximum of 18 points, including "Party organizations" (membership, services,
leadership style—7.5 points), "community self-government organizations"
(different committees, participation, level of education of employees, participation in training—5.5 points) and "volunteer and associations" (5
points). The quality of services provided by the community amounts to
more than a quarter of the total score (27 points), a total that includes employment and social welfare services but also 7.5 points for infrastructure,
most notably the requirement that office size be at least 400 square meters
for communities of more than 1,500 families and at least 300 square meters
in other cases. "Democratic self-government" counts for 17 points, divided
up into the categories of "democratic elections," "democratic decision-
making," "democratic administration," and "democratic supervision" of
cadres' work. Finally, a maximum of 13 points is assigned for educational
and cultural activities and 25 points for "community functions" such as
hygiene, security, environment, and family planning (the latter, surprisingly, only 3 points).

Each of these items is further broken down into subcategories, each
containing very detailed instructions for the scorer. This evaluation exercise can result in positive or negative outcomes both for the cadre's career

and for the funding that particular communities will receive in the future. The result of the evaluation is, unsurprisingly, dependent on the attitude of the visiting scoring official. While some criteria might be possible to assess mathematically (a 90 percent reemployment rate in the community, for example), others, like a "good" leadership style, depend on individual qualities or behaviors and can be assessed very differently by different inspectors. It is therefore clear to community cadres that maintaining good ongoing relationships with the officers in the Street Office is as important to their careers and success in the system as is achieving good results. They therefore try their best to be present at all initiatives of the "office," to be as visible as possible in the initiatives they organize, and to reflect as much as possible the language and ideas they hear from the "office." In the case of cultural activities, for example, the inspectors are asked to assess whether the office is "organizing activities that improve the community's civic environment, enrich its cultural life, and raise the civic quality of the residents."

Much of this evaluation will also depend on how well community cadres contribute to the promotion of the priorities and discourses of the local state. While hegemonic discourses of "harmony," "responsibility," "self-government," and "quality" are produced and sanctioned far away from the communities, they continue to be elaborated and adapted down to the lowest-level cadre and are internalized in the way cadres see reality. What makes these rhetorical tools so powerful is that they are both justified by political slogans and applied to daily experience inside the communities.

Cadres, for example, see their own "quality" as crucial to the success of their activities. As one cadre put it, "Let me tell you what the most important thing is. Those who have no culture have no business doing community work. Earlier, one needed simply to be in total control of the situation. This is still important, but today one also needs organizational and management skills and the ability to express oneself [in public]. Without these skills you will never succeed." The idea of a population of "insufficient" *suzhi* also clearly underlies the explanations given for many of the problems in the community.

> You can't pretend to raise the *suzhi* of the people by too much, but at least you can get to a point where people do not just think about themselves and where neighbors help each other. . . . "High-*suzhi*" means that people are virtuous and sincere. For example, we used to have a lot of bad behavior and

people fighting on the street, but now with community administration and education it is much better. If something happens now, it is almost certainly because of the migrants.

This powerful discourse of *suzhi* is one that places the ailing Shenyang working class in a specific position in the civilization ladder of Chinese society. On the one hand, due to its traditional privileges, it remains above and beyond the rural migrants, perceived by the local workers as the ones who steal their opportunities and by the local authorities as troublemakers, because of their low *suzhi*. On the other side, the ex-workers are also placed below the new social groups that are rapidly colonizing gentrified Tiexi, where large chunks of what used to be industrial land are now becoming prime real estate property and attracting the middle classes. One community employee expressed this shared feeling very directly: "This neighborhood is very run-down, and the *suzhi* of the people is low. I live in a commercial estate, and the situation there is much better than here. I think the *suzhi* of people depends on their economic circumstances. If you are poor, you are of poor *suzhi*."

The Shenyang working class finds itself trapped between those who are seen as low-*suzhi* and dangerous and those who are seen as high-*suzhi* and wealthy and whose lives are treated by the state as the social and behavioral benchmark (see chapter 5). Saving Shenyang's working class means not only keeping them alive with subsidies or keeping them quiet by social control. It also requires raising their "quality," which in turn will raise their ability to govern themselves. The penetration and contestation of such dominant discourses inside the communities results in a specific governance outcome, monitored through a close and personal scrutiny of cadres.

The Cadres' Crossroads

This chapter has described some of the experiences of community cadres and workers in Tiexi's poorest communities and found that they stand at a crucial crossroads between the providers and the recipients of state subsidies, between the subjects and objects of social regulation. One can easily be both a cadre (or figure of some authority) and a member of the disenfranchised working class that the system is committed to serve or, in Shenyang, to save.

In such situations, in cities that are striving to shed their industrial history and secure a postindustrial identity, the stories of these people reveal how the governing practices that individuals experience (or are at times called to implement) depend on those individuals' long-lived personal experiences and social positions. As former state workers, they have suffered a dramatic decline in status and have found limited alternative resources to deal with the new situation.

In her study of poverty among former state workers of the rustbelt, Mun Young Cho emphasized the need to "historicize poverty" in these communities and showed that the workers' constant reference to the signifier of "the people" prevents them from "being entirely converted into 'numbers,' that is into a regularized population without history."[12] The historically constructed frames adopted by workers and by cadres conflate with the everyday experiences of these communities in ways that expose the contradictions between the ideology and the practices of poverty management, between the obsessive, rigid definition of poverty relief (and other governance goals) and the perceived need for a fluid and bargaining approach in governing practices.

The state perpetuates the nostalgia and recreates dependencies by reproducing the rhetoric of "saving the working class." It relies on the often-overstretched administrative structure provided by the communities, both to beef up legitimacy and to contain the risks of systemic crisis. The state needs to be seen as fulfilling its commitment to the working class through the work of these cadres. Paternalism in these struggling neighborhoods is claimed and expected by the residents.

Self-government, which is the ideology behind the "community building" campaign, suggests that the state wants to produce more reliable citizens, but the suggestion that it wants to do so only by abandoning the more pastoral forms of government characteristic of the socialist moral economy does not fit the picture I have painted here. The conventional wisdom that the state is becoming less intrusive and radically changing the justification of its policies to adapt to the demands of the market does not seem to apply to these examples. Here, the idea of the state, its role toward individuals, its responsibilities, and its legitimacy are all produced and contested very close to the realities of daily struggles. The discourse of state responsibility is indeed being continuously elaborated and adapted to changing situations. For anyone who is dependent on the state, either as a subject or as one of its agents (and sometimes as both), its significance is expanding, not contracting.

Stability thus relies on both dependency and social control. The legitimization of paternalistic and pastoral practices of governing is both discursively and practically different from what I encountered in middle-class residential communities, with their embrace of the national rhetoric of reform and consumption and their emphasis on *suzhi*. Nonetheless, the different ways in which the rhetoric of "saving the working class" is performed and mobilized also lead to a convergence of perceptions on practices and values. In no other character of this story is such convergence clearer than in the community cadres, called to perform the role of savior, while in fact they are still themselves in need of saving.

3

Housing and Social Engineering

Governing has always implied, for the Chinese Communist Party, the aspiration to create citizens in harmony with the existing developmental project of the nation and willing to support it. Social normative institutions such as the household registration system or the work unit have greatly contributed to stratifying society along lines useful to the dominant social-ist ideology (collectivization, class struggle, and the creation of "cities of producers") on the one hand, while, on the other, organizing population and resources to achieve the important economic goals set by the planners. In the context of a development strategy that puts heavy industry first, as in the first decades of the People's Republic, the control of population movements was a necessary precondition to force the transfer of resources from the rural economy to the industrializing cities. Similarly, strict cel-lular organization of the urban population and control over distribution of resources was aimed at rationalizing (and rationing) consumption.

In the reform period, on the contrary, the new citizen is called on to consume more and more, to support the new economic imperatives. The need for China to engineer new kinds of citizen has stimulated different types of policy and institutions. Even the emergence of an awe-inspiring Chinese middle class that excites and concerns the boards of global companies all over the world is, to a significant extent, a result of this social engineering (*shehui gongcheng*).[1] While social engineering generally refers to the control and manipulation of ideas and behaviors, here I suggest a very concrete form of engineering: namely, the specific policies and practices through which the state selectively promoted the creation of a middle class. Housing and neighborhoods in the last two decades reveal how these new members of a high-consuming class have built their housing careers.

Dogs, Housing, Wealth, and the State

Dogs on a leash are a common sight in Hopetown, one of Beijing's first "new cities," a cluster of residential compounds for the professional middle class.[2] Hairy and generally noisy, dogs are not allowed to grow beyond the 35-centimeter limit set by the city government for the inner suburbs. Nonetheless, residents here were ready to pay a registration fee of 5,000 yuan (US$730) plus a 2,000 yuan (US$292) annual management fee to the city and to spend between 800 and 10,000 (US$116–1,460) yuan to buy purebred puppies from the *zifa* (self-organized) market that rural breeders set up every Sunday in Beijing's peri-urban counties. Dog food, dog health magazines, and dog clothes fill the shelves of supermarkets.[3] The *New York Times* reported in 2010 on "dog-treat stores, dog Web sites, dog social networks, dog swimming pools—even, for a time recently, a bring-your-dog cinema and a bring-your-dog bar on Beijing's downtown nightclub row."[4] Dogs become attached to the household registration of their owners and are issued a document with a color photo. In what is almost a metaphor of today's urban China, nonresidents are not entitled to the privilege of walking a dog.

Until three decades ago, there were ordinances against the possession of pet dogs, in recognition of China's poverty and out of concern for urban health issues. Their recent reappearance indicates a new affluence, embodied in an item that—unlike the modern electric appliances of previous years—can be showcased in the neighborhood's playground as a way of displaying who has "made it." Pet owners now have associations that defend animal rights and are developing an increasing sensibility for animal welfare. According to its website, the Chinese Companion Animal Protection Network, launched in 2004, has over 700 members in 48 pet protection groups and is part of the larger Animal Protection Network (*Zhongguo dongbaowang*), which has over ten thousand members and conducts campaigns, for example to stamp out the consumption of dog and cat meat.[5] As a vegetarian for over two decades, used to long explanations and occasional lies about my religious beliefs when presented with meat at a dinner, I confess to being glad that this new sensibility has made my own social relations in China easier!

What was puzzling, however, was that those walking the dogs were often not the prototypical new rich whom we have come to associate with the opportunity for quick money offered by transitional economies in largely unregulated markets. Instead, they were mostly public employees, for whom the main driver of status enhancement had been the policies of the state. In this and the following chapters, I will try to explain how this has happened, why housing and residential spaces have mattered, and what the consequences of these trends have been for both new social hierarchies and practices of governance.

Hopetown, the pseudonymous residential area where the next two chapters are set, is in northeastern Beijing. It is part of Chaoyang district and has officially been described as an area developed "with the support of the central authority." The planning of the whole area is therefore influenced by the directives of the city planners. The developer of these two enormous gated communities is one of the largest state-owned construction corporations in the country.[6] Nonetheless, it is a "commercial" (*shang-pin*) residential area.

The residential district where Hopetown sits, a long succession of high-rise buildings just outside of the fourth ring road, has become one of the largest residential developments in Asia and is home to around 230,000 registered inhabitants, with more residential space becoming available every year. It is a high-density residential area, covering about 3 percent of the city's total area, but it accounted in 1999 for about 13 percent of that year's housing construction in the capital.[7] It is today also home to a large international population and hosts the offices of a high-tech industrial park.

The area I call Hopetown encompasses two gated communities and, so far, a total of about 25,000 people. The first neighborhood of 26 buildings—each of 20 to 29 floors—was completed in 1997 and was hailed as the first fully commercial high-standard apartment block made available to the Beijing middle class, with its increasing purchasing power. The largest part of the almost six thousand units in this housing development—which I will call Hopetown 1—was sold on the open market by the end of 1998 to people who did not need bank mortgages, which did not exist until the second half of the 1990s. Already in 1996 the People's Bank of China had lifted the limit of five years on mortgage lending, but the 1998 housing reform regulations can be taken as the beginning of the mortgage market in China. One of my interviewees claimed that his 1998 loan agreement carried the Beijing serial number 001 and that he "received from the bank 90,000 yuan [US$10,000] in cash" to buy his first apartment. Although I am not sure whether I should formally credit him with having such a rare document, the narrative among this early generation of homeowners is one where they describe themselves as "mortgage pioneers."

Buyers at this stage had to have enough cash in hand to pay an average price of 5,017 yuan (around US$600) per square meter. Despite this being fairly high in absolute terms at the time, housing prices here were, in 2002, around the city's average (4,764 yuan per square meter, about US$580). The affordability of housing became a much greater issue later in the decade, with prices in the area averaging 17,000 yuan (US$2,500) per square meter in 2008, resulting in hefty gains for local owners and investors.

The second neighborhood (Hopetown 2), completed in 1999 by the same developer, is smaller (around 3,000 units) and includes both market-price "commodity" apartments (*shangpin fang*) and "economy apartments" (*jingji shiyong fang*) sold at a subsidized price. The prices of these units varied at the time of their construction from around 4,000 yuan (US$480) per square meter for the subsidized units to 5,500 yuan (US$660) per square meter for the "commodity" units, despite a remarkable similarity in quality, location, and services.[8] Buyers in this second development are generally mortgage payers. During a recent visit in spring 2013, I noticed real estate agents standing outside the gates of the two communities offering "good deals" to people who wished to purchase a unit in the community. The prices, even of the subsidized units, had by then skyrocketed to 32,000–35,000 yuan (US$5,200–5,700) per square meter!

Both areas were built with the intention of attracting a relatively well-off and educated group of residents by providing high-quality apartments, high levels of services, and a green(er) environment a short distance from the city. Today, the area is connected to the transport network by one of the lines of the Beijing light railway (*qingtie*). The general manager of the state-owned enterprise that developed the complex described it, upon completion in 2000, as a "modern and culturally advanced" project that should become "a model for other residential developments in Beijing and the rest of the country."[9]

At the time of my first periods of fieldwork between 2002 and 2006, residents of Hopetown were mostly nuclear families, typically young couples with one child or no children. Household composition often included retired parents. They were generally employed in skilled positions, especially in the public sector, but in some cases also in private or international ventures.

Housing and Status

This chapter argues that social engineering aimed at creating a propertied middle class is one of the foundations of the neighborhood consensus, as it aligned the interests of the propertied middle class with those of the state, while property also gave them a stake in the preservation of stability and social order. A dramatic status enhancement for wage-earning professionals has been among the major determinants of social change in the late 1990s and early in the new century, and it happened more despite the market than because of it.

The development of a high-consuming urban society has been as much the outcome of the social engineering project of the contemporary reformist state and its agencies as it has been a consequence of the opening-up of the economy and society.

My understanding of social stratification is based on the different abilities of social actors to access resources more than on their relations to the means of production or their relative wealth and income. The term *salaried middle class*, as used in this chapter, therefore refers to the popular image evoked by the expression (educated people enjoying a comparatively well-off and modern lifestyle), which can be used to pinpoint and identify a certain group in the urban social landscape; this includes many from the ranks of those in employment who have recently experienced a dramatic improvement of their living standards and purchasing power. Although these groups might appear amorphous and might lack the cohesiveness required by the traditional definitions of class, they appear increasingly to shape their status around a new set of locality-based collective interests, especially in their modes of consumption and access to resources.

The idea that, in post-Maoist China, wealth is not for everyone at the same time has been embedded in the reform policies since 1979, when Deng Xiaoping formulated the target of a "well-off society" (*xiaokang she-hui*) and the strategy of allowing some to "get rich first" (*xian fuqilai*).[10] In the 1980s and early 1990s, the people who benefited from this strategy were especially those with the ability to extract public resources from the economic system and to reinvest them in productive activities in the form of private or collective enterprises. In the 1990s, however, the image of the high achievers became more complex and began to include a larger group of urban professionals and skilled employees, especially in the public sector, whose economic situation had improved beyond the average.

Early analyses of the high-achieving sectors of urban society have focused on the challenges that the emergence of this group—armed with social capital composed of money, knowledge, and social relations—poses for the authoritarian state. Some authors have assumed that the upward social mobility of high-consuming social clusters is the outcome of the self-serving manipulations of resource-controlling bureaucrats and of the osmosis of state resources through the economic apparatus into the hands of the new entrepreneurial elites. Attention has been devoted to the emergence of independent entrepreneurs and "cadre capitalists" as the "new rich" and "new middle class."[11] They have been considered "inherently more entrepreneurial" and deemed to be the section of society that the Communist Party was most willing to coopt into its ranks.[12]

Because of their apparent inability to profit entrepreneurially from the improved market conditions, professionals were for a long time excluded from the image of the high achievers. To testify to their belated economic mobility, professionals came to be seen as "the fourth generation of those who got rich first." The first three generations were hard-working agricultural entrepreneurs in the late 1970s, entrepreneurs in rural township and village enterprises in the early 1980s, and successful entrepreneurs in speculative activities such as construction and the stock market in the 1990s.[13]

If the Chinese salaried middle class resembles in any way the popular images of middle-class lifestyles that have been experienced and studied in industrialized countries and if this group has some collective form of social identity, then Hopetown and the other gated communities that have sprung up in recent years are the ideal kind of environment in which to observe it.

A large number of middle to high income earners are concentrated here. Residents share the relatively new experience of homeownership, are generally highly educated, devote substantial resources to education, and are largely employed in positions that imply some level of responsibility, either managerial, technical, or administrative and often in the public sector. They have in common a well-defined consumer identity and, as will be explained, share the benefits of privileged access to the real estate market and an awareness of the rights to which this gives rise. To borrow an evocative expression, Hopetowners are overwhelmingly "salary men"[14] and are vociferous about the difference between those who have earned a deservedly high salary thanks to their skills and their loyalty to an employer (often the state) and those who earned early riches through means that were corrupt, at least in the view of these professionals. As with other communities, the origin, life history, and career of homeowners are very important elements in defining their status. Hopetown's salary men despise corruption and lavish consumption, just as entrepreneurs are often critical of the advantages enjoyed by public servants in their social mobility.

For the moment, however, I wish to stress the often-overlooked relevance of the emerging professional urban population among the new urban elites, which is there as a consequence of its exposure to policies aimed at stimulating consumption. Successful entrepreneurs might in some cases have accumulated greater capital, but the salaried professionals have been better positioned to extract the most out of recent efforts by the central state to create a consumer society. While the progressive privatization of the economy and growing urban unemployment have meant "downward" mobility in society and an "informalization" of their work situation for many in the traditional urban working class, with less job security and fewer guaranteed benefits, those who have managed to maintain a good position within the formal employment system can take advantage of policies aimed at increasing their consumption.[15] In the emerging market environment they have also cashed in on status privileges inherited from the socialist distributive system.

Marketization amplified the original policy intentions. My analysis of status enhancement strategies among the residents of Hopetown suggests, for example, that early access to the privatization of housing has become a major discriminant between social actors and that it often determines social status more than income does. In the words of Wu Fulong, "The privatization of real estate itself becomes a source of socio-spatial differentiation, because through the real estate market households are able to capitalize properties that were not distributed equally during the socialist period."[16] But beyond the macroscopic effects of a differential access to housing, the emergence of a professional middle class has also been the consequence of intensive and ideologically justified and coordinated policymaking, which manifested itself in a steep rise in public sector salaries and a protection of the welfare privileges of the skilled, publicly employed urban population. In remarking that consumption became a policy priority not only for the middle classes but also for the new migrant workers during the 1990s, Pun Ngai observed a transition in the national rhetoric "from the glorification of productive labor to an incitement for all to indulge in a 'high tide' [*gao-chao*] of ostentatious consumerism."[17]

The Liberation of Consumption Forces

This change did not happen by chance; it was part of a significant shift in China's economic priorities. The 16th Party Congress in November 2002 marked, in the words of Jiang Zemin, the strengthening of a policy of "building a well-off society in an all-round way."[18] Among the features of this strategy, the idea of coopting private entrepreneurs into the Party has been the most eye-catching, because of its revolutionary implications for the very foundation of Party ideology. Nonetheless, while the role of entrepreneurs as power brokers and supporters of economic liberalization must not be underestimated, the project of a middle-class society is of even greater importance, as it has focused on expanding the purchasing power and status of significantly larger groups of urban employees and professionals.

The rationale behind the policy of stimulating consumption stems first and foremost from the need to sustain economic growth. Just as the initial stage of reform in the 1980s entailed a "liberation of productive forces," the long move away from "heavy production and light consumption" (*zhong shengchan qing xiaofei*) was hailed as a necessary "liberation of consumption forces." A recurrent opinion in China's academic literature is that the traditionally low consumption rate has constituted a major bottleneck for economic development.[19] As late as 2008, the *People's Daily* lamented that China's consumption rate stood at a mere 35.3 percent of GDP, "not only far lower than the 70.1 percent in the U.S. but also below India's rate of 54.7 percent."[20] Despite some international observers hailing 2011 as a breakthrough year, with consumption for the first time edging past 50 percent of the GDP, official data still suggest that consumption was still at 35 percent in 2012.[21]

A second and possibly equally important reason, however, is embodied in the argument that a large middle class improves social and political stability. The idea that "only if a large number of people will enter the middle income strata will it be possible to protect the existing stability of the social structure" has repeatedly appeared in the recent public discourse and academic research on stratification.[22]

A book-length study of stratification in China that was published in 2002 by the Chinese Academy of Social Sciences proposed a definition of the characteristics of the middle strata that seems tailored to salary-earning professionals and employees in the public sector.[23] It suggested that six elements identify members of the middle strata: (1) the type of work (intellectual labor in a safe and clean environment); (2) rights and duties at the workplace (including responsibilities, and the right to speak up, make suggestions, and exercise some form of control); (3) income, including all perks, patrimonial assets, and other benefits directly or indirectly deriving from employment; (4) skills, especially education higher than high school, training, and experience; (5) lifestyle and consumption habits; and (6) moral and civic consciousness.[24]

The description of the middle strata often emphasizes the moral and civic consciousnesses that help to produce the image of the middle classes as both "civilized" and "advanced."[25] I will deal with the discourse of an exemplary middle class in chapter 5. For the moment, I wish to concentrate on the practices of social engineering that lie behind the production and distribution of new wealth among the salaried middle class.

In identifying middle strata characteristics, this now-classic CASS study carefully separated the effects on individuals of their participation in production, on the one hand, and of their participation in consumption, on the other, suggesting that members of this group now have access to a broader range of possibilities, beyond their employment choices, to build or raise their status.[26] Over the last decade, sociological literature has continuously acknowledged the far-reaching impact of the consumption variable on social relations, at a time when urban dwellers are changing from being *danwei ren* (work-unit individuals) to being "more modern" *shehui ren* (social individuals) or *shequ ren* (community individuals).[27]

A focus on consumption in developmental policies, however, has not resulted only in a greater reliance on market mechanisms, and it has not reduced the importance of employment situations (in particular, employment in the public sector), as many of the resources to stimulate urban consumption have been channeled toward employees "within the system" (*tizhi nei*).

Increasing the Purchasing Power of Urban Public-Sector Employees

The most significant improvement of living conditions for public-sector employees took place during the second half of the 1990s. After seeing their income stagnate during the early reform years, they started to experience a sharp increase in salaries. Employees in the health care sector, for example, saw their salaries rise by 168 percent between 1995 and 2000, reaching around 40 percent above China's national average salary for all sectors of employment (their salaries were equal to the national average in 1995). The same thing happened for employment in tertiary education and in scientific institutions (increasing 158 percent in five years, reaching 31 percent above the national average, whereas in 1995 they had been below average).[28]

Government policies played a major role in picking winners and in lifting the living standards of skilled personnel in the public sector. Even as they enjoyed a shorter working week after 1995, employees in the public sector have seen their salaries raised four times between 1999 and 2003, in what Premier Zhu Rongji himself described as attempts "to boost consumption demand."[29]

Over the last decade, public employment in both urban state-owned enterprises and government administration and service agencies has experienced a higher average increase in cash earnings than employment in other sectors, and this does not even consider the nonmonetary part of the remuneration, which is generally much more generous in administrative units and even more for public servants. According to Beibei Tang's elaborations from the China General Social Survey 2005, not only do government offices offer salaries 35 percent higher than average (17,003 yuan, or US$2,000, per year, comparable to the highest benchmark set by mixed ownership enterprises with 18,488), but public employees also have much easier and consistent access to medical insurance, pension funds, and housing subsidies as part of their salary package.[30]

Several recent studies have highlighted the continuing importance of and significant advantages offered to employees by public employment.[31] Research inside state-owned institutions has also revealed, for example, that workers in high-status institutions not only are receiving better benefits, welfare, and salaries but also have access to opportunities for private extra income through market activities made possible by the status of their employers.[32]

In Beijing, where more than a third—36 percent—of the registered population is still employed in the public sector, public-sector yearly average remuneration in 2007 (enterprises, public services, and agencies) was still higher than the average salary in the city (50,524 yuan vs. 46,507 yuan, or US$6,568 vs. US$6,045) and higher than the remuneration in other sectors of the economy, including the collective and private sectors. Nationwide, in the midst of what is perceived as a period of substantial privatization of wealth, salaries in the public sector outgrew all other sectors between 2000 and 2007, with an increase of 278 percent in state-owned units, whereas the private and international sector grew by 219 percent.[33]

It is therefore hardly surprising that in 2012 the number of candidates who participated in the public service admission examination was nearly 1.3 million, with some positions attracting close to four thousand candidates for a single job.[34]

In a time of dwindling employment opportunities and high pressure on the growing numbers of university graduates, *wending* (security) and *gao fuli* (high levels of welfare) remain attractive commodities for young job seekers.

For some positions in the administration of public affairs, the call for a clean and efficient government modeled on Singapore and Hong Kong has also been behind the policy of paying a "high salary to foster honesty" (*gaoxin yanglian*).[35] While many of the 67 million employees in the urban public sector are benefiting from this boost, some especially sensitive categories, such as judges, have experienced a fourfold salary increase in the ten years starting in the mid-1990s.[36] Honesty in public administration came to be positively associated with higher payment, to the point that certain local public administrations have even established an "honesty guarantee fund" (*lianzheng baozheng jin*) where honesty is rewarded with regular payments equal to a 5 percent bonus above the regular salary, which can be drawn on at retirement by public servants who have remained honest have avoided any involvement in corruption throughout their careers.[37]

The years after 1995, after China reemerged from the economic slump that followed the events of the democracy movement of 1989, were particularly significant in the trends toward higher income for public service employees. In Beijing, the city with the largest concentration of officials, the effects on public employment have been remarkable: The capital's employees in public administrative units (*shiye danwei*), who today are recruited on the basis of examinations and educational credentials, saw their average salaries more than double in the 1995–2000 period (increasing by 133 percent).[38] Increasingly, employment is education-driven, as evidenced by the soaring number of graduates produced by China's tertiary institutions.[39] After universities' budget constraints hardened, with a consequent need to recruit full-tuition-paying students to stay afloat, the bargaining power of well-known scientists and teachers has also rapidly increased as academic institutions compete to recruit them.

Another indication of a state commitment to increase consumption is the post-1995 policy to provide additional leisure. With the declared aim of increasing consumer spending, in May 1995 a compulsory five-day work week (*shuangxiuzhi*) was introduced, which suddenly brought the number of non-work days in a year among urban employees to 115, while major national festivities were progressively extended to week-long holidays.[40]

This move jump-started both domestic and international tourism. According to one study carried out in three major cities, the average amount of leisure time available to urban employees had already surpassed actual working time in 2003.[41] Those who enjoy the greatest amount of leisure time happen to be skilled employees (in the cultural, health, research, and education sectors) as well as Party cadres.[42]

After being portrayed as perennial under-achievers until well into the reform era, public employees, professionals, and skilled employees in the decade between 1995 and 2005 have shared the experience of sudden upward economic mobility. This encompassed more than simply higher salaries. Equally important are their perquisites in accessing resources such as education, welfare, and housing, which depend on their type of work unit and their administrative status. It is thus not surprising that in high-income households in Beijing, a higher-than-average number of their members are employed in the state sector and also have a higher level of education and professional training.[43] This emerging social class enjoys the economic stability that is increasingly slipping from the hands of the working class at a time of massive layoffs of unskilled and redundant personnel. During the end of the 1990s, while professionals were jumping on the reform bandwagon, industrial workers in Beijing's manufacturing sector were, instead, at the sharp end of a growing income gap. Their salaries expanded less than the average (up 72.5 percent, against a general salary growth of 93.1 percent between 1995 and 2000). The manufacturing sector lost over 520,000 employees in the same period.[44]

Housing Policies and Residential Segregation

The state's social engineering to enlarge the ranks of a consuming middle class has had the most visible effects in housing policies, especially during that same decade. The continued involvement in housing distribution by the state and its agents has affected the patterns of class formation in two fundamental ways: (1) residential segregation determined by the commercialization of housing is shaping the urban environment around gated communities, where residents enjoy relative autonomy from traditional workplace relations and engage in new forms of autonomous and interest-based collective activities; and (2) state intervention to subsidize homeownership has favored public employees and provided them with easier access to status-enhancing homeownership.

The apparent freedom to decide where to reside is limited by economic as well as cultural and social dynamics: in any country, it is not enough to say that people with better incomes tend to have a higher number of possible housing choices, because other factors such as administrative barriers, economic competition, and ethnic and cultural divisions can affect the possibilities of accessing residence in a particular area.

This social division of space within cities has attracted the interest of the social sciences from their very beginning. Friedrich Engels's portrayal of the conditions of the British working class included a fierce attack on the segregated nature of cities, which are often organized to prevent the working class from getting too close to the better-off elements of the urban population. Engels's work lies at the foundation of socialist anti-urban ideals and of the (often unsuccessful) attempts by socialist urban planners to avoid the degeneration of large cities and to overcome their embedded social segregation.[45]

In the 1920s, from a different perspective, the Chicago School set the course for urban sociology by resorting to the idea of "human ecology." This explained segregation via recurrent cycles of migration (invasion) into peripheral areas and the progressive movement of upwardly mobile groups from those areas to better locations in town, with the new invaders then taking their place. Robert Park envisaged a structure of the city resulting from the "biotic" competition for scarce resources and described the organization of a city as the product of competition in a "natural" environment.[46] For sociologists differently inspired by human ecology, the effect of this competition was a city structure made of concentric social areas or competing social sectors or multiple nuclei.[47]

Later studies increasingly stressed the relevance of social factors in the city's residential segregation. One approach based on social stratification is that of "housing classes," utilized by John Rex and Robert Moore, for whom cities are divided along the lines of a differential and spatially informed access to housing. Following Max Weber, they argue that access to housing (ownership, private tenancy, public tenancy, and so on) is a determinant of class position and is largely decided by employment.[48]

The relationship between access to housing and class position has also been linked to the availability of other resources. Ronald Van Kempen has pointed out that the resources available to households in the competition for scarce housing are not limited to financial ones (income, security of income, and capital assets) but also include cognitive ones (education, knowledge of the housing market), political ones (a reference to the "possibility of attaining and defending formal rights in society"), and social ones (membership in social networks).[49]

Residential segregation has also been associated, importantly for my argument here, with the "localized" factors of class formation. In Anthony Giddens's formulation, for example, the process of class formation and reproduction would only be traceable if inscribed within what he called structurations: a "mediate structuration" that refers mainly to the "distribution of mobility chances in societies" (the more open the mobility chances, the less demarcated the classes) and a "proximate structuration" based on the division of labor, authority relations within the enterprises, and the influence of "distributive groupings," that is, "relationships involving common patterns of the consumption of economic goods," of which "community or neighborhood segregation" would be the most important.[50]

According to Giddens, class has both objective and subjective determinants (or "overall" and "localized," to borrow his words) and is the outcome of a complex structuring process that involved both economic and authority relations as well as their subjective perception. Class structuration occurs, in Giddens's view, not only within the production arena but also outside of it, in the field of consumption, and among people who share a common style of life. Distributive groupings such as segregated communities "interrelate with the other set of factors . . . in such a way as to reinforce the typical separations between forms of market capacity."[51]

During the decades of Maoist radicalism in China, the socialist urban planners tried, more or less successfully, to design cities free of segregation, in the belief that different housing conditions could determine social inequality. The administrative and economic control over population, production, and consumption and the fact that the state controlled the processes of building and distributing housing and owned the urban land—all of this contributed to make the project relatively successful. With restrictions in place against migration into cities, for a long time urban resources could be concentrated on a relatively small and stable population, and cities were organized in self-reliant cells (generally around or within the work units, in integrated residential/productive neighborhoods providing essential services and controlling consumption and distribution) rather than as functional areas (residential, industrial, service, and commercial). Transport was left underdeveloped in large cities such as Beijing and Shanghai, since the problem of moving the working population was solved, at least in theory, by placing residential areas so close to the workplace.

Due to the nature of the *danwei* system and its dominant role in the construction and allocation of employees' accommodation, housing quality largely depended on the resources available to the different work units, and a certain level of egalitarianism worked to limit differences among members of the same work unit. In an era when the work unit constituted the basic administrative, production, and social unit in the cities, the resources and status of the employer dramatically influenced one's overall social status. Units' choices with regard to housing quarters affected the nature of urban "social zones" more than socioeconomic or cultural stratification patterns. Victor Sit's study of Beijing in the early 1990s revealed, for these reasons, a much lower level of residential and functional segregation than was the case in East European socialist countries in the 1970s.[52]

Since then, much has changed. China has embarked on a pattern of urban organization that recognizes a correlation between status and housing consumption patterns, and residential segregation can thus become a fundamental marker for the analysis of social stratification and the emergence of new classes.[53] The rapid growth of homeownership in Beijing is determining a new skyline of buildings and lifestyles, one dominated by the imposing presence of neighborhoods of high-rise developments for the newly affluent middle class.

Today, the Soviet-inspired low-rise concrete buildings of Beijing are rapidly being replaced by modern, colorful, high-rise housing projects that can accommodate a larger number of homeowners in much-sought-after locations.[54] While the fancy up-market villas out of town remain a dream that only the truly rich (plus some Western and Asian expatriates) can afford, an increasing number of apartments of good quality have been built in the immediate suburban areas. The new institutional blend, where state agents and market forces interact, has made it more likely for social groups with a similar mixture of administrative access to housing and relative affluence to concentrate.

Hu and Kaplan have attempted to map Beijing's affluent population.[55] Using a survey of residence and income characteristics, they mapped out a concentration of well-off households in the suburbs between the northern sections of the third and fourth ring roads. They also showed that the areas where the more affluent people are settling down correspond to those that the municipality had zoned—since the 1982 master plan—to "specialise in culture, education, scientific research and government" activities.[56] This is a sign of the shifting focus in the long-term planning of the capital city—from an industrial and administrative center toward a modern, service-based urban economy, reaching its high point with the reconstruction effort in preparation for the 2008 Olympics—but also of the relevance of culture and education in the housing choices of the new rich.

Subsidizing the Neighborhood Consensus

The effects of the housing reform, however, were not only geographic. At the present stage of China's development, rising salaries and greater bargaining power in the labor market would not be enough to account for the dramatic surge in status and consumption levels experienced by some employees and professionals. The patterns of housing acquisition have also proved to be decisive in changing the lifestyles and consumption abilities of at least the first generation of Chinese reform-era professionals.

Even after the dismantling of the virtually free allocation of rented accommodation, which prevailed through the early 1980s, both housing and the financial tools necessary to make purchase of housing possible have been circulating in a less-than-perfect market. The administrative role of urban gate-keeping institutions and the interest structure inherited from the earlier socialist modes of distribution have helped to decide who was going to "get housing first." Despite the progressive decline of traditional redistributive institutions such as work units, other agents of the state's project to "create" a middle class, such as state-owned real estate developers and state commercial banks, have contributed to shaping this strategy. Citizens who managed to maintain a relatively high-status position within the public sector appear to have been privileged (either directly or indirectly) with respect to access to these assets and today form what is popularly known as the *fangchan jieji* (propertied class). Decades of policies aimed at the subsidization of homeownership for groups "within the system" may well have contributed to increasing, rather than decreasing, the overall affordability of housing.

The massive sale of public housing to employees throughout the 1990s occurred at highly subsidized prices for the existing housing stock. Alternatively, employees were given the option of buying newly built houses, while the work unit would carry the lion's share of construction or purchasing costs. Although the share of housing directly built by work units declined from the early 1990s (to the advantage of major real estate developers), public employers remained an important engine of the real estate market, buying extensively to cater for the needs of their professionals and other employees or undertaking homeowners cooperative schemes.[57] Hopetown 1 was an early example of this attitude: Large state-owned enterprises and public institutions purchased blocks of private apartments and then resold them at very low prices to some of their key employees. Contracts often included clauses linking property rights to a long-term working relationship with the employer. This practice of rewarding loyalty and substituting real estate for higher salaries continued in the years after the 1998 housing reform, especially in organizations such as universities that depend on the retention of key human resources.[58]

Beijing's experience is emblematic. By the year 2001, three years after the formal end of the *danwei* housing allocation, about 58 percent of the city's resident families had purchased properties from or through their work units.[59] Almost 90 percent of all residential housing units sold by Beijing work units to their employees by 2001 had gone for less than 100,000 yuan (around US$12,000), a very low price considering the average costs of commercial housing in the capital at that time.[60] While subsidized selling had started in the late 1980s, the purchase of commercial housing did not pick up until the second half of the 1990s. Even as late as 2004, only an estimated 2.5 percent of the Beijing population was living in private commercial dwellings, while 68 percent was living in "reformed" public housing (*fanggaifang*). In 2012, slightly more than a third of the resident population (33.8 percent) were living in private commercial dwellings, while about 42 percent were still living in *fanggaifang*, with about 5 percent owning other types of housing. This brings the percentage of registered families (such statistics never include the migrants, who are mostly tenants) who own their apartments to over 80 percent. A smaller proportion rent public (11.5 percent in 2008) or private housing (4.1 percent).[61]

This sale of public housing stock at very low prices enabled well-placed employees to obtain cheap entry into the real estate market, effectively boosting the new owners' wealth.[62] Not everyone benefited in the same way, though, and housing careers remained path-dependent. According to a 1988 survey, the housing situation at the beginning of the labor market and housing reforms was greatly affected by employment status: cadres had a per capita living space about 30 percent higher than that of workers, Party members did better than non–Party members by a margin of 20 percent, employees in centrally administered units had more space than those in locally managed units, and the housing of state enterprise employees was more spacious than that of employees in the collective sector.[63] Since the housing reform was carried out on the basis of actual housing conditions, rights to subsidized sales of existing housing or newly built apartments varied greatly among employees and between work units.[64] Its effects were to amplify an old distortion with the help of a new market environment.

In the early days of housing reform, buying the apartment one was already living in (virtually for free) seemed like a waste of money to most people, but in the second half of the 1990s and even more after 2000, a speculative rental market, an emerging mortgage market, and a secondary property market eventually turned these properties into wealth multipliers. In order to boost the secondary market, the Beijing government progressively reduced restrictions on property rights, and properties that had been bought very cheaply became marketable at increasingly inflated market prices.[65]

In 2005, employees in the public sector (government offices, state-owned enterprises, and administrative units) still had the best chance of being homeowners, as compared with employees in other sectors of the economy. By 2005, 69 percent of SOE employees had acquired real estate, against 31 percent of those who worked in private enterprises. Within the public sector, government officials had access to higher-quality housing, as their family average living space reached 92.98 square meters, whereas it was only 81.32 square meters for employees in administrative units and 65.81 square meters for employees in state-owned enterprises.[66]

The introduction of housing provident funds (*zhufang gongjijin*) in the 1990s, formally to foster homeownership, did not enhance egalitarian distribution of housing assets either—quite the contrary.[67] The funding schemes ended up further expanding the housing affordability gap, which favored employees in the financially and economically most viable enterprises; within this group, it privileged employees with a high level of employment stability and prestige who could rely on a long-term relationship with the enterprise and were less at risk of sudden unemployment. Enterprises with better economic performance were able to make higher contributions to the funds, helping the accounts grow faster, and higher salaries attracted higher contributions. Collective and private enterprises largely did not participate in the scheme, thereby excluding most of the urban employees who were not employed by the state sector.[68] In developed areas of the country, participation was very high (as high as 90 percent in Jiangsu and Zhejiang), while in less developed areas it often did not reach 50 percent. Contribution by the enterprises also varied, from below 5 percent of salary to the 10 percent generally seen in Shanghai and Beijing.

Funds were also redistributed to a small minority of well-placed borrowers: According to one source, in the early 2000s about 80 percent of the fund's total lending in Beijing was directed to the purchase of high-cost commercial housing, while in Shanghai 44 percent of the funds went to just 4 percent of the fund's contributors.[69] Since how much one could borrow from the fund depended on the balance of the accumulated individual account and on the borrower's income, only high-income earners could afford to borrow enough to purchase an apartment, while younger or lower-income contributors could not take advantage of the low-interest loans, thus supporting with their compulsory savings the purchase of high-end apartments for their more fortunate colleagues: Only 5.4 percent of participating employees nationwide accessed their entitlements between 1998 and 2004.[70]

A further policy step to improve the chances of middle-income earners becoming homeowners was enacted in 1998, when all major cities were instructed to begin construction of "economy housing" (*jingji shiyong fang*). This is a subsidized form of commercial buildings rather than public housing, comparable in quality and location to commodity housing, with the price kept in check according to an agreement between the local government and the developer. The scheme took different forms, but in general it followed this logic: when assigning land use rights to the developers (in many cases state-owned companies), the local land-controlling authority stipulated that, in exchange for free or cheaper land and reduced fiscal charges, the developer must sell a portion of the units at a discounted price, which would be decided by the local authorities.[71] In Beijing, access to this indirectly subsidized housing in the early 2000s was formally granted only to households with a yearly income below 60,000 yuan (US$7,200) with no property of their own and living in substandard rental housing.[72] About 12 million such units were built nationwide until 2008, while even as late as 2011, about 13 million square meters of subsidized apartments were under construction in Beijing.[73]

Despite formally aiming at middle-income families, the policy outcome favored, again, the usual groups. During my fieldwork in Hopetown 2, where most of the homes are of this type, evidence surfaced that the income limits, which are enforced very loosely, are easily circumvented by higher-income families or by families with preexisting properties, a situation that has caused lower-income families to criticize the system.[74] Those in Hopetown who had access to this form of subsidized housing are often the same people who had earlier bought public and work-unit apartments. Among the reasons that lower-income families have been kept out is that, while the units are subsidized because the land is leased at favorable prices by the local state, apartments are often sold privately by the developer, whose agenda is to maximize the return on each development. This has produced a tendency for the developers to build larger apartments to cater to richer (and therefore more profitable) customers.[75] This practice was so widespread that in 2006 a new regulation forced all developments to include at least 70 percent of the space for smaller apartments (defined as under 90 square meters). In 2009, the fixed size of "economy" apartments was reduced to 60 square meters; despite the discounted prices, these subsidized apartments often remained beyond the reach of lower-income families who qualified for them.[76] According to one source, in 2008 a subsidized unit was still worth an average of 780,000 yuan (US$113,880), a price higher than the city average.[77] As one author suggested, they risk becoming "the weekend residences of the rich" instead.[78]

Also stimulated by government policy, a commercial mortgage market emerged rapidly after 1998. In China as much as anywhere else, mortgages typically reward those with stable incomes and preexisting property. Ownership of assets and an employer's endorsement are important credentials in securing commercial bank loans, so the chances for the usual suspects are enhanced. Reformed commercial banks in search of relatively low-risk

private consumption markets began to enter the arena aggressively starting in 1998, relying on the long-term consumption-stimulus policy of the
central bank. The outstanding balance of individual housing loans issued
by commercial banks countrywide had increased from 19 billion yuan
(US$2.28 billion) in 1997 to 750 billion yuan (US$90 billion), a thirty-nine-
fold increase, by October 2002.[79] The residential construction sector has
maintained an annual growth of over 20 percent since 2000.[80]

The Neighborhood Reward

As we have seen, the importance of income levels, at least in this transitional phase, is overshadowed by the distorted access to housing. This, of
course, does not mean that high-income earners do not enjoy an advantage in the competition for better housing. Rather, it means that, in a situation where the gap between housing prices and income remains wide,
people with privileged access to the state's distribution policies have managed to carve out lifestyles well beyond their means. This phenomenon has
been more significant to the housing careers of this group than have their
personal resources or their skills and their capacity to acquire wealth. The
high rates of homeownership claimed by local authorities seem otherwise
not sustainable in terms of disposable income.[81] On the open market, in
2002 an average apartment of 80 square meters cost around 33 times the
average yearly disposable income of a Beijing household. In the first half of
2009, this figure had skyrocketed to 61.5 times![82]

Buying a home is a fundamental concern for anyone wishing to climb
the ladder of social status, and the experience of "becoming a homeowner"
is central to many of the conversations of Hopetown neighbors. Buying an
apartment is considered a life-changing experience, and many expressed
surprise at how quickly this had become an opportunity. Several times
I heard the phrase "Five years ago I did not think this was possible."

In the older neighborhood (Hopetown 1), only "commodity" apartments were available. People who bought here in 1997 had to face high
costs and virtually no access to commercial credit. Provident funds, helpful
for some, were often not sufficient, and some resorted to family savings
while accessing extra income sources such as second jobs. Many of them
used resources that had become available to them during the initial phase

of the housing reform, especially apartments they had bought from their work unit.

As one illustration, Mr. Wang used to work for a state museum. He keeps using his old work unit's identification card ("it is easier to introduce myself to people"), but he actually works as a consultant for a private museum and an auction house. His wife, who used to work in public administration, received what she describes as a "generous early retirement package" that grants her almost the same income as before. They bought their old apartment, in a very central area, from his work unit after they had both retired. When they moved to Hopetown looking for a more comfortable residence to spend their retirement, they relied on the extra income generated by the first apartment, which they renovated to "make it suitable for a foreigner." The social capital earned on the right jobs gave them access to the right people (renting a *danwei* apartment to a foreigner generally implies an agreement with the local police station) as well as to material benefits.

The links connecting public employment, the state, and achieved status were often explicitly central to the mobilization of Hopetown homeowners. During a dispute with the developer over the state of one specific building, written materials prepared by residents were signed "Old Communist Party members of building X." "I have been a Communist Party member for thirty years," said an elderly woman prominent in this "defend your rights" (*weiquan*) protest, "and when I had to decide where to buy an apartment I thought that buying here would have been like buying from the state itself." Others, especially younger employees, also saw the role of the state in the development of this area as assuring the protection of their equity. This included the confidence that the relevant transport network and the promised infrastructures would soon be completed. That the area became a hub of the new fifteen-line network of the Beijing rapid transport system built before the 2008 Olympics was a guarantee for both the investment value and the convenience of their properties.

Many residents see apartments as their principal means of investment, and they use their privileged access to acquire property not just to live in but also to rent out. Despite the limitations imposed by law on the purchase of Hopetown's subsidized "economy apartments" (Hopetown 2), families with second properties generally manage to circumvent the regulations. At the time of my fieldwork, only 60 percent of the subsidized apartments

in Hopetown 2 were occupied by their owners, indicating that a considerable proportion of them had ended up in the hands of people who owned
multiple properties.

As one example, a middle-ranking cadre in a state financial conglomer-
ate obtained her apartment in 1997 at "a fraction of the cost"; the company
covered the rest. The contract she signed with her employer denied her the
right to sell the unit for fifteen years, but she and her husband, who works
as a public accountant, lived in the apartment for only two years and then
moved to an "economy" apartment in Hopetown 2 that they purchased
at a 30 percent discount from the developer. They have been renting out
the first unit ever since, making a good profit and plowing part of this
back into the mortgage. A year later they purchased a third apartment,
in the "economy" building where they live. In the case of this family, the
properties were made accessible to them as a result of their work-unit
affiliations and a loose interpretation of state policies to subsidize urban
homeownership.

In addition to receiving money from rental properties, the disposable
income of Hopetown professionals is often higher than their salaries, because of moonlighting in addition to their state employment. Many even
see the community as a potential "marketplace" in which to sell their expertise and special skills. The growing demand for insurance policies (car,
life, home), for example, has provided some with an easy way to boost their
family income by selling policies to their neighbors in their spare time.

Household budgets of 8,000 to 10,000 yuan (US$960 to US$1,200) a
month were most common at the time of my fieldwork in cases where
both members of the family earned a salary. This placed them in the high-
income cluster of Beijing's employees, considering that in 2001 only about
11 percent of the city's employed population had salaries above 2,000 yuan
(US$240) a month.[83] The average Hopetown 2 family paid 2,000 to 3,000
yuan (US$240 to US$360) per month in mortgage repayments, a very high
rate for the average Beijing resident but less than the monthly rent I was
charged for my apartment in the neighborhood.[84]

For well-off Hopetown residents, this burden was small enough to
allow a high level of consumption as well as additional real estate investments. Status-related consumption is generally in line with newly acquired prosperity. One young woman who earned a salary of 9,000 yuan
(US$1,080) a month as an accountant at a major state company complained

to me that Beijing does not offer enough for her as a consumer and that she ends up "buying a new mobile phone every time I get bored." Despite a mortgage, this Party member and middle-ranking professional owns her own car (her husband uses the company car), pays 250 yuan (US$30) a month at the local gym, and has traveled overseas several times: "When we traveled to the U.S., they only took us to cheap stores, where most of the goods where made in China. They did not think that we could buy expensive stuff too!"[85]

In addition to the services provided by the management company and by the local government (a primary school, sports and recreational facilities, a clinic, security guards, and women who operate the elevators twenty-four hours a day), Hopetown 1 has a much larger and more mature commercial network than Hopetown 2. The large community of high-spending residents has stimulated the establishment of all sorts of businesses. The large basements underneath each building have been rented out to all kinds of commercial activities, from 24-hour restaurants to laundromats, beauty salons, and fancy teahouses.

Buying a car is a high priority for Hopetown's residents, and the growth in the number of vehicles often outpaces the construction of parking facilities. While car sales had grown dramatically in 2002 (133,000 vehicles were sold in Beijing in the first six months of that year), cars became an even hotter consumption item in 2003, with the SARS outbreak convincing many to speed up the purchase of a private car to prevent risks from public transport and taxis.[86] The number of cars circulating on the congested roads of the Chinese capital had already reached the 2 million mark and would surpassed 5 million by 2012.

Hopetown residents are no run-of-the-mill consumers. Restaurants privilege the rediscovery of traditional Beijing cuisine over junk food. International retail chains like Starbucks started appearing in 2006. One of the two supermarkets runs a well-frequented bookshop that includes translated books of translation, poetry, and art books, together with textbooks for MBAs and the still extremely popular Chinese versions of such American business management books as Spencer Johnson's *Who Moved My Cheese?*

Electronic goods are also a top priority, with some families owning more than one personal computer; mobile phones, having become an everyday accessory, have lost some of their cachet as status symbols. Hopetowners have a high level of technological awareness, and many of them are computer geeks who use the internet extensively. Most of the apartments were equipped with a broadband connection at a relatively low cost. Hopetown in 2004 was one of the hotspots in one of the first internet-based "home-owner clubs" (*yezhu julebu*). Hosted by Sina.com, at that time it already hosted over 270 forums as the collective members of the club. Each corresponded to one gated community and was a forum for the discussion of collective conflicts, or disputes with the management companies inside the community, although some had less traffic than other. The provider required an individual registration and a forum moderator, while there were also self-imposed rules about politically and culturally sensitive material. Nonetheless, discussions about ongoing conflicts affecting the communities were generally very open and heated. The same provider also hosts a citywide forum on real estate conflicts. Today there are dozens of providers offering platforms for *yezhu* discussions, often on a city-by-city basis. The model still remains that of community-based membership, and most of the discussion going on in these forums is about specific issues of concern to the organization or conflicts in the individual communities. The provider's interest is in offering his advertisers or customers access to a very significant market of affluent consumers who are also heavy internet users. The internet is also used for mobilization of collective and locality-based interests, while some community activists have also become well-known bloggers.

Despite the role played by consumption in shaping status in the neighborhood, the nominal incomes of some residents do not suggest an ability to buy expensive housing or to lead an expensive lifestyle. One of my neighbors, a man named Fang, had recently been named director of a state-run chamber of commerce in Beijing. Nonetheless, his monetary salary remained only around 2,000 yuan (US$240) per month. Despite his low salary and his youth (he was in his mid-thirties), he owned an apartment and had recently bought a small car. His father was a well-known academic who had bought the work-unit apartment where he had lived for decades before retirement. Fang was later successful in buying a subsidized apartment in Hopetown 2. His parents moved into that apartment and rented out the old one. With the income obtained from the first, Fang bought a third apartment, which he shared with his fiancée.

Xiao Du was a young technical employee for a state-owned TV production company in the capital. His salary was not particularly high, especially because, as he often complained, he was a self-taught technician and did not have a university degree. Nonetheless, due to the nature of his job, he enjoyed long periods of free time, which he could spend at home as he waited for the next episode of the soap opera to be shot. This gave him the chance to take up additional work for other production houses and to devote time to social activities in the neighborhood. His wife, who had a degree in industrial chemistry and worked for a Taiwan-funded company, earned more than he did. Together they made around 5,000 yuan (US$600) from their salaries, and they spent about half of their income on the mortgage for their small apartment. Their parents, however, were well placed to benefit from the housing reform: The parents of both Xiao Du and his wife are cadres from the railway ministry. Both sets of parents have been able to buy homes from their work units and secure an extra income from them. The young couple, however, did not seem to fit the general picture of Hopetowners: Their consumption was much lower than others in the neighborhood, and they were not planning, for the time being, to get another loan to buy a car or to have a child. Their presence in the community is a result of their entitlement to economy housing in Hopetown and to their families' early access to the property market. Xiao Du found himself at the forefront of the homeowners' association in the neighborhood, mostly because he had time available, felt a significant pressure to protect his housing investment, and had good communication skills.

Cooptation and Social Engineering

More than their monetary income, what made these early residents of Beijing's first gated communities a homogeneous group was their (or their families') ability to access valuable resources from the public system and their ability to maintain this privileged relationship until these resources could be turned into private assets.

In this chapter, I have presented some evidence of the process of social engineering that has resulted in a cooptation of new social groups through targeted housing and consumption policies. The social makeup of these neighborhoods reveals the effect of a structure of opportunities that is built on the traditional distinction between citizens inside and outside the system of public employment. In the emergence of these new privileged urban clusters one can see, much more than the effects of the market, the very visible hand of the *state* and the strengthening of a stratification that had already been created during the socialist period. There is a visible convergence between the interests of new high-consuming groups (often dependent on specific policy orientations of the late socialist state) and the interests of the local and central state in maintaining order while fostering economic growth. This process is among the concrete drivers of the consensus, as it provides these emerging groups with a stake in the redistribution of the wealth produced by the reform project. It is also very visible in the neighborhoods, where the new urban residential segregation is often a consequence of both policy measures (widespread housing subsidies for urban residents and public employees) and market factors (the abnormal growth of real estate prices) that have produced sudden wealth for those who were catapulted into the real estate market by the privatization of public housing.

This specific process of accumulation results from more general objectives of the state, such as the creation of a consumer-oriented professional middle class, which has been among the stated objectives of the economic reforms in recent years. Public policies, economic conditions, and resource allocation have all contributed to the rapid upward socioeconomic mobility of the professionals.

After years in the doldrums, public employment has again become a top preference among job seekers.[87] The need to boost consumer spending, the quest for social and political stability, and a desire to foster a more efficient and dynamic bureaucracy have convinced the state to raise salaries and improve conditions for officials and to professionalize processes for their recruitment, with educational credentials becoming increasingly important.

The middle-class strategy of the Chinese government has employed a redistribution of public assets—especially of housing—based on the interest structures that existed during the years of planned socialism, in a way that has greatly favored sectors of urban society with strong ties to the state and to public employment. The social legacy of the traditional distribution of welfare and of the housing patrimony has put those with skills who "held on" to the state in a position of earning higher incomes and of profiting from a relatively inexpensive acquisition of valuable resources. A significant generational gap (which surely deserves further and more detailed research) also characterizes these groups, with those who entered the public labor market before the end of housing allocation in 1998 gaining much better conditions and assets than the younger public employees.

In the production of a consensus, the creation of a more responsible citizenry and a conservative middle class has played a central role.[88] This strategy has indeed been selective, targeting specific groups that had a bigger stake in the developmental trajectory of China's economic reform and that are more likely to be aligned with the government. Nonetheless, it is hard to predict whether this strategy will begin to backfire once the economic and political system allow for more participation, and these groups, increasingly representing private wealth, find it hard to align themselves with the interests of the regime that made them in the first place.

One of the direct consequences on the urban environment of a housing reform oriented around middle-income citizens has been the deliberate re-zoning of urban space, with the emergence of gated communities and segregated residential neighborhoods populated by new homeowners. The stories of my Hopetown neighbors point up how strategies of housing acquisition have provided a path for status enhancement and how administratively granted access to ownership of subsidized housing (and its skillful manipulation) has not reduced, but has rather increased, segregation and stratification.

Housing developments such as Hopetown produce a complex social fabric that is becoming a new arena for class formation. While employment remains the major condition of status enhancement, consumption patterns and family socialization and lifestyles tend now to evolve outside the purview of the workplace, in a relatively autonomous space shaped within the neighborhood's gates. As we will see in the next chapter, conflicts at this level are restricted and localized and generally do not challenge the political legitimacy of the state. Nonetheless, they provide a testing ground for independent forms of social organization.

4

CONTAINED CONTENTION

Interests, Places, Community, and the State

> In the community the idea of home has to be expanded: your home is not
> only your bedroom, living room, kitchen, and bathroom; it also includes the
> stairs, the gardens, and the parking lots. We live in the same neighborhood;
> we have to build our home together!
>
> LEAFLET DISTRIBUTED BY HOPETOWN RESIDENTS

An increasing number of disputes related to collective housing accompanied China's housing reform. In 2000, just two years after the reform
that greatly accelerated the growth of homeownership, housing-related
disputes reached the courts in about 166,000 cases nationwide, a 42 percent
increase over 1997.[1] Disputes concerning housing sales more than tripled
in 2001, prompting the popular press to call it the "year of the high-rise
disputes."[2] Conflicts about housing in urban neighborhoods were not a
passing phenomenon. Between 2002 and 2006, Beijing's Chaoyang district
court heard 5,931 housing-related cases, while nationwide in the first half
of 2009 there were more than 260,000 legal disputes involving "management companies, rent issues and other housing related disputes."[3]

Seen from the point of view of the neighborhoods, these conflicts are
about very specific but very important interests, amplified by the collective and geographically enclosed nature of the gated communities and sustained by the central role of real estate investment in defining status and
producing wealth for the families. This chapter, however, will challenge

the assumption that an assertive middle class is coming of age through the experience of neighborhood conflicts and investigate the nature of the collective interests inside the communities.

A Geographic Mismatch

On a warm evening in May 2002, a group of exasperated homeowners in Hopetown gathered in the courtyard of the neighborhood in response to an urgent appeal distributed through their own internet forum.

A few weeks earlier, a brick wall had been erected around a square area within the compound. Instead of protecting the children's playground, as promised by the area's master plan, the wall encircled a parking lot. In the previous weeks the white painted wall had been sprayed with protest slogans: "Give us our green back" (in red, with only the word *green* in green paint), and "You cheated us, keep your promises!" That night the apparently harmless mob was determined to take further action. The little crowd entered the parking lot and—under the helpless gaze of the compound's baby-faced security guards—pushed the thin brick wall down. They took good care that none of the expensive imported cars parked inside were damaged in the process, that the rubble fell outside the encircled area. No police were visible in the compound, and no formal attempt was made by the local authorities to intervene. The rubble of the wall remained for several months on all sides of the area, with the exception of a small portion of the wall facing the main walkway that became a message board for this "protect your rights" (*weiquan*) movement. Residents began removing the pavement stones and replaced them with trees purchased from donations they had collected from the internet community. Some of these trees were labeled and named after the individual donors. For a couple of months, residents met regularly every Saturday morning to work on the site. They printed yellow T-shirts with protest slogans that they sold for 10 yuan (US$1.20) as a form of fundraising. After a couple of months of physical work, however, this group of salaried middle-class men and women grew tired of using up their valuable leisure time on the plot. They resolved to hire some of the unemployed migrants hanging around outside the compound's gate to keep working on the reappropriated "garden." As one of the neighbors told me: "They can do three times the work that we can, and we don't need to waste our time, which is much more valuable."

It took, eventually, many more headaches, the resilience of a smaller group of residents, repeated fundraising, and private initiative to achieve a result. During a visit to Hopetown in 2007, fully five years after the beginning of the conflict, a group of neighbors proudly showed me the garden they had built through their own private investment (after repeated failed attempts to get trees to survive in the dry soil, they finally hired a private landscaping firm). All of this was accomplished over the objections of the developer.

While they have the potential to impact on social stability, conflicts of this kind generally involve private stakeholders. Typically, they arise from commercial disputes and from noncompliance by the developer with the terms of the contract (land allocation, discrepancies between the promised level of services and the delivered reality, the quality of the buildings or the environment, misleading advertising, excessive fees, and so on).[4]

Figure 11. Homeowners take the situations into their own hands, pulling down a wall surrounding a parking lot during a dispute.

Figure 12. A garden in Hopetown

Figure 13. A van used by homeowners during a protest against a local developer

Sometimes they go as far as a lawsuit; in other cases they stop at popular forms of individual resistance such as nonpayment of the monthly management fees. Resistance to what is perceived as the tyranny of the management companies is so common that some companies have been forced to act to protect their right to be paid a fee for services. In one famous case in Beijing, a large developer who built and manages twenty-four estates in the city took 568 individual residents to court for not paying their fees, complaining that the losses had exceeded 30 million yuan (US$3.6 million) over three years.[5]

Numerous collective conflicts begin with the misappropriation or embezzlement of land use rights, which often change hands when projects are well under way, damaging the economic investment and lifestyle expectations of the owners. On one occasion, a group of Hopetown owners organized a public demonstration against the construction of a new gas station in a lot originally allocated to a recreation center serving several neighborhoods. An angry but well-organized crowd, including some still wearing their power suits and high heels after a day at the office, gathered at the scene, pulled down the walls of the building, and left it in rubble. Despite the destruction of private property involved, the developer's reaction was not to seek prosecution or compensation. Instead, the company obtained formal approval for the project, rebuilt the site, and had it protected by private guards (not the police) to prevent further destruction. The residents' response was then to turn to what they called "legal weapons"—that is, to bring the developer to court.

In another dispute concerning a building illegally erected by a state-owned developer, residents turned to a mix of legal and direct "weapons." They combined a class action lawsuit with a series of demonstrations to expose the "corruption" of the developer and to request the closure of the construction site. The same residents also picketed the entrance of the building site twenty-four hours a day for several months and participated in large numbers in the public hearings of their case before the local court. Despite the growing frustration over the issue, the demonstrations, which were widely publicized in the press, remained largely peaceful. Although no proper permission was ever granted (residents repeatedly applied at the local police station but never obtained a reply), law enforcement officers were unwilling to intervene to disperse what would formally be classified as an unauthorized demonstration. The authorities intervened on only one occasion, when the residents tried to bring their banners outside the walls of the gated compound. Scuffles followed, and the bitter lesson of a spatially limited freedom of demonstration was rapidly absorbed. Since that episode, neighboring communities involved in similar conflicts have carefully avoided pushing demonstrations outside their privately owned ground.

In yet another "economy housing" estate, the developer sold on the flourishing black market the land use rights of a portion of the land that had been obtained from the local land bureau at a subsidized price. Residents realized the swindle when they noticed a few buildings of highly priced apartments were already under construction on some of their own land. As a consequence, they found themselves deprived of all the wonderful services and public spaces originally included in the planning and advertised as the main feature of the community. In this case also, many months of collective standoff followed and the matter ended up before the local court.

In Beijing's outer suburb of Chanping, residents of a gated community organized numerous rounds of protest against a developer for changing the planned destination of a lot of land from a garden to a new high-rise. During the long dispute, a group of 150 residents also protested at a local exhibition, in front of the developers' stand. Later that day, some senior residents were attacked and beaten by a group of migrant workers employed at the building site, an action condemned by the residents as the developers' revenge for the public shaming imposed on the company by the residents' initiative.

The list of such conflicts is almost endless, and virtually none of the Beijing developments I visited between 2002 and 2010 was entirely exempt from some kind of conflict with the development or management company. Reports on this type of conflict also fill several folders on my shelves, showing the growing interest of local media in this type of dispute. According to one Renmin University survey, 80 percent of all new residential neighborhoods between 2001 and 2005 experienced some kind of property management conflict.[6]

What do such conflicts mean? They are less dramatic and touch much smaller issues than many large-scale social conflicts among workers or peasants that have been studied in recent years, but their ubiquity both in the press and in the lived experience of new homeowners cannot be underestimated.[7] In her book *In Search of Paradise*, Li Zhang suggests the importance of what she calls "regimes of living" in the process of identification and formation of the middle class. Beyond the material impact, new housing compounds contribute to altering "the way in which Chinese people live and think about class, status, social space and selfhood." Private homes thus become the "physical and social ground on which the making of a new middle class becomes possible."[8]

I suggest here an interpretation of these neighborhood conflicts as the visible sign of a process of formation of collective interests among people who do not identify themselves with a class or for whom class is, as Ira Katznelson once wrote, "only one of a number of competing bases of social life."[9] Such recently formed locality-based interests determine patterns of cooperation between neighbors as well as their strategies with regard to private actors and the state. As discussed in the previous chapter, through a complex process of cooptation that was a direct result of state policies, homeowners in Hopetown have become members of a "status community," in which "the life-style of one's neighbors becomes the social context for one's own life-style."[10] These are communities of consumers, not of producers, and their status is at least as much formed in the context of local socialization patterns in the neighborhood as in the workplace. The enclosed and cohesive spaces they inhabit also play a central role in drawing the boundaries of their autonomy: They would hardly have any chance for (or interest in) collective action without the protective and magnifying effects of the neighborhoods' walls.

Simply put: the motivation of this or that Mr. and Mrs. Wang to mobilize in defense of the common garden is driven by the concentration of their interest in a specific community and in a specific place and is framed not by class consciousness but by a certain understanding of justice and a higher moral ground attached to their status as responsible citizens. Unlike patterns of middle-class segregation studied in other countries, the factors that in the years after 1995 led thousands of Mr. and Mrs. Wangs to move into a certain middle-class neighborhood in search of a distinctive lifestyle are not race, gender, income level, or religious belief. While an apartment in this neighborhood means an improvement in their family's status, the possibility of living here often derives from their exposure to well-targeted state policies. Many are likely to have spent the first thirty years of their lives in a work unit–managed compound instead of having inherited "middle-class" values to take with them into the new community. Rather, it is in the community of propertied individuals that their interests as consumers have become separate from their interests as producers in the workplace. This process is the result of interactions (and conflicts) with neighbors, institutions, economic and social actors, and, not least, the state.

The practices of this interaction, including the conflicts generated by dissatisfaction and frustration, are performed within the boundaries of the community and appeal to familiar narrative repertoires and to publicly sanctioned discourses of *suzhi* and responsibility. The ground rules of this confrontation are ones in which the hegemonic frame of social order plays a central role, and they are used to legitimize the actions of all of the different players (be they individual, collective, private, or public). Social order is part of the understanding that these owners have of the neighborhood they inhabit, which was sold to them with the promise of a superior lifestyle. As a group of Beijing homeowners wrote in a public document: "What is a 'lofty neighborhood' [*gaoshang xiaoqu*]? To speak simply, it is a civilized, orderly, neat neighborhood, that makes people happy and proud and bolsters high moral standards."

The spatial, enclosed dimension of the neighborhood conflicts as well as the ubiquity of such hegemonic frames point not only to a narrow definition of these homeowners' societal autonomy but also to clear limits to the potential for a class identification. Also, while a loose homeowner (*yezhu*) identity provides membership in a status group, divisions within their ranks are not class-based either. The relative position of individuals and families with respect to "the system" reproduces significant loyalties, as it defines a more crucial separation between groups. Public servants, professionals, or private entrepreneurs often tend to see each other as sitting on different sides of the social fence and as maintaining contradictory interests, ethical foundations, and social identities.

The eruption of spontaneous collective action suggests that we need to consider new neighborhoods less as administrative entities in a changing political environment than as arenas of complex social interaction and, potentially, as breeding grounds for a particular type of social change and interest formation. With the shift in the role of work units and mass organizations from agents of distribution to paternalistic employers and consumption facilitators, affluent Chinese urban dwellers now seem to enjoy a wider range of independent decisions that relate directly to consumption and that affect their perception of status and awareness of private interests.

The public discourse that surrounds consumer rights and the rhetoric of "community building" that dominates urban policy making provide the new homeowners with the legitimacy to build a collective consumer identity and a cultural "framing" that motivates collective actions; the spatial form of the gated community enhances the perception of autonomy that is necessary to undertake informal socialization and to "mobilize" resources and material interests.[11] In the context of this changing relationship between administration and private interests, my questions here concern how such interests form and organize, what moves individuals to action, how people sharing the same courtyard act in defense of what they perceive as a threat to their way of life, what the structure of their material interests entails, how these interests contribute to a collective need for action, and how groups achieve a certain level of cohesion.

Neighborhood Politics and China's Gated Communities

Both Marxist and Weberian approaches to neighborhood-based political activism focus on interest formation, but the two differ in their understanding of where interests are formed. Authors maintaining Marx's focus on production-related "objective interests" have argued that conflicts in the realm of residence are, for example, a form of "displaced class struggle," taking place when the dominant capitalist relations of production extend their tentacles to issues of consumption or distribution.[12] While acknowledging the importance of production relations in the process of class formation, Weberians also draw our attention to the importance of the relations of consumption in determining interests.[13] Class cleavages therefore emerge not only from the struggle for the control of production factors but also in the realm of consumption.

The class approach incorporates Marx's analysis of the formations of objective interests, which in this case would be "rooted in the property relations of the home place rather than in those of the workplace," and the idea of "housing classes," which is based on the assumption that the relation to domestic property is one of the determinants of social status.[14] John Rex and Robert Moore understood Weber's idea in such a way that "class struggle was apt to emerge wherever people in a market situation enjoyed differential access to property [and] might therefore arise not only around the use of the means of industrial production, but also around the control of domestic property."[15] Peter Saunders has suggested that a more significant distinction is to be found between those who have access only to the housing's "use value" and those who also have access to its "exchange value."[16] Those who have access to housing as a form of capital accumulation might well become a class in the original Weberian sense. What holds them together as a class is the protection of the exchange value of their property, a motivation to act that would differentiate their collective interests from those of tenants.

Later critics pointed out that the protection of use values (qualitative and not directly economic) also plays a role in motivating homeowners to act. John Emmeus Davies included them in his idea of a "bundle of interests" encompassing interests of exchange and interests of use.[17] The solidarities forged to protect these interests are based on "the place where they have their homes, raise their children and relate to each other more as neighbors than as co-workers."[18]

While the tradition of western sociological debates provides us with valuable tools, we cannot explain activism in Beijing's residential gated communities in the same way as if they were in, Los Angeles, Chicago, or Sparkbrook, near Birmingham, England.

A fundamental difference is that areas like Hopetown include mainly new residential compounds in the form of gated neighborhoods (*fengbi shi xiaoqu*) and commercial developments managed by property managers, not the socially complex areas that have generally been the object of sociological research on neighborhoods. Their geography is decided by blueprints, walls, and fences, not (or not yet) by complex networks of social interaction. These new human communities are superimposed on a static design that is supposed to engender lifestyle expectations but lack a shared tradition of social trust and cultural, economic, racial, or ethnic characteristics derived from historical experience. Beijing's gated neighborhoods have existed for a very limited time and are not "memorable places"; they artificially concentrate people in a plain social terrain created and designed by a real estate developer as a product for new abstract aspirations and consumption demands.[19] They are providing new, appealing lifestyle models but also reshuffling the cards of social complexity in the post-*danwei* cities.

As explained in chapter 1, gating is a tool for spatial segregation and social classification, a device to classify and govern society, and its result is a concrete representation of the adaptation of urban social governance to a more complex social fabric: While high-end walled compounds become home to "high-*suzhi*" citizens entitled to self-government, other, "lower-*suzhi*" groups struggle to resist the increasing pressure from the state to control their autonomy and their need for informality.[20]

A second difference is that homeownership is a new experience. Until the early 1990s, almost nobody in Beijing could aspire to be a homeowner. Purchasing an apartment has been, until recently, an opportunity enjoyed by a very small number of people. The situation has changed dramatically with the policies initiated in the mid-1990s and with the emergence of a commercial mortgage market starting in 1998. The number of people sharing the experience of buying a home has increased dramatically. The already mentioned steep decline over the last decade in the percentage of the population living in public housing and the corresponding increase of the homeownership rate after the subsidized sale of massive quantities of *danwei* housing suggest that novelty is indeed a factor in determining what interests are more relevant to Chinese homeowners.[21] For these first-generation homeowners, issues such as "salability" and "legacy" are less relevant than status-related "use-values."

A third difference is the level of public intervention in the privatization of housing and its impact on the social fabric of these communities. Housing welfare assumed a very peculiar form in China, for at least two reasons: (1) the long-term commitment to providing free housing to a limited number of public employees in the city gave some people earlier and better access to ownership once the public housing stock began to be sold in the 1990s; and (2) housing welfare during the reform period has privileged subsidized mass ownership (following the example of such places as Hong Kong and Taiwan) over the public tenancy administered by housing councils that is typical of many Western welfare systems.

Finally, the new neighborhoods ushered in a structural change in the organization of urban society. The de-linking of work and residence, which came about as a consequence of the housing reform, effectively compelled China's urban dwellers to acquire their own house but also increased the complexity of their patterns of dependence.[22] Compared to the traditional housing system—in which a large number of urban residents lived under the social, political, and administrative control of their employers and resided in compounds attached to or owned by their work units—the environment where urban dwellers reside, socialize, and manage their consumption today enjoys greater independence.

For a section of urban dwellers, affluence and commoditization have increased the opportunities for autonomous decisions (for example, job-seeking, residence, status-related and durables consumption). A shift away from dependence on a single source of status formation has become possible, while consumption has assumed an important role in the process of status enhancement. An individual's potential to relate to others and to build tangible networks of interest creates opportunities for independent judgment on neighborhood decisions, while collective conflicts and the related social activities provide opportunities for practicing individual and social skills that might earn individuals a reputation, and therefore status, within the communities.

Assessing Homeowners' Interests

Purchasing an apartment in Hopetown is expensive, which makes the protection of equity a central concern for the new homeowners. They have been encouraged—by rising prices and the government's intervention to facilitate homeownership—to speed up their investment, but they are often unsure about the long-term sustainability of the value of their houses. Equity not only depends on the market prices but also on location, the characteristics of the built environment, the services available in the neighborhood, the quality of management, the availability of transport, facilities, and commercial networks. When purchasing an apartment in Hopetown, residents, mesmerized by the promises of green-hued ads and the plastic dioramas, generally agree to buy an apartment in a yet-to-be-built area. When the developer slows down completion of the common facilities or introduces changes to the original plan, the residents' reaction is first and foremost to protect the value of their investment.

For example, the prospective construction of a thirty-story residential building just outside of Hopetown 1, in an area originally designated as a park, sparked angry protests by those who would be directly affected. The residents of one building complained that their view would be blocked by the new high-rise, eventually reducing the value of their investment. They grumbled that they had agreed to pay a premium to buy apartments in the most prestigious building in the development, and now the only thing to distinguish it from the other buildings was the appealing neon-illuminated word "HOPE" on the roof. Residents now saw the prospect of their apartments' uninterrupted views being blocked by the new building as a serious threat to their investment. The developer was responsible for changing the destined use of the land and subcontracting its development to another firm. In March 2002, residents organized a demonstration within the gates, but their attempt to leave the compound with banners and loudspeakers resulted in police intervention and minor scuffles.[23] The entrance to the allegedly illegal building site was then picketed for months with the help of a small "propaganda van," and women and elderly men from the neighborhood took shifts around the clock. Physical confrontations between the residents and the migrant construction workers at the site were also reported. The risk that the real value of their investment would decline was a concern strong enough to bring together a large number of neighbors, including those from other buildings not directly affected by the new plan. Eventually a class action suit signed by over three hundred petitioners was filed; the local court ruled in favor of the residents.[24]

State involvement in the development is also generally perceived as a guarantee of stability and equity. In the case of Hopetown, the municipality has endorsed the development and has planned substantial infrastructure for the area. Also, that the developer was state-owned fueled the owners' disappointment over its failure to deliver the promised high construction quality. In an open letter at the height of the conflict, they wrote:

> We believe that a company such as yours, managed by the Beijing government and owned by the state, that ranked at the top of the list of the hundred largest construction corporations in the country, should be the most honest and guarantee the best quality and the best services. But what you have done in our neighborhood has made people unhappy![25]

Public support for the construction of transport, medical, and school facilities is also very important to the market value of properties. The position of the area as a hub in the newly planned system of underground and light railway lines boosted the prices and was a magnet for buyers. At the same time, however, the failure to provide those services as planned was a blow to the residents' value-related expectations. Shortly after completion of the compound, Hopetown 2 suddenly received the news that the school that should have opened within the neighborhood was no longer to be funded as a public school. Nine thousand people, many of them young couples with young children, found themselves in the position of having to enroll their children in the existing school in Hopetown 1—but at a much higher cost. A spontaneous committee was formed to meet with representatives from the local education commission, and at the end of the confrontation an agreement was reached that the Hopetown 2 school would begin operating the following year.

The value of an investment is determined not only by the selling price of the property but also by the collateral income that it can generate. In Hopetown, which was built in the early years of the construction boom, for example, the quality of the apartments was good enough to attract a community of expatriates unwilling to pay the high rents that are generally necessary to live in purpose-built international residential compounds. Because this was from the beginning classified as an "open development" (*kaifa xiangmu*), foreigners have been allowed to live in Hopetown from the early days without the specific police authorizations required in other urban areas. In the early 2000s, at least thirteen hundred Korean nationals were already renting from local owners in the area, a situation that gave Hopetown the nickname of "Korea City" (*hanguo cheng*) and a reputation for the best Korean food in town. Despite the limitations imposed by housing regulations on access to subsidized housing (see chapter 3), many of the families who live in Hopetown 2 own another apartment, usually the one they purchased from their employer. For many middle-class families, the real estate investment is the most important of their economic activities, often generating a real income higher than that earned from employment.

Problems that produce conflicts between owners often arise with the value or profitability of the new properties for reasons independent of managers or developers. "When the developer or the manager infringes on your rights," wrote one in a blog post, "it is a superficial violation, but when neighbors abuse other neighbors it is a mortal sin." "Uncivilized" (*bu wenming*) or "undisciplined" (*bu zilü*) behaviors by certain residents sometimes produce the harshest reactions from neighbors, who see them as a sign of the low "quality" of some new rich. On one occasion, a dispute with the property manager led to some residents refusing to pay their fees and to the subsequent suspension of crucial services for the community. The result was a long standoff that reduced the level of services for everyone, making apartments in the community less desirable and therefore less valuable. Some angered residents have dubbed the actions of these neighbors "community terrorism" (*shequ kongbu zhuyi*).

In one document, a homeowner noted: "A new neighborhood means new property but also new people. New physical property is a positive factor, but new people can be a negative one. New owners come from all different walks of life, from different social strata, different economic, social, and cultural backgrounds, different moral and educational levels—they are like fishes and dragons."

Because housing regulations are often subject to manipulation, apartments built and sold as first houses for middle-income families often end up in the hands of families who intend to use them as investment. Although owners are compelled by regulation not to rent or sell economy apartments for at least five years, according to the management company, many of the apartments in Hopetown 2—where "economy housing" is predominant—were not occupied by their owners.[26] This mix of owners and tenants is seen by some as a destabilizing factor for the collective advancement of neighbors' interests in the case of conflict. As one owner once told me,

> Owners and tenants have completely different interests in the neighborhood. The majority of the owners have made this place their home, cherished it from the beginning, and thought about all aspects of life in the neighborhood. Tenants are indifferent. They only think short-term and move to better places if the opportunity presents itself. It is not their fault; it is just how it is.[27]

One issue potentially affecting salability is that of existing limitations on property rights. In China, urban land for residential developments is owned by the state and then leased for periods of up to seventy years. This limitation did not seem to bother Hopetown owners, who were generally confident that the state would never exercise the right to reclaim its property. Policy steps to reassure owners and stimulate the housing market have gradually supported this conviction. In the initial years of the reform, some forms of limitation on property rights were in place, especially for the sale of public housing, on the assumption that highly subsidized prices should benefit owner-occupiers rather than speculators. The need to develop a secondary market has, however, prompted the elimination of many of those restrictions and in the mid-2000s the market began accommodating a large quantity of ex-public housing stock: Since October 2003, the owners of Beijing's 1.6 million ex-public apartments (half of which belonged to municipal work units and half to state units) have been formally allowed to put their houses on the market (*shangshi*), overturning previous limits imposed upon the ownership rights of these properties.[28]

Finally, only very few Hopetowners have had the experience of inheriting property. Recent real estate investments, however, are often family businesses involving multiple generations. In addition to the traditional burden-sharing between parents and children when purchasing a new property, the earlier employment situation of the parents is often a factor in determining the children's ability to acquire subsidized housing of varying quality. Also, in many households the decision of the parents to move in with the newly formed family is not only a sign of respect for the elderly (and a way to use their home and child care services) but also a purely economic decision: By freeing up the house that the parents acquired from their work unit, they allow it to become a very substantial contribution to the well-being of the extended family.

Interests of Use

The formation of collective interests and the willingness to act to protect them also derive from the expectation for security and lifestyle engendered by homeownership.

As an example, for many people, owning a home in these compounds means the assurance that individual and family needs (shelter, protection, personal security) will be fulfilled. The social entropy of metropolitan social relations, the increase in the visibility of urban poverty, the focus of the local media on criminal activities, and the end of a clear-cut geographic and administrative separation between local residents and rural migrants in the city have all contributed to make security a central psychological concern affecting housing choices. Not surprisingly, according to a survey among potential home buyers in Beijing, the reputation of the neighborhood and the security of the built environment are the two factors that most influence the decision on where to buy an apartment (particularly among white collar workers).[29]

In Hopetown, security is often associated with walls encircling the blocks of residential buildings while a private corps of young guards—generally recruited from the migrant population—protects the gates of each building. Residents need an electronic card to pass through the building gate, while guests must be identified by the guard or by their host through the video entry phone. Each guard takes a six-hour shift, and this "vigilance" is maintained around the clock. A four-hour shift is reserved for an additional traditional social control tool: the ladies who operate the elevators day and night. Access by car is also regulated, and visitors pay a fee to enter. The local management claims that, when it was built, Hopetown was a state-of-the-art security compound, "the most secure in the whole country." While the official rates of violent crimes in Beijing is low, the perception of risk is very high and is, as we saw earlier, supported by an official discourse of security that formally supports segregated regimes of residence. As in cities that experience a much higher level of violence, as in the São Paulo described by Teresa Caldeira, violence and fear generate "new forms of spatial segregation and social discrimination."[30]

Because segregated communities are expected to provide a measure of protection from the dangers of the outside, their appearance and organization are a focus of continuous anxiety. While shops selling expensive Italian furniture have mushroomed in the vicinity of these neighborhoods to cater for the demand for quality inside the house, the appearance and functionality of the neighborhood is a concern that arises from individual expectations but that can only be fulfilled by acting collectively. For example, the commercial use of the basements in most buildings has been a concern for the security and tidiness of the area. Some residents have complained that "the neighborhood has become a garbage dump" and that with commercial vehicles coming and going all the time, it is "dangerous for the kids to play outside and even for cars to reach the exit in the morning."

The failure to complete the garden was thus perceived as particularly ominous, especially because the availability of open or green space is a fundamental component of the difference in lifestyle between insiders and outsiders, between the green dream and the grey reality of the rest of Beijing. In Hopetown 2, at a time when 90 percent of the units were already occupied, work on the outside facilities and the central courtyard had only just started. The area was already highly populated, but heavy construction was still under way, and it looked disappointing, especially when compared with the emerald compound depicted on the advertising posters. Residents organized "tree-planting activities," but the results were meager, as the soil was too poor to sustain large plants. When shooting a home video of the compound during Beijing's infamous spring sandstorms, one neighbor commented, "What really makes me sad is that the sandstorm will soon be gone, but all the rest will still be in this desolate state!"[31]

One enemy of socialization is the segregated nature of residence. Apartments in guarded buildings in very large communities with little chance for external activities provide families with security and autonomy in their daily life, but many regard such security measures as hindering the residents' ability to care for their community, to "love our home."

In this respect, conflicts emerging from common interests help to overcome the architectural barriers and become a very important source of socialization, nursing the first steps of spontaneous community-making. The effects of interest-based conflicts on socialization have been visible while I have been in Hopetown. When I first arrived in the neighborhood, the conflicts had just started to bring people together, drawing them out of their houses and into the gardens. I experienced the transition of the group from an anonymous ensemble of individuals who barely knew each other to an organized cohort of neighbors who shared both recreational activities (a swimming association, a soccer league, a basketball league, an excursion group) in addition to the increasingly complex issues related to the neighborhood conflicts. Lacking a framework for their organization and with local neighborhood institutions unable to cater for the socializing demands of neighbors, conflicts are providing the glue for a group of people who would have otherwise been dispersed and atomized in their guarded beehives.

If the developer is held responsible for whether or not the neighborhood is up to the standards of the envisaged lifestyle, the management company has the unpleasant task of absorbing the day-to-day complaints of local residents. Reflecting a widespread custom in Beijing's real estate market, the management company, often directly owned by the developer, is therefore perceived as fundamentally biased.

The growing relevance of public discourse on consumer rights gives a powerful logic to the owners' discontent.

As one of them put it:

> The basic nature of the management company should be "service," not "management." . . . [Its] services are a kind of commodity. If we buy a fake product, we have the right to return it and obtain a refund. We can decide to choose a product from a different producer next time. . . . Security, tidiness, and order are what all of us in the "new city" hope for. And all residents in the neighborhood want the management company to change its muddle-headed management and to improve the quality of its work.[32]

In Hopetown 2, increasing numbers of car owners staged a protest for several months against the high costs of the underground parking (an average of 280 yuan, or US$33, a month). Despite the availability of spots in the convenient new guarded facility, car owners were filling every inch of common space (and often gardens), which sometimes provoked tensions between garden-loving and car-dependent residents.

In addition to the number and variety of conflicts and lawsuits, another indication that homeownership is bringing together the interests of an increasing number of upwardly mobile Chinese is the popularity of housing topics on the internet. In Hopetown, each of the compounds (all buildings are connected to a high-speed broadband network) runs a well-frequented forum that devotes most of its space to exchanging information on issues of common interest, including new regulations, information about ongoing conflicts, SARS cover-ups, food safety issues, collective activities, and the like. All relevant newspaper articles are forwarded and discussed on the forum, although an explicit and self-imposed ban on politically sensitive material is in place. But housing disputes—and the social disturbances that they sometimes stir—do not to fall into that category and are reported widely and proudly. A special section of the website hosted on an overseas server even featured pictures and home videos shot by the residents during the different moments of their socialization experience, including everything from card games to demonstrations in front of the local courthouse to meetings with the representatives of the developer.

The Pains of Self-Administration

Residents generally disagree about the most efficient form of organization for their interests. Hopetown 1 was among the earliest to establish a "homeowner committee" (the new form of self-elected representative body established in 1997 at the neighborhood level), but in Hopetown 2 residents have long delayed setting one up, preferring more informal groups to lead protest activities.[33] One possible explanation points to the fact that the younger population of Hopetown 2 was less attracted to the traditional forms of organization promoted by the local authorities. More important, though, homeowner committees were seen in this case as actually reducing—rather than increasing—the independence of residents' activities without dramatically improving their effectiveness. By 2006, only about 18 percent of the new neighborhoods had formally established homeowner committees, while informal forms of organization or resistance remained very popular in the capital.[34]

The impetus to establish the new organization generally comes from government institutions (the district government, through the Construction Commission's neighborhood office—*xiaoquban*—in charge of community-level affairs, street offices, and neighborhood committees) in the attempt to reestablish institutional control over the now atomized and networked interests of the residents. Many groups have resisted that pressure and opted for different strategies, while others who have taken the "institutional" path encountered frustration. Even fundamentally commercial relationships like those with management companies are often stuck in a web of official regulations that frustrate individual participation. As a member of a homeowner committee once told me: "You and your neighbors, in your country, don't need to seek approval from the city government when you want to change your property manager. Well, we do!"[35]

In the governmental discourses of contemporary urban China, as we have seen, the traditional hierarchical structure between street offices and neighborhood committees (the *jie-ju* structure) has been replaced by the "community system" (*shequ zhidu*). In the new situation, the different players in neighborhood politics (from elected cadres to management companies to homeowner committees and community-level associations that perform mutual support functions or services) all work in "partnership" (*huoban*) with the government, providing services, oversight, and often even funding to nongovernmental organizations that must be formally registered.[36]

This "partnership" is one of the ways in which the autonomy of community-level organizations is both fostered and kept under control. Regulations in Beijing specifically state that, once they are elected by owners and endorsed by the neighborhood office, the homeowners committees are entitled to sign a new contract with the management company and to undertake supervision of the company's budget and management practices. The reality, however, is much more complex, because in many cases the management company and the local officials have been accused of conspiring to prevent the approval of the homeowners committees in the first place.

In Hopetown 1, the first elections for the homeowners committee took place in 2002, but by 2004 the neighborhood office had not yet formally approved (*pizhun*) the elected committee. The neighborhood office contested the outcome of this election because it was organized through a meeting of representatives (about 80 of them) from owners, mass organizations, local authorities, and the management company instead of taking place through the general assembly, as prescribed by the regulations. The chairman of the elected committee claimed that it was the only way to get things done, in a neighborhood where almost five thousand families should have been summoned to hold the election, and that it was impossible for participation to be as high as the regulation prescribed.

The first application for approval to the neighborhood office was sent back because four of the elected committee members had yet to pay their management fee (as mentioned, a common way by which homeowners protest against the management company during a conflict). In order to remove this obstacle, the four were later asked to resign, but a second application was also denied approval, this time because the neighborhood office wanted a change in the original charter, requiring a two-thirds majority in the owners' general meeting for all motions to revoke the management company's mandate.[37] This clause, which is regarded as "unrealistically democratic," especially in such big communities as Hopetown 1 and 2, was later introduced in the new regulations on homeowners committees that came into effect on September 1, 2003.[38]

The head of the neighborhood office, who met the homeowners' representatives in person, also requested that the four resigning members be replaced by individuals nominated by the street office and the management company. Despite the repeated assurance of homeowners that it was not at all their intention to replace the management company, the stand-off remained unresolved and left the homeowners with a deep sense of frustration.

Angered by their unsuccessful applications, the elected members of the committee later argued publicly in favor of direct action. In a document distributed to neighbors in February 2003, they wrote: "A beautiful slogan with ten thousand words does not match a tangible action! Let's move, respond to the call of our committee, and act to defend our threatened interests!"[39] Frustration about the committee's effectiveness spilled out of the gates, to affect Hopetown 2 where the establishment of a similar owners' committee was put on hold.

Even when the neighborhood office formally endorses a committee, its effectiveness is often limited by strict controls. In another community in the area, the approved committee had called a general assembly to vote on important issues relating to the management company. But while the turnout had been encouraging (almost 300 families out of a total of 1,000), the committee chair opened the meeting by saying: "We have made it clear to the neighborhood office that we consider this vote to be representative [*you daibiao xing*] of the owners' will, but they responded that they will overthrow any decision which is not made with the prescribed majority."[40] While these votes appear to be a genuine exercise of long-withheld rights of participation at the grassroots level, their effectiveness in governing the neighborhood is still very limited and contributes to mounting frustration, which, in turn, often leads to direct action.

The dialectic of the residents' relationship with the developer is even more confrontational. As one Hopetown resident said, "It's us, the independent owners, versus them, the powerful corporation; it is the law on the side of the weak versus the unsound regulations made ad-hoc for them; it is a loose and hesitant group of activists versus a predatory group of professional merchants."[41]

Resorting to direct confrontation is often seen as the only option to get the residents' voice heard. The traditional street offices are perceived as marginalized actors in the new, market-dominated environment and as constrained within outdated power relations: "The director of the street office is a grassroots cadre. How can we expect him to stand up to the general manager of the development company, who ranks as high as a vice minister?"

Autonomy and Contained Conflicts

Despite the attempts by the local authorities to transform the old structures of social control and manipulate them to adapt to the changed social and spatial structure, the emergence of informal organizations and confrontational discourses among residents suggests that, on the back of property rights and community interests, a relatively autonomous space for socialization and limited action is being created, safeguarded by the walls of the gated communities. From my analysis, however, it appears that these activities, maintained within the gates of the neighborhood, are shaped by the interaction and "collective" nature of local interests and by the struggle for recognition more than by a significant cross-societal middle-class identity.

The peculiar histories and social composition of homeowner communities spreading around Beijing offer an opportunity to discuss class and space as different, though not alternative, interpretations of social organization in postsocialist neighborhoods.

Neighborhood action has often been explained by the concentration of "class" interests. A similar class background would be among the reasons that certain social groups sharing values, lifestyle, and interests—end up under the same roof, behind the same gates, sharing the same protest slogans. In Beijing's new cities, however, things appear different. Neighborhood action and the creation of autonomous spaces are among the consequences of the explosion of mass ownership ignited by the housing policies of the Chinese government. By resorting to a mix of marketization and subsidized ownership, these policies have favored ownership among people who maintain ties with the state. For them, real estate investment is often a more important economic activity than employment, thereby greatly increasing their sensitivity to and awareness of housing-related rights. One could assume that, because they share a relationship with the state, they also hold a similar class position. Such a position, however, produces interests that only materialize in the spatial and economic space of the neighborhood and thus remain localized and limited.

The importance of both equity and lifestyle-related interests in the individual homeowner experience; the novelty of China's gated communities; the active role of the state in determining access to housing properties; the reduced interference in social organization by traditional neighborhood organizations; the limits still imposed by the state on society-wide catalysts for values and interests in the form of cross-societal independent associations, organizations or political parties (that in other countries are generally believed to coalesce around status groups and class interests); and the dominant rhetoric of community empowerment have all contributed to turn China's "new cities" (*xincheng*) into shielded oases of social interaction and interest formation.

Gated neighborhoods amplify the reasons behind individual grievances and collective mobilization by highlighting the collective and practical nature of real estate interests and of the rights engendered by property. Privately owned spaces within the community provide residents with an autonomous arena for social organization and resistance.

The existence of a self-perceived spatial and organizational autonomy inhabited by a socially heterogeneous group of individuals suggests that the "new cities" not only are breeding China's new consumer culture but have also become an active catalyst in the formation of collective identities. These identities come as much with the rights to protest as with the responsibilities of self-government: Rather than simply "containing" homogeneous groups that owe their class position and status to external factors, their relatively autonomous environment improves the chances of individuals and groups becoming aware of and defending their rights. Their peculiar spatial form, however, also works in favor of a redefinition of the relationship of certain social groups with the state. By shielding socialization from the excesses of institutional control, gated spaces also provide an environment where individuals are entitled and encouraged to govern themselves. Conflicts and protests are "tolerated" and "contained" and easily reoriented toward intermediate players (local institutions, developers, property managers) rather than toward the state.

As I have shown earlier and will continue to reveal in the next chapter, this autonomy limited to the "space within" is one of many ways in which consensus is produced. The setting of boundaries, whether physical, administrative, or discursive, contributes to managing and containing conflicts. Such contained conflicts, rather than stimulating an alternative worldview, resort to legitimizing frames that borrow from public discourses of social stability. By accepting the exclusive rights of homeowners and the social distinction that comes with living in gated areas, boundaries also reinforce the technology of classification and of social inequality that are central to the state's legitimacy.

A Contagious Civilization

Community, Exemplarism, and Suzhi

The final practice of the neighborhood consensus is the promotion, through exemplarism, of urban and civilized practices of community. Classification, segregation, and place-specific manifestations of the activity of governing happen in the context of a civilizing effort that permeates much of the governing rationalities in contemporary China.[1]

The legitimacy of the post-Mao communist regime has relied on the simultaneous development of two aspects of civilization (*wenming*): the material (*wuzhi*) and the spiritual (*jingshen*). In the words of Børge Bakken, "Roughly, 'material civilization' represents the growth aspect of the model, and 'spiritual civilization' the social control aspect of it."[2] Mainstream interpretations of governance in reform-era China are fundamentally geared toward the material side of the equation. The spiritual side—individual behaviors and the commitment to the values of civility, order, and stability—has attracted less attention. The legitimacy of the present regime has overwhelmingly been associated with the quantitative elements of its government strategy (capacity), and predictions have abounded about the impact that an economic slowdown could have on the stability of the regime. But while this material interpretation is certainly important, it fails to clarify why empirical studies show that legitimacy and levels of support for the Chinese government have no evident link to economic performance.[3] China's quest for modernization, economic development, and a more appropriate place in the world has been accompanied by a "civilizing" project that aims at producing a strong correlation between the *suzhi* (quality) of the population and the strengthening of the nation, between the "responsibilization" of the citizenry and the goal of an orderly and productive market society. With social order central to the governing rationalities of the current regime, it is no surprise that civility features prominently in what has sometimes been called "moral regulation" and in recent years has been named, in the official jargon of the government, "social management" (*shehui guanli*).[4] While the tools of this regulation are the cultural representations of the mass media and other forms of public expression promoted by the authoritarian government (including, still, capillary political campaigns to tackle social evils), the target of such campaigns are at times apparently harmless everyday practices, as in the case of the sanitization of the "uncivilized" street-side mahjong games described by Paul Festa.[5] The emphasis on civility amounts to an emphasis on the technologies of self-regulation, so the system of community governance—as well as the citizens themselves—are often called upon to implement the practices that derive from government slogans.

The benchmarking of "what it means to be civilized" is difficult even for the powerful machine of Chinese propaganda. Despite the difficulties of defining the size and nature of the Chinese middle class, as discussed earlier, its heralded growth and widespread association with "high *suzhi*" provides one way to benchmark civility. In common parlance, official rhetoric, and academic discourse alike, the middle class is associated with the highly mobile, educated, and professional groups that constitute the backbone of the "advanced forces of production" (*xianjin shenchangli*). The middle class I refer to in the remainder of this chapter is thus a large, loosely defined social group whose members share the potential or the experience of enhanced access to resources (education, information, and wealth) and rapid upward social mobility, one that is becoming the object, inspiration, and exemplary yardstick for the contemporary version of traditional governmental discourses of self-improvement.[6] The rhetoric and practices of the middle class are also easily embedded in community practices. The segregation mentioned in the previous chapters allows local governments not only to tailor governance strategies to different types of residents but also to build an exemplary hierarchy in which citizens are positively or negatively portrayed, depending not on their contribution to society but rather on their assumed level of quality (*suzhi*) compared to the optimal behavior of the responsible middle class.

Such use of the middle-class discourse (independent of whether a middle class in China exists or not, or how big it is) is central to three governmental objectives associated with the new forms of community governance: (1) the making of new subjects who are autonomous enough to choose what to consume (and therefore stimulate economic growth and China's integration in the global market) but also responsible enough to contribute actively to the maintenance of social order; (2) the benchmarking of social aspirations and behaviors, with the creation of models for individual self-improvement; and (3) the production of value in the city by associating the middle class and its practices and "quality" with the material worth of public and private goods.[7] In China's drive toward modernization, middle-class professionals, entrepreneurs, intellectuals, and administrators are viewed as avid consumers who will spend more than the average person and thereby keep the engine of economic growth going. They are also assumed to be the most educated group, and as such will help to make China a member of the club of the most powerful nations. Yet they are also held to be the most responsible citizens, who, by virtue of their "higher *suzhi*," will secure the reproduction and strengthening of Chinese civilization as well as social and political stability in a time of growing economic inequality and social complexity. Such middle-class, "civilized," "high-*suzhi*" subjects play their role actively, espousing the late socialist state's objective of civilizing China's population and embodying the model of a modern and responsible citizen. As such, they challenge the widely held assumption of a normative role played by these groups in the country's envisaged transition to democracy. Instead, they appear as the most desirable type of subject for an authoritarian state: politically docile but willing to participate in an ethical and moral community in the name of social stability, consumer rights, and virtues. But these new subjects do not just happen. As I mentioned in the previous chapters, they are being engineered, stimulated, and rewarded; nurtured by economic opportunities; empowered by a rhetoric that justifies their privileges and highlights their responsibilities; and, finally, restrained in their "natural" aspiration to more freedom and autonomy by the ever-present threat of disorder and chaos.[8]

This characterization has materialized in the context of a changing opportunity structure (new forms of social stratification, marketization of labor relations, liberalization of consumption and of personal mobility, a growing range of personal liberties), but it is certainly not immune from political conditioning. The temporality of this phenomenon is enclosed between two political moments and two associated slogans: Deng Xiaoping's call for a *xiaokang* (affluent) society in the 1980s and Hu Jintao's trademark evocation of a "harmonious society" (*hexie shehui*). The stress on harmony as a rationality of government at this stage of China's social transformation is not coincidental. Chinese society today is described by the political elites as "complex" (*fuza*), as it incorporates diverse and often conflicting interests (*liyi duoyanghua*), all striving for representation. However, in the dominant ideology, these interests are no longer portrayed as being at opposing ends of "antagonistic" class struggle, as were those of the capitalist and working classes during the Maoist period. They are "non-antagonistic," and the objective of government is to accommodate them and to avoid conflicts. Although "harmonious society" does not appear to constitute a departure from traditional paternalistic patterns of governance, as a goal of social policies the search for "harmony" is essentially different from the simple call for "order"—it argues for the conscious and rational removal of the causes (be they economic, social, or behavioral) underlying conflicts rather than for their institutionalization and repression. It is therefore accompanied by a stress on individual conduct, self-improvement, virtue, and responsibility. It also defines a disciplinary regime, which is different from the capillary penetration of society generally associated with the institutions of authoritarian rule. This disciplinary regime increasingly adopts governmental techniques that envisage the active participation of subjects and the agency of a wide array of players in a virtuous scheme based, whenever possible, on self-discipline.

Governing Rationalities

China's post-Mao reforms are generally seen in the framework of a "transition," and the numerous manifestations of the market in today's China have led many observers to surmise that the final stage of this transition will be a liberal democracy. In reality, it is increasingly becoming clear that the political apparatus of the socialist hierarchical state is still in place; after more than three decades of marketization, there is little sign of the system that would successfully supplant it. Its role in defining the practices of power is still overwhelming, although perhaps more fragmented and not felt as directly by some of its citizens as in the years of mass campaigns and class struggle. Nonetheless, even the apparently monolithic state adapts. The rationalities of government and the subjects they attempt to produce today are different from those of thirty years ago. Today, the state requires citizens who are both "autonomous" (so that they can participate in the market) and "responsible" (so that they will maintain the political status quo).

Analysis of governmental techniques in liberal systems insist on their increasing reliance on techniques of governing that privilege less *intervention* but not less *government*. Mitchell Dean and Barry Hindess, for example, observe:

> The victory of liberalism over the earlier views of government involves a shift in the meaning of "government," from a pervasive activity of regulation rooted in a multiplicity of agencies across the social body to a more focused, top-down activity of the government and its agents, acting on and through relatively autonomous domains of social interaction. The earlier concern on the "happiness of society" has not been abandoned here, but on both normative and prudential grounds it is no longer seen as best served by the activities of government.[9]

While it is not at all my intention to argue that China is—unbeknownst to its leadership—becoming "liberal," the transition away from the "pervasive activity of government" can be noticed there as well. In particular, the emergence of "autonomous domains of social interactions" and the transition toward a more ethical form of government is taking place in China alongside the emergence of new agents of governmental practices. The call for "small government big society" (*xiao zhengfu da shehui*)—formally a downsizing of government structures and an empowerment of society—also seems to indicate that China's political elites share with Western political rationalities a "fear of governing too much" that is not "so much a fear that the population is governed too much, but that the state is doing too much of the governing."[10] In other words, the activity of governing remains the goal of governments, but it can take place with other means or through formally autonomous agents, as this book has already revealed. The question here, however, is not whether the neoliberal demand for a smaller state is being heeded in China but rather how the governing mode has been shifting under the impact of economic liberalization. The actual size of the Chinese state has, in fact, hardly shrunk, despite the continuous restructuring and reorganization of the bureaucracy, the latest announced in March 2013. In fact it has grown steadily since reform, in particular at the sub-provincial level.[11] The reliance on external agents of government during the liberalization of the economy has therefore gone hand in hand with an increased public presence in the realm of regulation and administration.

The Chinese government is vastly more present in activities of government and social control and cultural engineering than most of its "liberal" counterparts. Nonetheless, a multiplication of governing agents is taking place here too and, increasingly, requires the involvement of citizens. When this analysis is extended to the realm of actual practices of government, it connects with my idea of a consensus: the legitimacy of certain ways of doing things depends on the acceptance of certain fundamental principles of social and political action, primarily the fundamental role of social stability. The promotion of "stability-enhancing" behaviors that often points to the middle class as a benchmark (educated and responsible) contributes both to coopt the highest-*suzhi* citizens and to justify the deficit of citizenship rights imposed on less accomplished social actors (migrants and uneducated workers being the most visible examples).

New forms of self-governance as administrative self-management in the residential community are framed within the expectation that "high-*suzhi*" citizens will be responsible enough to play a constructive role in maintaining social order.

Quality, Harmony, and Community: The Official Discourse

On February 19, 2005, President Hu made what has been labeled, in the tradition of Communist Party propaganda, an "important speech" on the need to build a harmonious society (*hexie shehui*). The speech listed the institutional and moral pillars of a harmonious society: "democracy and rule of law, justice and equality, trust and truthfulness, amity and vitality, order and stability, and a harmonious relation with nature."[12] In this speech Hu preempted accusations of idealism by reaffirming that "realizing social harmony and building a happy society are the social ideals constantly pursued by the whole of human kind and the social ideal of Marxism, including the Communist Party of China."

Despite the idealistic flavor of the rhetoric on harmony, this was not the beginning of a new wave of political reform. On the contrary, it was a strategic call for the resolution of some of the tensions in society that risk leading to unrest and delegitimizing the Communist Party's rule over China. The rationale behind this new rhetoric appears to be one of incremental development. Once the objective of a *xiaokang shehui* is reached (a relatively affluent China with US$1,000 per capita GDP, as predicted by Deng Xiaoping in the 1980s), it becomes important that the additional wealth earned goes to rebalance the significant inequality that the initial phase of reform has created. It is equally important, however, that this takes place not as a consequence of the conflicts that inequality has created but as a rational and orderly process, which involves all elements of society and is led by the ruling party. The "harmony" Hu talks about is, indeed, not idealistic but rather a political project that aspires to rationally integrate and reinforce the ruling capacity (*zhizheng*) of the Party while "responsibilizing" autonomous social players in the management of social contradictions. In no way is it an ideal condition where social harmony is substituted for the need for authority. But the choice of words suggests a political realm swinging toward the "spiritual" (moral, ethical, and behavioral) construction of the nation, which a focus on economics would, allegedly, disregard.[13]

The word *community*, as we have seen in earlier chapters, is generally associated with both a level of administration and a spatial subdivision of the city. Yet in its meaning of a tight human group (sometimes rendered as *gongtongti* instead of *shequ*) with a shared ethos and shared values, the term has been mobilized by such different groups as real estate developers marketing their housing projects and neighborhood associations protesting their rights. As such, the discourse of community has often transcended its administrative meaning to define an environment where residents live together as neighbors and fellow consumers, mobilizing resources collectively to protect or valorize their entitlements. With this meaning, community refers to social cohesion and solidarities as well as horizontal networks of mutual responsibilities among stakeholders.

From the official discourse we can infer that the preconditions for "harmonious communities" (*hexie shequ*) and successful self-government are a sufficient economic base, a sufficient moral base among residents, and a willingness among high-*suzhi* residents to act as exemplars in the construction of harmony. These elements are commonly intertwined. For example, in one article in the *People's Daily*, harmonious communities are described as "strategic spatial units in the construction of a harmonious society."[14] Self-government is, however, only possible where there is "an economic base and sufficient economic capacity to guarantee consumption and continuous development. [It is] therefore not suitable for poorer areas."[15] The members of a harmonious community should also be blessed with high ethical and traditional values, have a balanced relationship with their neighbors, "speak truth and harmony," and have a strong sense of belonging: "a community that is not truthful and lacks morality will hardly become a harmonious community."[16]

One author, arguing the need for a "moral foundation" (*daode jichu*), affirms the importance of cultivating virtue and morality in social relationships in the community as well as in the workplace and the family. "Behavioral standards informed by truthfulness and morality," he argues, "will define relationships between husband and wife, between generations and among neighbors."[17] Exemplary behavior should be the outcome of this morality, and the affluent and the educated who have gained advantages during the initial period of reform bear higher responsibilities in the edification of a harmonious society.[18] Another official commentator writes:

> State, society, and individuals will have to share duties and responsibilities. For individuals the most fundamental task is to respect moral and social standards. This implies protecting the fundamental need for order in society. "Those who got rich first" and those who have a privileged position in society will have to accept even more responsibilities and duties in the process of building a harmonious society.[19]

This proactive role expected from the middle class and "advanced forces" in moralizing society contrasts sharply with the attitude toward the "vulnerable groups" (*ruoshi qunti*). These include *xiagang* (those laid off from state-run enterprises who nevertheless still enjoy social welfare benefits), people "outside of the system" (*tizhi wai*) who have never belonged to the state sector, and rural migrant workers. These groups are said to have a "very low ability to represent and pursue their own interests," to have few resources and, "despite their sheer number, not [to be] able to voice their interests."[20] The solution suggested for these groups is not to facilitate organization of their collective interests but rather "to rely on the government and the media to express their concerns."[21] So while the "advanced forces" of the middle class are given "extra responsibilities" in the creation of the harmonious society, the disadvantaged groups are deemed to require extra patronage from the state, so that they do not resort to "unreasonable methods" (a euphemism for violence) to represent their interests.[22]

Residential segregation and spatial zoning produce the effect of projecting this distinction between those who govern themselves and those who are governed by others onto the urban landscape. Communities of middle-class owners with access to resources are expected to practice self-government and achieve autonomy, but the urban underclass is still very much dependent on the direct institutional discipline exercised by neighborhood institutions through the social service network. So while an increasingly wealthy middle class can shut the gates of its residential compounds and avoid the interference of state-sponsored mass organizations such as community committees, in Shenyang's working-class areas, badly hit by years of industrial restructuring, state-sponsored community organizations have been revitalized and are becoming increasingly central to the well-being of large numbers of unemployed and needy citizens.[23] Faced with a declining standard of living, a growing risk of unrest, and the closure of many work units, the welfare system has shifted to a more localized, residence-based form of delivery.

Converging Discourses

In the debate on *suzhi* and community self-government, the middle class often endorses the governmental discourse of exemplarism. Indeed, use of official rhetoric on the morality and exemplary role of high-*suzhi* groups is often part of the way in which middle-class community organizers frame their actions. For instance, at a seminar organized in April 2005 by the neighborhood office of the Beijing Construction Commission, administrators and community activists were placed around the same table to discuss "harmonious communities." Two of the most popular homeowner activists in the city, Shu Kexin and Bei Ye, both heavily involved in a wide range of property-related conflicts, provided some of the strongest arguments in favor of ethical self-government and the need for economic and ethical bases for harmonious coexistence.[24] In presenting his view of social relations, Shu Kexin stated:

> The differentiation and individualization of needs has destroyed the traditional stability of social relationships. [. . . We now experience] a problematic relationship between "groups with different interests." This [situation] is not the same as the "contradictions between us and the enemy" but presents a problem for the creation of a harmonious society.[25]

Shu places a "sense of civic responsibility" at the center of the construction of harmonious communities: "A widespread civic education, which stresses both freedom and the responsibility one bears for the consequences of one's actions, is necessary. A sense of responsibility must be continuously promoted."

He also accepts that *suzhi* is a precondition for the creation of a rational and responsible society and that only those who possess "high *suzhi*" are capable of the rationality and responsibility necessary for civilized coexistence: "Rational [conduct] requires a civic quality of the citizens, a sufficient level of education and civilization [*wenming suzhi*]. Only those with both wisdom and abilities can act rationally. This is why we say that peasants are not rational, because they haven't achieved civic education."

Bei Ye also stresses the role of the "elite" (*jingying jieceng*) in shaping a sense of civic responsibility at the community level. His argument focuses on the need for harmony, self-cultivation, and behavioral norms. In commenting on what he sees as inappropriate and unreasonable conduct on the part of some homeowners, he says:

> We have to be responsible, because chaos is bad for everyone. [. . . Society] is like a body that can only be healthy if all of its organs are healthy. Communities today are therefore very important. [. . . They] are the best school for citizens and without communities it would be impossible to educate citizens. In the communities you learn to have respect for the rules and to love

your neighbors. Can someone educated in this way become a bad citizen? Chinese already know how to get along with their leaders, how to get along with friends and relatives, what they don't know is how to mix with strangers, and this is the reason why we haven't had communities. This is the role that modern communities are playing today.[26]

During interviews and in community materials I collected in Beijing and Chengdu, the ethical community is described in phrases such as "the best school to build citizens," "the cornerstone of society," or "the foundation on which the nation is built." This argument comes to the fore in the numerous conflicts involving homeowners, developers, and management companies. The discourse justifying actions against greedy managers or developers puts communities on the side of the government's wish for a stable and harmonious society: "There are over 100,000 communities in the country," notes a document from a community organizer in Beijing. "If each community succeeded in training its residents to be reliable citizens, consulting each other and participating [in community life], then what would China become if not a harmonious society envied by all?"[27] This unofficial discourse of reliable, responsible, self-disciplined, "high-*suzhi*" citizens justifying their grievances by the need to improve the nation and contribute to its advancement and modernization signals the emergence of new subjects, self-disciplined and in tune with the goal of the "community" project. These subjects are essential for a transition to a form of government relying on the "responsibilization" of private stakeholders in the management of society. New middle-class neighborhoods often project the image of virtuous human organizations that will contribute to social stability and nation building—a step forward in the civilization of urban China. Yet such convergent rhetorical turn does not prevent conflicts, and in fact it has the potential to be both *structural* (components of a long-lived and elaborated "mass frame," as mentioned in the introduction) and *strategic*, to take advantage of the discursive opportunity created by the strategies of the state while legitimizing the short-term objectives of social action.

The Exemplary Practices of a "Middle Class"

In the context of China's civilizing project, advanced and educated elites have become more than just a factor in maintaining social stability. What the state rhetoric calls the middle class or the middle stratum is now also an exemplar of population improvement and of responsible self-government.[28]

The promotion of the middle class as "exemplary" occurs at various levels—in official state campaigns, the media, and, not least, neighborhood institutions but is also echoed in the marketing pitch of real estate developers, the self-promotion of commercial property managers, and among middle-class communities. Academic discourse also often reinforces the assumed centrality of these groups in China's contemporary developmental path. One author, for example, gushed, "Our country needs the middle stratum [*zhongchang jieceng*], because it is the political force necessary to stability, it is a regenerative force of production, it is the scientific force behind creative production, it is the moral force behind civilized manners, it is the force necessary to eliminate privilege and curb poverty, it is everything. . . ."[29]

At the top of the state apparatus, campaigns to promote spiritual civilization are in the hands of a "Central Guidance Commission for Building Spiritual Civilization" (*Zhongyang jingsheng wenming jianshe zhidao weiyuanhui*), established in 1997. The commission is in charge of nationwide campaigns to promote the values of civility in a process often labeled "cultural engineering" (*wenhua gongcheng*). Communities are the targets of many such campaigns, including those promoting the standards for harmonious communities, the "communities of four advancements" (*sijin shequ*, rewarded for showing advancements in technical, physical, legal, and hygiene education) and the "culturally advanced communities" (*wenhua jin shequ*). The Central Guidance Commission for Building Spiritual Civilization, through its local branches and community organizations, aims at stimulating "morality building" (*daode jianshe*) and the cultural advancement of Chinese society. In practice, these campaigns propagate stereotyped models of "quality" comportment and take middle-class behavioral modernity as exemplary.

In its drive to improve the image of the city and the civility of its people before the 2010 World Expo, the Shanghai Municipal Committee for the Construction of Spiritual Civilization published a book entitled *How To Be a Lovely Shanghainese: Instructions for the Shanghai Citizen*.[30] The book first enumerates all the ways in which the spirit (*jingshen*) of the Shanghai people differs from that of people in other cities—Shanghainese are said to like quarrels, to be parsimonious and cold-hearted, and so on. It then proceeds to define "moral standards" (*daode guifan*)—at the center of which are the seven key commandments ("don't spit, don't litter, don't damage public property, don't destroy public greenery, don't dress in messy clothes, don't smoke in public places, don't use coarse language")—and adhere to a reevaluation of "relationships" (with the other sex, with your family members, and with your neighbors). Later in the text, under the rubric of "civilizing education," readers are provided with a meticulously detailed description of how to dress (the section "how to wear a Western suit," for example, informs the reader about the difference between a two- and a three-piece suit and the importance of choosing an appropriate shirt), how to stand, how to sit properly, how to behave in a public toilet (*wenming shang cesuo*), the civilized way to travel on a bus, to drive, to address other people, to shake hands, to ask and give directions, to be a good guest, and so on. While the main concern of the committee might have been to improve the image of the city by standardizing (*guifan*) Shanghainese behavior in anticipation of the large number of international visitors expected for the Expo, the result of this process is to set the educated urban citizens as the standard for everyone and the adaptation to their civilized way as a prerequisite for membership in the Shanghainese community. As in the handbooks for rural maids described by Sun Wanning, in order to become a member of the community of the "lovely," the uneducated and uncivilized are encouraged to adopt the manners of the middle class.[31] The message of the campaign inundated the city with the intention of "civilizing" (*wenminghua*) public places and specific public behaviors. In one instance, a public service announcement at a pedestrian crossing in downtown Shanghai calls upon people to create "a civilized crossing," that is, one where the traffic rules and the traffic lights are actually respected, without the need for crossing guards to police the intersection. In the lead-up to the 2008 Olympics, Beijing authorities staged "queuing days" (*paidui tuidong ri*) on the 11th day of each month, in which volunteers patrolled subways and bus stations to educate users in the civilized etiquette that the Olympic status of the city required.

Urban districts in wealthy cities also invest in a "civilizing" popular education. Starting in 2003, for example, Beijing's Haidian district has organized "schools for civilized citizens" and in 2010 claimed to have expanded this educational effort to every rural level in the district (a central school plus local schools down to each village). An "*à la carte* quality courses

supermarket" allows people to choose from a wide array of courses, ranging from cooking, tea ceremony, and psychological health to etiquette,
choral singing, and early childhood education. The model is one in which
the school books the services of "visiting professors" and "the state foots
the bill."[32]

Performing Middle-Class Value

The governmental effects of the rhetoric of *suzhi* and civilization do not
stop at setting moral standards inspired by the "civilized" middle class.
The impact of this discourse is also very material.

While visiting the old buildings of Shenyang's "worker village," which
were still standing but bearing the unmistakable marks of imminent demolition, we once met an old lady who rose from her mahjong table to ask
us, as rare visitors from out of town, whether we were willing to buy her
apartment. Smiling, she said, "250,000 yuan [US$30,000] would be enough.
At least I could buy an apartment in this area. It is becoming so expensive
now." She was still waiting for a good offer of compensation from the government for the small apartment she had obtained in the 1960s from the
Shenyang Electric Cables Company, one of the city's large socialist factories that had recently stopped production, putting twenty thousand employees out of work.

The progressive expulsion of workers from forcefully gentrifying areas
of the city suggests that, in urban settings, the functional relationship between a demobilizing working class and the new rich is much closer than
one sometimes expects. The resulting conflicts of such a process of gentrification, however, do not bear the marks of a traditional class struggle, as
the balance of such relationship is often decided by the heavy hand of the
city planners and by the intervention of the state. The unemployed may
still live in housing built for them when they were working in state-owned
factories, but they occupy land that the local state wants to reallocate to
more profitable use. The social landscapes created by urban "renewal"
(for which read: demolition and reconstruction) are therefore not decided
uniquely by capital flows and price gaps but also by the lifestyle choices of
a growing class of homeowners and by the powerful intermediation, planning, and decisions of the state.

The impact of the exemplary hierarchy produced by state and private discourses in each of the cities I have described in this book has, therefore, a very material side. Promoting the middle classes implies producing value that very often provides returns for the local government. The civilized ones are, to this end, endowed with an active, performative role. The intrinsic *suzhi* of civilized middle-class bodies is at times even portrayed as a contagious force, to the point that, like a new Midas, they can create value by reinventing physical and social spaces, often simply because they inhabit them.

One example of such practices comes from Chengdu, where the middle class is certainly underdeveloped with respect to other larger and more central metropolises but is, nonetheless, experiencing rapid growth and a consumption (and construction) boom. The new residential features of Chengdu's "leisurely" tradition are showcased loudly and proudly on the pages of a magazine called *Housing Weekly* (*Ju Zhoukan*).[33] Established as the weekly real estate supplement of the *Chengdu Daily* in 2003, *Housing Weekly* rapidly became very popular among homeowners and home buyers for its practical approach to real estate and for its representation of "the side of the consumers." While its pages are filled with advertisements for new developments, *Housing Weekly* also includes investigative reports on neighborhood conflicts, consumer reports on housing quality, and surveys on management quality in the different compounds; it even organizes an annual competition for the best management company in town. The editors and journalists (overwhelmingly female) employed by *Housing Weekly* are public employees, themselves militant members of a new Chengdu intellectual middle class catapulted into the housing market by generous subsidies and access to inexpensive credit through the housing provident fund (see chapter 4).[34]

In the summer of 2004, *Housing Weekly* launched a campaign to transform the existing perception of Chengdu's eastern district (*chengdong*) as backward, poor, and inhospitable and to improve its attractiveness to both developers and buyers. The campaign was called *zhongchan chengdong* ("middle class in the eastern districts") and was accompanied by the suggestive slogan "Go East!" The activity included excursions into the districts to discover their potential, public initiatives, and leisurely gatherings, including a community event named the "Eastern Districts' Middle-Class Summer Olympics." It also included a number of articles published in *Housing Weekly* in which the transformative power of the middle class was characterized. *Housing Weekly* explained the newfound enthusiasm of the middle class for changing the reputation of the eastern district in this way:

> With its material and *suzhi* advantages [Chengdu's three-million-strong] middle class already represents the search for a lifestyle based on virtuous character, healthy living, moral enlightenment, and dynamic practices. The eastern suburbs, which offer the potential for a better quality of life, are entering the line of sight of the middle class, and this is enough justification to expect that they will become Chengdu's middle class heaven of freedom, where "the high skies make the birds fly and the vast seas make the fish jump."[35]

In a campaign such as this, the relationship between the middle class and value creation is made explicit and actively promoted. It is the human quality attached to the advanced groups that will transform the area from an inhospitable suburb into a prosperous (and free) "heaven." This transformative aspect of the middle class, which is present in both public and private discourse, here becomes almost an act of colonization, as if the presence of groups of high-*suzhi* people would be enough to spread the virus of quality in the reclaimed wasteland.

Similar operations took place in several other areas of the city. In one case, a developer acquired a large plot of land that had been the site of a garbage dump. The company reclaimed the land and initially transformed it into parkland, adopting the slogan "We make the environment before we sell the homes" (*xian zuo huanjing hou mai fang*). For about a year it organized community events in the park for potential customers so that people could get used to the new, reassuring look of the area and thereby increase its value by populating it. People participating in those events were literally "making" a prime residential location out of a garbage dump. Only after this process of colonization was the land finally developed and were the apartments sold for top prices to members of the upper middle class. This process of value creation is therefore expressed not only in the ability of the middle class to consume but also in its ability to transform spaces from inhospitable and ungovernable places into pacified, morally superior, and governable consumer paradises.

This performative role of the middle class is even more apparent in Shenyang, where the homeownership boom is associated with the city's transition from its industrial tradition. A construction and residential economy has become central to the reorientation of the Shenyang inner districts as a competitive, global, and postindustrial city; the new rich, with their consumption habits and their hunger for quality lifestyles, are an essential factor in the city's rebranding effort. In 2005, to the surprise of those who know the dominant grey tones of its sky, Shenyang was awarded the title of "Forest City" (*senlin chengshi*), only the second in the country after (in another surprise) Guiyang. This was in recognition of the exceptional efforts made by the city to produce "urban forests," to improve the environment, and to increase the per capita green areas from 3.5 to over 12 square meters between 2000 and 2005. Shenyang's "greening" might have been affected by the experience of neighboring northeastern city Dalian, whose mayor Bo Xilai similarly remodeled it from an industrial hub into a "green city." In her study of Dalian's green remodeling, Lisa Hoffman observed that this effort is not only aimed at creating "new urban landscapes, but also . . . may call for a new way of thinking . . . [that] not only impacts the physical construction of green cities, but also shapes the citizens who fill them."[36] Along similar lines, the mayor of Shenyang at the time, Chen Zhenggao, also described Shenyang's greening as necessary to improve the city's competitiveness and its overall development: "If we don't pursue the transformation of Shenyang into a forest city, we won't be able to improve our condition; with no improvement we won't be competitive, and with no competitiveness we won't be able to develop and flourish."[37]

It is no coincidence that the greening of Shenyang had to be "built" and that the "forest city" reputation now heralded by the city government relied heavily on the demolition, reconstruction, and gentrification of the last decade. Forest "building" occurred to such a degree that in 2005, 38.9 percent of all urban green areas were located inside almost inaccessible private residential compounds. When asked about the most important consideration prior to buying an apartment in these communities, informants generally mentioned good management and a green environment as essential for maintaining the value of their investment. They also, however, associated efficient management and the green environment with the need for "quality neighbors." "Choosing where to live," said one, "means choosing a good living environment. This community is much better than where we used to live. The old community was dirty and filled with all sorts of people." Another remarked, "We have to think about the living environment, a good management, and a green community. We have to consider the *suzhi* of our fellow residents too. We are not going to live with those people at sixes and sevens. But I don't think that kind of people could afford to live here anyway."

The planning of a "forest city" therefore goes hand in hand with improving the quality of the population by providing a better living environment and matches the move away from the city's dirty industrial image and working-class tradition. With the loss of the working class, urban districts are become increasingly gentrified.

Gentrification in Shenyang, however, is not happening as a result of the revitalization of the existing neighborhoods. Rather, it involves a thoroughly planned demolition and reconstruction of residential spaces and a redefinition of land use (mainly from productive to residential or from public to private) with the specific intent of making such spaces available to a different section of the population and to obtain a better return on land usage.

This process is one that involves the middle class both as a subject of policies to increase homeownership rates (as seen earlier) and as a factor in the revaluation of the urban territory. The middle-class quest for a better lifestyle is more valuable to the production of a postindustrial Shenyang than a conflict-prone working class. *Value* here refers to both the commercial value of the land (or of the housing estates built on it) and the human and moral principles ("higher-*suzhi* people") that become attached to specific areas and that make certain areas more desirable than others. Changing the designation of a block of land increases the value of the land but, as in all processes of gentrification, it is the middle-class aspiration to live in a new place that changes the overall value of the area. In other words, the remaking of certain spaces changes not only the monetary value of that space but also the original moral geography of the city.[38] Specifically, higher-*suzhi* humans produce more valuable communities.

Observation of such processes of value making in Shenyang confirms this picture. In one gated community in Tiexi, for example, residents admitted their original skepticism about buying an apartment in an expensive compound located in a "low-*suzhi*" district. The developer, a company from Hangzhou, started with a small development on the dilapidated site of a glass factory that had recently been closed. The first development was intended to showcase the potential for the area to become a convenient and attractive living environment for middle-class residents and was then expanded to about eight times the original size (at more than double the price) after the success of the first phase.

The developer's main problem was to transform the perception of the place and improve the potential for the area to become attractive to middle-income home buyers from other districts. The developer's marketing philosophy, therefore, beyond building houses, was to "create an environment, a culture, and a spirit." A promotional slogan that was repeatedly used was:

> Real estate is not only a market for land, building materials, and services; it is also the product of its time, of cultural and spiritual change. A building is not only steel and concrete; it is also molded around the culture and spirits it requires.

The marketing of these compounds is therefore based on the idea of a spiritual and cultural recreation and valorization of the dilapidated industrial area, presented as a task not only for the developer but also for the residents. One resident said: "Who could even imagine that such a lush and modern new city stands on the grounds of what were the ruins of an old factory!" The discourse applied here to the promotion of the area also echoes the government's rhetoric of "harmonious communities" mentioned earlier. The "creation of a spirit" is explained on the developer's website in terms of planning principles that "place humans at the center" (*yi ren wei ben*—a slogan often used also by local government to describe the humanistic nature of community services) and that aims to achieve "harmony between residents and the built environment." A harmonious community of high-*sushi* people can also only be achieved, as the developer boasts on its website, by "building a beautiful space for spiritual and material life" where "the highest value is obtained only when it is shared with others."

While developers sing the praises of Tiexi and its new gated communities by mimicking the government's slogans, the government itself has been busy providing an overhaul of the district's infrastructure. During the celebrations of the fifth anniversary of the establishment of what was called "New Tiexi" in 2007, the speakers repeatedly proclaimed the grand progress of the district, which now features large parks, wide roads, and high buildings, and everyone can buy good-quality meat conveniently at the Carrefour superstore next door.

As recounted in chapter 2, Tiexi's old industrial heritage has been completely wiped out, together with hundreds of thousands of jobs once held by the socialist workers' aristocracy. The factory and traditional neighborhood life are all but gone, and there is no visible trace of industrial production in the whole district.[39] The planning strategy for the district has been "demolition and relocation" (*chaiqian*). Most of the old workers who lived in small and unsafe single-story houses were forcibly moved into high-rise crowded residential communities where they no longer live with their old workmates. At the same time, the residential developers for the new and expensive gated communities targeted the land that had been occupied by industrial sites. The result is, yet again, a high level of segregation within the district, with gated communities on one side and low-quality housing built with a substantial injection of public investment on the other. In Tiexi, the district government invested, in 2007 alone, 2.26 billion yuan (US$300 million) in thirty-five subsidized new housing compounds to relocate people who had been living in old, low-rise workers' compounds.[40] The new apartments were then sold at a price comparable to the average compensation that the inhabitants received for their old houses (an average of 2,400 yuan, or US$320, per square meter). The relocation of large parts of the population from central areas of the district has resulted in increased density and the freeing of prime real estate locations for more lucrative development projects. In addition, the local government also invested 300 million yuan (US$40 million) in infrastructure and 127 million yuan (US$17 million) to improve the living environment of the district.

These investments are only made possible by the generous injection of funds in the last few years from the central coffers into the cities of the northeast struggling to cope with industrial restructuring. The ability of the local levels of the state to fund these projects is significantly affected by the fact that large portions of Tiexi's now-valuable land use rights have been sold to private and public developers for the construction of new privately managed gated communities that sell for two to three times the price of the subsidized housing.

Tiexi's gentrification process therefore features the displacement of old residents, the improvement of the housing stock, and the change in character of the neighborhood (the three characteristics of a "classic" gentrification process) but also two significantly different features: the direct involvement of the state, as landowner and economic planner, in designing the transition and an increasing segregation and privatization of residential life, with high rates of homeownership and gated communities becoming the new dominant form of urban revitalization.[41]

After analyzing processes of gentrification in European and North American inner-city neighborhoods, Neil Smith concluded that the movement of the middle class into dilapidated working-class areas that begins gentrification and value creation was "a back-to-the-city movement all right, but a back-to-the-city movement of capital rather than people."[42] In a somewhat similar way, in the case of Ticxi, it is hard to imagine gentrification without the vested interest of the state and a substantial public investment to upgrade infrastructure and to facilitate and attract capital.

The transformation of this district into New Tiexi in 2002 therefore also corresponded to a dramatic reorganization of its geography and of its inhabitants. During the 1980s and 1990s, Tiexi was believed to be a dirty, polluted, and uncomfortable workers' area, physically separated by the railroad tracks from the more civilized and livable center and commercial areas of Heping and Shenhe. Still today it is not uncommon to hear demeaning comments about the "quality" of Tiexi from residents in other districts of Shenyang. But in the short span of five years, under pressure to find resources to fund the ailing social services for the mostly unemployed population, the city and district governments have refashioned the image of the district into that of an appealing and affordable middle-class residential paradise by moving all industries to the new development zone, eliminating any reference to a "dirty" industrial past, selling land use rights to private and public developers, and, finally, mummifying and gentrifying the few remaining spaces reminiscent of that past that still remain today.

To be sure, to speak of Tiexi as a well-established middle-class paradise is clearly an exaggeration. Large numbers of disgruntled workers and unemployed people living on subsidies or on informal employment opportunities still make up a significant part of Tiexi's population. Moreover, the transformation of this area is in fact also serving the purpose of reducing conflicts among the poorest communities of former workers now living off subsidies and occasional employment, as it has deprived the workers of all the elements of their identity, by demolishing the factories that were the focal point of the numerous conflicts of the late 1990s.

In *Against the Law*, Ching-kwan Lee argued, based on research in the late 1990s and early 2000s, that the unemployed in the northeast would be able to sustain their conflicts for a longer time because their work unit–based communities would maintain a certain level of collective identity.[43] Today, after the physical transformation and "gentrification" of Tiexi, this possibility seems less likely. The destruction of any potential reference to industrial production, the increased direct control over community life, and the progressive disintegration of the social texture of these communities have drastically reduced the ability of these workers to organize around either industrial disputes or residential proximity.

On the one hand, New Tiexi's gentrification contributes to the prevention and dispersal of the conflicts that the final years of deindustrialization have inevitably created; on the other, it uses the rhetoric of the middle class as an exemplar to enhance Tiexi's reputation in the eyes of consumers and potential homeowners, and reposition the district within the city's new moral geography based on a diffuse understanding of "value."

These stories of value formation on the back of the discourses and practices of the middle class exemplify the many ways in which the subjectivity of "advanced social groups" becomes a useful tool for governing social change in the cities and show how the aspiration to improve lifestyles becomes a way to transform space and produce new values and norms. What appears peculiar in the Chinese case is not so much the use of moral and ethical discourses in the marketing of spaces and in the promotion of places, houses, and other goods but the convergence of governmental arguments with those of formally autonomous agents and, often, of individuals in the market.

International experiences of urban segregation have taught us that there is both a "global" dimension to how life in the city is segregated and how wealth and status are produced and protected through fortress-like residential spaces and a local and historically specific dimension in which segregation is understood, accepted as a natural evolution of established practices, or rejected as a part of a generally controversial tradition. The obsession of certain societies with security is generally a result of an exposure to the risk of violence, and the construction of "defensible settlements" has historically been a consequence of such concerns.[44] The wealth differences produced by the global reach of the market logic also make sure that segregation protects the privilege of wealth, privileged access to resources, and the living environment from decay and threat.[45] The emergence and popularity of such enclaves among upper-class South Africans, for example, has attracted wide public opposition, as the spatial form cannot be decoupled from the historical condemnation of the country's tradition of racial segregation—although today it is justified, at least in theory, by the soaring crime rates.[46] While security and violence appear constantly in the discourses that justify segregation around the world, the language of security and insecurity remains locally constructed and historically informed.[47] In China, spatial arrangements that feature some form of segregation and security are justified by the traditional socialist organization of urban life that is well known to urban residents and glorified in the recurrent call for social order. The palpable popularity of this spatial form also relies on the legitimization and reproduction of dominant discourses that praise self-improvement, *suzhi*, and distinction, that are supposed to be embodied in the civilized gated residential community more than in any other form of urban cosmopolitan tradition.

Value and Consensus

One of the broader consequences of the analysis presented in this chapter is that a more comprehensive and satisfactory explanation for the neighborhood consensus depends on consideration of both the material and spiritual elements of China's political culture and practices of power. The two, I suggest, are closely connected, and much of the spiritual civilization drive of the last three decades has been useful to a production of material value and to a containment of social conflicts.

China's educated, increasingly wealthy, conflict-prone, but reliably nationalistic middle class has become an agent (spiritual and material) for the development of a "harmonious society." Such a society requires a concentration of the activities of government on solving urgent and threatening social problems where they emerge (unemployment, migration, rural unrest), while more and more of the wealthier sectors of society preach and practice social stability. This requires the acquiescence and cooptation of the middle class, something the present government has dedicated three decades to achieving, not only through moral indoctrination but also through generous programs of subsidization of homeownership, the reduction of working time for employees, and the constant improvement of working conditions and salaries for skilled state employees.

A large middle class not only provides the backbone of a consumer society that has become so crucial to the economic development of the country; it also boosts support for the central campaigns on national strengthening and entrenches the values of civility and responsibility that undergird the legitimacy of the present regime. Considering the pervasiveness of contemporary civilizing discourses in China and the direct or indirect role played by many sectors of the middle class, we should therefore not dismiss their influence on how Chinese society adapts to the new forms of grassroots government promoted by the present leadership.

The discourses on civilization and on the role of the middle class converge with the subjective perception that these social groups are more "advanced" and thus constitute a vanguard in the struggle to build a "high-*suzhi*" nation. In terms of governance, this situation leads to increasing autonomy in the spaces inhabited by the middle class, while the potentially dangerous "weak groups" remain objects of political patronage and maintain their dependence on the state. For example, residential communities, by defining discrete units of socialization, contribute to classifying the population into "high-*suzhi*" clusters (those who are able to govern themselves) and "low-*suzhi*" clusters (those in need of state patronage). Different communities are also governed differently, with the rich enjoying higher levels of autonomy and self-governance.

In this process, the middle class serves an exemplary purpose. In the new social hierarchy, not only education and wealth but also virtuous conduct and spiritual civilization have come to be associated with this group. Their behavior is often essentialized and utilized as an example, while the rhetoric of *suzhi* is also internalized and mobilized as an identity marker for the new subjects. Most importantly, this dominant exemplarism associated with the middle class is not only about morality and stability. It also produces value, raises land and real estate prices, and increases the prestige, power, and cash flows of local land-controlling elites and local governments, while private actors also promote it as a way to increase the value of their investment. Lifestyles are both a governing tool and a commercial bait.

Conclusion

Arenas of Contention and Accommodation

This book is about political practices and the rationalities of government that produce them. Practices of everyday interaction between the state and society often challenge the understanding of this relationship as merely antagonistic. While political practices make governing ideologies concrete, tools of domination, as they move closer to everyday life, have the capacity to adapt and differentiate. A particular rationality of government, such as the need to maintain social order, can therefore produce a multiplicity of governing practices. The legitimacy of such practices can be accepted or challenged, or it can be the object of bargaining, without necessarily affecting the overall validity of the principle that inspired them.

Neighborhood life has the potential to incubate urban citizens' desire for political participation. As Ben Read shows in his research, while participation in grassroots neighborhood institutions remains relatively low, their existence as arms of the state and their focus on maintaining social order are generally perceived as legitimate.[1] Despite their role in extending the capacity of the state to monitor society, there is no generalized hatred against them, and it is widely felt that they perform an important role in society that could not be performed by anyone other than the state. The increasing variety of lifestyles produced in urban China by the reorganization of residential patterns, however, also suggests an increasing graduation in individuals' experiences of the state. Besides more or less knowledge of, engagement with, or dependence from neighborhood institutions, citizens also learn to interpret and evaluate their relationship to the state as a function of their position in society, which is concretely epitomized by their residential situation. The presence of the state in the neighborhoods, either in the form of formal grassroots mass organizations or as the concretization of hegemonic political discourses through private or nonstate agents, is a strategy of legitimization of the present regime. The government of residential areas is the result both of material practices and of the reproduction in everyday life, by a variety of actors, of the discursive rationalities that underpin the legitimacy of the Chinese Communist Party. The more the principles and discourses of a polity (in China monopolized at the center by an all-powerful Party and elite) become embedded in everyday conflicts, the more significant such discourses become to individuals and groups, who interpret, adapt, and internalize them according to the fundamental demands of their situation.

Sebastian Heilmann and Elizabeth Perry have already argued that "China's governance techniques are marked by a signature Maoist stamp that conceives of policy-making as a process of ceaseless change, tension management, continual experimentation and ad-hoc adjustment" that sets it apart from most other polities.[2] This adaptation by design, resulting from China's peculiar political culture, accounts for much of the variation encountered in this book. The range of variations visible in the neighborhood also shows that this quintessentially Maoist repertoire of techniques is extending to tactics and principles typical of liberal systems, like ideas of community, *suzhi*, efficiency, scientific management, and value production. For this reason, they also involve nonstate actors.

The ability of citizens to withstand or adapt to the power of the state changes depending on their position in society, in the labor market, in the economy, and even (as a consequence of these "positions") in the built environment. Political legitimacy is, at least partially, the result of how overarching governing principles and discourses are elaborated and internalized in the context of these everyday experiences. In other words, flexible practices, rather than rigid institutions, populate the contested ground between the priorities of state authority and the interests of the citizens.

How Is Consensus Different?

In the introduction to this volume on the practices and politics around neighborhoods, I suggested that *consensus* is a possible way to characterize state-society relations. It is also my way to suggest how existing characterizations of state-society relations can be modified.

What I call consensus has, first of all, little to do with active political support. There are, in China, only very limited avenues to express formal consent to or dissent from institutions or political ideas, but, as the literature on contentious politics has taught us over the last two decades, there are many ways in which local practices are resisted or, indeed, accepted.[3] Consensus suggests that both resistance and acceptance are accommodated within a legitimate framework of discursive and practical rules. Neighborhood conflicts, for example, are instances both of resistance and of consensus, as they reflect active organization by aggrieved homeowners but also reproduce and amplify the dominant discourses of the state (primacy of social order, *suzhi*, even patriotism). The resistance paradigm, in the tradition of social movements research, is properly concerned with how (and what) resources are mobilized in the process of overcoming the domination of the state or of other forces. Scholars have been divided on how to interpret contention, with some suggesting that claims about rights could develop into a consciousness and a "counterhegemonic project," while others believe that, as earlier in history, contention is the result of a consciousness of the rules of engagement with the state rather than of universal or widely held rights.[4]

Whether in the form of "rights" consciousness or of "rules" consciousness, arguments about contention tend to reveal the concern of social groups with playing the system in a strategic manner. The awareness of rights or the capacity to manipulate the system within its own rules to protect individual or collective interests both point to a strategic intervention in the system to remedy one's misery or to advance one's social position. I interpret the framing of resistance not as an occasional and strategic

manifestation but rather as the consequence of a structural condition, resulting from experiences that are embedded and can vary among places
and social groups. I also suggest that the struggle for social recognition
(either as a result of a conflict or of social mobility in general) is a process entrenched in one's relationship with the state and is often mediated
through the hegemonic discourses that it produces. Neighborhoods are
places where such mediation is most visible, as they provide a catalyst for
the formation of social status, an institutional and cultural framework for
a relationship with the state (one that can imply more or less autonomy),
and an environment for the crystallization of collective interests, conflicts,
and resistance.

Consensus is also not a tool of deliberation. Consensus decision-making
has been popularized by writers of deliberative democracy as a direct, locally contained way to increase citizens' involvement in local issues that
directly affect their livelihood.[5] While China has introduced, with great
fanfare and effort, forms of "self-governance" in urban communities and
rural villages, participation and the search for consent is, at best, imper-
fect and greatly affected by the awesome power and resources of the local
state. According to one estimate, China already had over 450,000 grassroots organizations involved in different types of deliberative processes
in 2004, from village committees to consultative budgeting committees.[6]
Such formal consultation is, however, tightly regimented, and the limits of
what can be decided (and how) are firmly policed. The recent nationwide
crackdown on independent activism in the lead-up to the 2012 leadership
succession is a sign that the central political entities in the center are unwilling to surrender their imperative of "social stability above all else" or
to change their emphasis on the preeminence of CCP rule. At the same
time, localities are often allowed to adopt different and creative strategies
to maintain social stability that are the result of availability of resources,
economic capacity, and local political economic conditions.

This situation suggests that once the political boundaries for contention
are set, the political system is capable of tolerating a significant amount
of local and specific contention. Conflicts, in turn, while limited in their
systemic impact, do contribute to determining the direction of political
change and adaptation in the political system. Chen Xi finds that social
conflicts in China are increasingly routinized and that, despite the inad-
equacy of institutions of representation, the pervasive presence of conflicts

"serves as an indicator of the remarkably elastic character of the Chinese system," to the point that "beneath the surface of noise and anxiety, the whole political system remains stable."[7]

When I talk about consensus, then, I refer not to a deliberative process but rather to the existence of a space where bargaining between state and society and within society is made possible through formalized institutions, routinized practices, and discursive boundaries. It is an arena of political interaction among the state, individuals, and private or local actors in which the state's hegemonic discourses act as the confines but contention is allowed to emerge—and does. In my analysis of neighborhood politics, contention is often amplified when interaction within the community is "deep" and problems are territorialized and close to the special interests of the neighbors. It is, however, also contained by the tight limits of sanctioned political agency and moral rhetoric. In this arena, neighborhoods constitute a metaphor (a bounded space where interaction is enhanced but its effects contained) but also a practical environment for a multitude of interactions. In such interactions, formalized spaces also contribute to the agency of neighbors, for example by shielding them from state repression. As we have seen, activists often adopt, almost verbatim, the (different) discourses of the state; at the same time, cadres can be both arms of state policy and discontented members of a destitute working class, that is, providers and receivers of the same public assistance. State actors can use completely different and often contradictory rhetorical arguments and social strategies depending on the subjects they are trying to rule and the result they are trying to achieve; spaces, representing the concretized manifestation of power relations, often determine the limits and strengths of the different social groups and their autonomy; power relations and the attitude of the policing institutions often change when one exits the glorified and protected boundaries of the neighborhood to challenge established forms of authority. Even conflicts cannot simply be seen as challenges to the state while advancing specific interests. They can also highlight issues that require policy or disciplinary intervention by the state to deter more widespread effects on social stability and therefore avoid a deeper crisis or contribute to improve governance of social change.

The idea of a consensual arena of interaction is also different from that of a civil society. As Read has observed, the growing associational space in Chinese society potentially competes with the controlled and somewhat corporatist associations created by the neighborhood organizations. By providing possibilities of interacting in collective endeavors and "a sense of taking part in an important civic project and a national mission," neighborhood organizations may "soak up the citizen's participatory energies like so many widely dispersed sponges."[8] In the civil society model, the rules of interaction are provided by legal regulations, formal organizations, autonomy from state influence, and a free representation of interests across society. In consensual arenas of interaction, the state is not necessarily confronted, "rules" can be quite different in different spaces, and interaction is limited to local and practical problems. Autonomous mobilization is constrained and is often unable to transcend the limits of material interests or to achieve broader territorial coordination at a level higher than the limited autonomous space of the single neighborhoods. Coordination among homeowners to organize public action has been observed on the occasion of some significant public conflicts.[9] Such forms of "beyond the border" activities have, however, rarely materialized as either movements or higher forms of organization, which are strongly opposed at all levels of government. Activists have decided to run for office as independent candidates in the local people's congresses, while homeowner associations have at times undertaken public advocacy and attempted coordination at the municipal and even national level, but the government has systematically defused these attempts. While, as we have seen, individual activists have become prominent in the public debate about property rights, even the most spectacular initiatives have failed to bring about higher levels of organization among homeowners or in a homogeneous social movement. This was the case, for example, for a homeowner-initiated petition to the NPC suggesting changes to the property management regulations, which was signed by over 180,000 people in 2007.

The state being strong and present, social activism is always in danger of overstepping its boundaries, whether spatial, discursive, or political. Consensual arenas of interaction may be seen as a typical product of a totalitarian state, promoting atomization of societal interests. Social conflicts in a consensual arena, however, also produce limited but significant agency. This agency has repercussions on social policy innovation and the efficiency of governance mechanisms but carries limited potential for systemic political change. Restricted as they are by their shared boundaries of political interaction, conflicts result in strengthening the governmental rationale through the daily performance of hegemonic ideas and practices.

This is, admittedly, a pessimistic view of the direct impact of neighborhood organizations. What is interesting, however, is not how much impact conflicts in such consensual arenas have on democratization or the substantial reform of China's political system but rather how they contribute to reconfiguring the practices of power and authority. In other words, while political change might not be going in the direction of a broader, institutionalized participation and a proactive and rule-bound state-society relationship, change might nevertheless already be here, in the form of a state that is less and less able to dominate society and must increasingly participate in shaping and regulating contention.

Here I return to the original five governing strategies that have guided my analysis of neighborhood politics and discuss their significance in this context. I will then, by way of a conclusion, outline what questions remain unanswered and where research could lead us from here.

Social Clustering

Social clustering is the reproduction and concretization of governing rationalities on the territory through the use of space, capital, and social classification to achieve clearer definition and legibility of social groups and allow the government to put tailor-made policies and governmental strategies in place.

While it is not surprising that an authoritarian regime would decide to adopt such a strategy, in the reform period the reorganization of the urban territory has been the result of the convergence of state interests with those of private actors under the condition of the state's monopoly on land. Chinese cities have become the places for competition and accommodation of different interests, private and public, individual as well as collective, framed by political, social, or economic imperatives.

As I have shown, this clustered repackaging of residential areas is therefore not simply the result of public planning, it is both facilitated and regulated by the state in three different ways. First, the residential space is institutionalized, as rules and systems of self-government are put in place by the state in accordance with the need to maintain social order under different conditions. These institutions are imposed on the territory to define and enforce the rules of membership in a specific community. The recognition and organization of such membership has become even more important with the decline of the role of employers in the administration of the urban population. Administration, provision of services, and participation are all organized territorially and extend the clustering produced by gated spaces. Institutions also graduate their intervention, depending on the degree of privatization of neighborhoods, with privately managed areas allowing greater autonomy than poorer neighborhoods.

Second, through the public control of urban land and an explicit support for gated spaces, the state facilitates residential *segregation*. The active intervention of local bureaucracies in the real estate market is a consequence of both the financial and speculative interests of local officials that lead to strategies to maximize short-term returns and fiscal revenue on locally controlled land. Urban governments are dependent on land sales: a recent central government audit of the debt structure of thirty-six major cities found that most of the debt since 1979 was repaid through the increasing sale of land use rights, while 86 percent of all debt was used to pay for infrastructural projects.[10]

Local governments also intervene to contain governance costs by privatizing service provision and governance functions inside residential spaces. By controlling the lease of urban construction land, local states maintain (indeed, increase) their say in what is built and where and favor the building of large and segregated residential areas on the territory they control. Urban regulations also explicitly encourage the use of gates and security systems.

Third, the state promotes a discursive rationalization of such structural segregation by disseminating the language of "security" and (human) "quality," which is re-broadcast through all other involved players, from real estate developers to individual citizens, from local cadres to urban governments, in order to advance or protect their vested interests and social positions. When seen from the vantage point of the community, such discursive repertoire becomes part of the process of community building and is reproduced by residents and private and public players alike.

Micro-Governing

The result of such clustering is that, while the state is using numerous different nonstate actors to promote and implement its governance strategy, it still requires an administrative organization that describes the territory and reflects the social segregation that allows governing to happen. Social order is too important to the legitimacy of the Chinese Communist Party as ruler of the country to be left completely in the hands of private actors. Postindustrialization, deindustrialization, and the growing role of the urban service economy have transformed the nature of China's cities, not without significant implications for the governance of social change. The "advanced" groups of the middle class provide the strongest support to the contemporary regime, and their social careers are often bound hand and foot to the state, but the Shenyang workers who entered in a downward spiral after reform see the state as the only significant remaining guarantee of their entitlements as socialist citizens. In cities suffering from the decline of public industries, communities and neighborhoods are hubs of the public effort to maintain stability and "save" the working class and to prevent this situation from becoming endemic and chronic. This strategy requires not the retreat of the state but a transformation of its governing action.

Working-class communities like those in Tiexi described in chapters 1 and 2 reveal three strategies of the state deriving from this rationale. First, an extensive infrastructure is deployed inside the communities to provide services to the weaker groups of the population; wherever the state needs to cope with social decline and risks of unrest, the state makes itself visible. Second, cadres coopted from the ranks of the unemployed working class become a local bridge between the logic of assistance promoted by the state and the claims of disenchanted community members. Third, community governance, far from reflecting the principle of self-government, is ceaselessly monitored and audited. Its effectiveness is benchmarked against the community committee's capacity both to uphold its role as service provider and to guide participation.

In chapter 2 I focused on the fact that, while governance has changed, these traditional tools of socialist governing that I named "micro-governing" are still alive and widely employed. This term points to a visible structure of governance in the community that reflects the reliance of the state on practices of governance that are recognized as legitimate, especially in these communities of ex-workers. These practices suggest that intense interaction, direct intervention and bureaucratic supervision are not at all a thing of the past and that "governing too much" is a risk the state is still willing to take wherever an acute social crisis is looming.

All three characteristics point to the continuity and unexpected survival, despite the marketization of residential spaces, of a paternalistic form of governance. While the state promotes practices of self-governing by calling citizens to participate (and sometimes even to vote), it does so by placing its own rhetoric of social order at the very center. In other words, to resort to the analogy used so far, it allows for a consensual arena where interaction is intense and bargaining is conducted very close to the ground. By doing so, it also aims to produce dependencies among the poorest citizens, who have access to subsidies only through the channels of their community and no longer through their employers. The result is a convergence between the rhetoric of "saving" the left-behind working class, victim of the economic reform, which the state itself is producing, and the long-term rhetoric of the "lost generation" that dominates the narratives of ex-workers.[11]

This specific aspect of the consensus both confirms and challenges arguments about China's neoliberalization.

China's waning urban working class becomes marginalized for its "socialist" interpretation of economic and social relations. Proud workers, who are defending their identity as members of a disappearing socialist elite, expect the state to stay true to its ideological commitment to defend the interest of the working class and refuse to conform to the principles of efficiency and competition promoted by the new ideology of the reformist state. This situation fits the bill of a state that is willing to produce a classification and "graduation" among social groups through its intervention in society as a consequence of the need to conform to the logic of global capital.[12]

At the same time, however, a street view of governing practices also reveals the importance of continuity and shows that governing by other means often translates as governing by a familiar strategy, especially in situations that might be dangerous for social and political stability. A neoliberal logic of government, which relies on the action of external agents and on self-government, does not satisfy the primary need for stability and a reliance on moral and ethical principles imposed on the population against the apparent interests of the global market. My surprise at the intensity and visibility of the state made me think that any analysis of China in this framework would need to consider what Neil Brenner and Nik Theodore called the "contextual embeddedness of neoliberal restructuring projects" and to highlight not only the importance of path-dependent factors in the formation of "actually existing neo-liberalism" but also the variety of outcomes that can be achieved within the same system, at different scales of analysis.[13] Despite the country's central role in the global flows of capital and goods and its acceptance of the logic of optimization associated with neoliberal practices, its governing practices also remain deeply rooted in a traditional political culture that might determine their success or failure and that often contradicts the expected trajectory of evolution that links marketization with the decline of the role of the state.[14]

Social Engineering

The third set of practices highlighted by housing and community reform I call "social engineering." In chapter 3 I drew a link between the emergence of an urban middle class and the policy of privatizing housing provision that began in the 1990s. What this analysis reveals is that housing policies have actively shaped the social structure by granting certain groups in Chinese society, in particular those traditionally employed by the state, privileged access to significant private assets. The rationale for engineering a salary-earning, nationalistic middle class is underpinned both by the need to promote domestic consumption as an alternative engine of economic growth and by a similarly important need to maintain support among the socially mobile groups who inhabit China's postindustrial cities.

Housing privatization, which began with a massive transfer of housing stock from public to private hands in the 1980s and 1990s, has provided an opportunity to engineer a middle class systematically, through selective incentives and subsidization. It also built on the converging interests of local governments and developers in selling and developing their land, which remains the main source of income for urban governments to balance their budgets and finance infrastructural projects. These policies have inevitably favored those who had already been privileged by the unequal redistribution of housing in the socialist period because of their employment in the public sector. The resulting boost for a property-holding middle class went therefore mostly toward employees and families actively employed in the public sector, who became the first large cohort of Chinese homeowners during the housing reform of the late 1990s. This original connection between public-sector employees and the first broad-based privatization of public assets is among the reasons that my middle-class neighbors appeared more as staunch supporters of than as challengers to the rhetoric of the Chinese regime, particularly with regard to social stability. Such an assessment is necessarily conversant with the liberal expectation that the middle class would constitute a harbinger of political change in the country, along the lines of what happened in other countries, especially in Asia, as well as with the broader analysis of the origin and political role of the Chinese middle class published in recent years.[15] It also suggests the need to go beyond characterization of the middle class as "moderate" or "conservative."[16] While there are many reasons, some of which are outlined in this book, that the new middle class is likely to have a positive impact on regime legitimacy, simply thinking of such impact as the result of an alignment with the conservative tendencies in the government would miss the complexity of the interaction. I see the symbiotic relationship between the state, its policies, and its discourses and the middle class as a dialectical process. In line with my understanding of consensus, homeowners' support for social stability does not prevent such groups from having agency in their social and political interactions. In fact, consensus implies that social and political change can happen without the disruption of the fundamental rules of engagement or in an environment that tolerates and at times even encourages limited conflicts. While I see the production of the middle class as the result of a political and economic project of social engineering sponsored by the Chinese leadership, I do not necessarily see the resulting social formations as unequivocally supporting the Party's monopoly of power or entirely coopted into its ranks. Their opinions about the need for stability seem to be more the result of long experience with the regime. As a result, anyone willing to pursue further the study of the role of the middle class in China's political change might need to ask different questions, for example about the role set out for the wealthy and the educated in the program of social reform in China or about what directions such change might take and how the regime might be affected by the emergence of a social elite that has had a taste of contention and participation. In consideration of a dialectic, rather than an oppositional, relationship between the government and the middle class, these questions might be more productive than those focusing on the advancement or stalling of elsewhere-defined democratic ideals among the Chinese middle class.

Contained Contention

Such dialectic understanding also requires a new look at conflicts. Neighborhoods, as I showed in chapter 4, are places of contention. They are places where interests are formed and where contradictions among different interests are ripe. In neighborhoods, however, contention is both facilitated and contained.

First, just as neighborhoods are governed through a multiplicity of actors, conflicts around housing also involve more than just the state. Much of the contention inside and around residential neighborhoods is the result of conflicts among nonstate actors—or actors that do not perfectly overlap with the state—which the state is at times called upon to resolve. Second, and by the same token, contention can be very intense and can involve large numbers of people, but have no immediate repercussion on social order, because it targets specific and very local issues; here the state can afford merely to play the role of the adjudicator. Third, the gated nature and territorial administration of residential areas also contribute to the containment of such contention, so that conflicts are tolerated in their local form but are not accepted if they present a challenge to the authorities or the legitimacy of the state. Finally, local contenders often frame their claims through the moral rhetoric of the state, where the priority of social stability prevails over chaos, thus resulting in an amplification of hegemonic discourses (on *suzhi*, patriotism, morality, and corruption) and enhancing the legitimacy of its governing rationality.

When seen in the context of the rising number of social and collective conflicts in China, contained contention implies the existence of an acceptable frame for the representation of grievances. The systemic challenge they provide is limited, but they are not irrelevant to the regime's governance strategy. Typically, my description of such conflicts as part of a consensus does not discount the social and political change that can be generated through them or as a long-term result of such constant frictions and the counterhegemonic discourses they can reproduce. The state is, in fact, constantly required to react and adapt to the discursive and practical challenges provided by these situations.

Neighborhood conflicts do reveal, however, that contention is part of an accepted dynamic of a dialectic relationship between state and society and within society and that the capacity to feel aggrieved and to protest is now built into the governing strategies of the present regime. The different solutions and multiple actors involved also suggest that institutionalization of contention through administrative bodies coexists with more pastoral practices of bargaining aimed at limiting the reach, rather than the emergence, of conflicts.

So how does this idea change our understanding of contention? The institutionalization of conflicts has been largely seen as a factor that strengthens regime resilience.[17] Unlike traditional institutions of accommodation, like courts or the "letters and visits" system, which aim at simplifying conflict resolution by placing rules and practices around them, contained conflicts in the neighborhood are institutionalized through a definition of the rules of interaction, territorial borders, and the shared imposition of political boundaries to the rhetoric used to claim rights and protect interests as well as through the presence and involvement of neighborhood institutions.[18] I suggest that consensual arenas of contention are a form of institutionalization that, rather than simply relying on a set of rules, depends on a set of local practices and still requires the state to maintain a significant presence at the grassroots to shape the dominant rhetoric and to strengthen control.

In Chen Xi's analysis, the recent upsurge and "routinization" of collective conflicts is puzzling mostly because petitioners have preferred certain forms of action, namely "localized collective petitions with the use of a variety of 'troublemaking' tactics that can keep a balance between defiance and obedience."[19] Chen's argument is that such routinization is directly facilitated by the actions of the state and that, besides the functions of social control, it significantly affects the structure where such contestations take place, including the historical and political narratives that frame them.[20]

In this book, I have provided some evidence to support Chen's argument, and there is no denying that the state maintains a direct or indirect presence in the way conflicts are framed. As discussed in the introduction, I am attracted to explanations of conflicts that look at the everyday and lasting effects of the state on enduring social structures, rather than only at its capacity for social control and domination, and see contention—either within the state or between state and society—as a dialectical process rather than as a zero-sum game.[21] Only such interpretation, it seems to me, can bring us a step closer to explaining the paradoxes and complexities of the role of contention in an authoritarian system and understanding their relationship with China's regime legitimacy.

Exemplarism

One such embedded dialectical mechanism is exemplarism, both a long-lasting discourse of the socialist state and a well-rehearsed marker of social mobility in Chinese society. By reproducing differences and social hierarchies, neighborhood practices reveal the way that the Chinese state uses exemplars, in particular by reifying the role of the middle class as the moral and economic fulcrum of the country's development and social stability. At the same time, it explains how such exemplarity (either the middle class or more traditional socialist exemplars such as the Shenyang working class) features in the long-term strategies of neighbors and is built into the conflict frames.

The exemplarity of the particular conduct, morality, and political "quality" of a highly essentialized "middle class" is promoted as part of the state rhetoric at all levels. What is interesting, however, is that, at the local level, such discourses produce two very important and tangible effects. First, the state uses the middle class as a benchmark reproduced across society to indicate how a "good citizen" should behave, while it relies heavily on the reproduction of discourses of morality within wealthy neighborhoods by real estate developers who market lifestyles and housing compounds as middle-class paradises. Second, the rhetoric of the middle class produces "value" in the city, as it is often associated with vast programs of urban regeneration that result in significant advantages for both local leaderships and real estate speculators. The production of "middle-class paradises" is the most powerful tool to achieve an appreciation of urban land and the real estate built on it by making sure that both private investors and the state (the ultimate land-holder) have an interest in promoting a middle-class lifestyle.[22]

The involvement of the state in such processes of top-down gentrification, resulting in the construction of higher-quality housing and gated spaces, also assures that the idea of social order is upheld, with the marginalization of the lower-*suzhi* population and the injection of more "responsible" middle-class subjects into these urban spaces.

·

Translating in the Local: Where To from Here?

The stories one learns in neighborhoods reach much further than the neighborhoods themselves. Residential communities are complex social bodies that tell stories of how social change has been managed and produced. Housing and spaces are not neutral actors; they have an impact on social relations and help in the action of government. The state is present in all processes and in many different ways: The action of governing happens sometimes through new actors in society, other times against them. Rationalities of government are visible in the ways that physical space is conceived and constructed, in the ways that state rhetoric describes and attaches meanings to social groups, in the ways that principles of social order are prioritized in all these interactions, and in the ways that these interactions are turned into positive or negative exemplars. Social actors use the limited arenas of political interaction provided by these new spaces to promote and protect interests, on some occasions strategically using the logic of the state, on others challenging the perceived state of power relations. Social mobility is constructed to the almost exclusive advantage of groups buying into China's social agenda and civilizing project.

Neighborhood politics also tells stories of a changing but resilient polity. Dialectical, consensual arenas of interaction are just one possible way of characterizing state-society relations. Consensus highlights how very local practices of government mirror higher-level political rationalities and hegemonic discourses. It identifies the convergence of such discourses with framing arguments and practical interests and infers that it produces legitimacy for the system. Rather than suggesting a single explanation for the resilience of this regime's political legitimacy, it shows how legitimacy is achieved through the continuous bargaining of local practices. Neighborhoods not only provide some insights on how the performance of practices and discourses produces or fosters legitimacy, they also reveal that the state is not retreating, but rather resorting to structural, historically informed and familiar political repertoires, which, while contradictory, can be mobilized to appeal to the demands of diverse groups in society. It can do so only by maintaining visibility or by imposing a spatial and political hierarchy on the territory.

An almost endless list of questions remains open at the end of this research. The main one is whether and to what extent the rationale of such consensus applies to other political arenas of interaction. The method that I suggest here is that such questions are more easily asked in areas of investigation that produce a concretization of governing discourses and can therefore be tested on the ways that these discourses are concretized into everyday practices. One could easily think, for instance, of labor relations as an arena of interaction that traditionally involves a spatial dimension, a mix of private and public actors, a recurrence of conflicts within a loose legal framework, and a rhetoric that is at the core of the state's legitimacy. One could also think of much more complex processes of transformation such as the land transfers that accompany urbanization. Here a central ideology of "the urban" (the rational representation of urbanization as a trajectory of transformation for the country's economy and society) is at work, together with a very local set of practices that includes forms of resistance and accommodation, significant and rapid transfer of resources among private and public actors, and a contested sense of place. Once again the priorities of economic growth and social order are likely to determine the rules of engagement.

Seeing such conflicts as simply the result of a pattern of domination and resistance risks blinding us to the processes of translation of the political ideology into the social, cultural, historical, and political economic conditions of the locality. While I am not intending to suggest that the hyperlocal context of this research is the only dimension that matters, the context where such "translation" of hegemonic discourses takes place seems to provide an important new possibility to our understanding of Chinese politics.

Further studies might also find it necessary to disaggregate ideology. Much recent political analysis has highlighted the widespread perception that the political ideology of the Chinese state is bankrupt and its political appeal limited, with an increasingly assertive public opinion revealing cracks in the sturdy ideal construction of the Chinese Communist Party. I found in my research much to agree with this position. I also found enough to convince me that it is not only the monopoly of the political ideology that makes China's elite resilient. The appeal of such ideology is in its promotion of social ideals of population improvement, national pride, cultural distinction, self-cultivation, and exemplarity, together with the promotion of a role for the government as the main agent of social reform and the main protector of social order. My findings suggest that there are ways in which by associating themselves with such principles and the practices they produce, the state and its agents gain in legitimacy. In such a situation, the practices and framing arguments of my neighbors, those of striking workers, or those of villagers protecting their land, or those of anyone else involved in social conflicts can reveal the penetration of social ideologies and their capacity to increase or weaken the grip of the Chinese regime.

NOTES

Introduction

1. One of the first investigations of these issues in reform China was Deborah S. Davis, Richard Kraus, Barry Naughton, and Elizabeth J. Perry, *Urban Spaces in Contemporary China: The Potential for Autonomy and Community in Post-Mao China* (Cambridge: Cambridge University Press, 1995).

2. David Bray, "Designing to Govern: Space and Power in Two Wuhan Communities," *Built Environment* 34, no. 4 (2008): 392–407.

3. Benjamin Read, *Roots of the State: Neighborhood Organizations and Social Networks in Beijing and Taipei* (Stanford, CA: Stanford University Press, 2012), 252.

4. Literature on residential neighborhoods includes Read, *Roots of the State*; Thomas Heberer and Christian Göbel, *The Politics of Community Building in Urban China* (London: Routledge, 2011); Mun Young Cho, *The Specter of "The People": Urban Poverty in Northeast China* (Ithaca, NY: Cornell University Press, 2013), 97–100; Robert Benewick and Akio Takahara, "Eight Grannies and Nine Teeth between Them: Community Construction in China," *Journal of Chinese Political Science* 7, no. 1–2 (2002): 1–18; Friederike Fleischer, *Suburban Beijing: Housing and Consumption in Contemporary China* (Minneapolis: University of Minnesota Press, 2010); Robert Benewick, Irene Tong, and Jude Howell, "Self-Governance and Community: A Preliminary Comparison between Villagers' Committees and Urban Community Councils," *China Information* 18, no. 1 (2004): 11–28; David Bray, "Building 'Community': New Strategies of Governance in Urban China," *Economy and Society* 35, no. 4 (2006): 530–49; Bray, "Designing to Govern."

5. David Bray, *Social Space and Governance in Urban China: The Danwei System from Origins to Reform* (Stanford, CA: Stanford University Press, 2005).

6. The best analysis of the early transformation of urban administration in the early years of the Chinese revolution remains the "Cities" chapter in Franz Schurmann, *Ideology and Organization in Communist China* (Berkeley: University of California Press, 1968), 365–403. See also John Wilson Lewis and Jerome Alan Cohen, eds., *The City in Communist China* (Stanford, CA: Stanford University Press, 1971).

7. Read, *Roots of the State*; Heberer and Göbel, *Politics of Community Building*; Luigi Tomba, "Residential Space and Collective Interest Formation in Beijing's Housing Disputes," *China Quarterly* 184 (2005): 934–51; Wang Bangzuo, *Juweihui yu shequ zhili* [Resident committees and community governance] (Shanghai: Shanghai Renmin Chubanshe, 2003).

8. Li Ruiyang, *Chengshi renmin gongshe yundong yanjiu* [Research on the urban people's communes movement] (Changsha, China: Hunan Renmin Chubanshe, 2006).

9. Andrew G. Walder, "Organized Dependence and Cultures of Authority in Chinese Industry," *Journal of Asian Studies* 43, no. 1 (1983): 51–76.

10. Jeremy Brown, *City versus Countryside in Mao's China: Negotiating the Divide* (Cambridge: Cambridge University Press, 2012).

11. Yanjie Bian and John R. Logan, "Market Transition and the Persistence of Power: The Changing Stratification System in Urban China," *American Sociological Review* 61, no. 5 (1996): 739–58; Nan Lin and Yanjie Bian, "Getting Ahead in Urban China," *American Journal of Sociology* 97, no. 3 (1991): 657–88.

12. Luigi Tomba, *Paradoxes of Labour Reform: Chinese Labour Theory and Practice from Socialism to Market* (Honolulu: University of Hawai'i Press, 2002).

13. For one example of how state-owned enterprises reacted to this change, see Jonathan Unger and Anita Chan, "The Internal Politics of an Urban Chinese Work Community: A Case Study of Employee Influence on Decision-Making at a State Owned Factory," *China Journal* 52 (2004): 1–26.

14. Jian Li and Xiaohan Niu, "The New Middle Class(es) in Peking: A Case Study," *China Perspectives* 45 (2003): 4–20. See also You-tien Hsing's analysis of the role of "Socialist land masters" in her book *The Great Urban Transformation: Politics of Land and Property in China* (Oxford: Oxford University Press, 2010).

15. Heberer and Göbel, *Politics of Community Building*.

16. Benjamin Read, "Democratizing the Neighborhood? New Private Housing and Home-Owner Self-Organization in Urban China," *China Journal* 49 (January 2003): 31–60.

17. Luigi Tomba and Beibei Tang, "The Forest City: Homeownership and New Wealth in Shenyang," in *The New Rich in China: Future Rulers, Present Lives*, ed. David S. G. Goodman (London, Routledge, 2008), 171–86.

18. A number of different theses have been put forward to explain the now three-decade-long puzzle of why China has not (yet) democratized. For some authors, democratization remains inevitable; see Bruce Gilley, *China's Democratic Future: How It Will Happen and Where It Will Lead* (New York: Columbia University Press, 2004). For others, what is inevitable is the collapse of communist rule; see Gordon Chang, *The Coming Collapse of China* (New York: Random House, 2001). Others have tried to accommodate the inexplicable resilience by theorizing China's success in such processes as the institutionalization of conflicts and political struggle; see Andrew Nathan, "Authoritarian Resilience," *Journal of Democracy* 14, no. 1 (January 2003): 6–17. Still others have highlighted the system's ability to adapt and to flex rather than break; see David Shambaugh, *The Chinese Communist Party: Atrophy and Adaptation* (Washington, DC: Woodrow Wilson Center, 2008). Finally, others see China as stuck in the middle of a process that it seems unable to complete, somehow not capable of moving either forward or backward from a "reform equilibrium"

trap; see Pei Minxin, *Trapped Transition: The Limits of Developmental Autocracy* (Cambridge, MA: Harvard University Press, 2006).

19. Teresa Wright, *Accepting Authoritarianism: State-Society Relations in China's Reform Era* (Stanford, CA: Stanford University Press, 2010).

20. Pierre Bourdieu, *The Logic of Practice* (Stanford, CA: Stanford University Press, 1977), 53.

21. Ibid., 54.

22. William Hurst, "Mass Frames and Worker Protest," in *Popular Protest in China*, ed. Kevin J. O'Brien (Cambridge, MA: Harvard University Press, 2008), 71–87; Doug McAdam, John D. McCarthy, and Mayer N. Zald, "Introduction: Opportunities, Mobilizing Structures, and Framing Processes—Toward a Synthetic, Comparative Perspective on Social Movements," *Comparative Perspective on Social Movements: Political Opportunities, Mobilizing Structures, and Cultural Framings* (New York: Cambridge University Press, 1996), 1–22; John Emmeus Davies, *Contested Ground: Collective Action and the Urban Neighborhood* (Ithaca, NY: Cornell University Press, 1991).

23. Hurst, "Mass Frames," 79.

24. Ching-Kwan Lee, *Against the Law: Labor Protests in China's Rustbelt and Sunbelt* (Berkeley: University of California Press, 2007).

25. Ibid., 8.

26. Gramsci defined cultural hegemony as the cultural domination of one class over subaltern social groups in *Quaderni del Carcere* [Prison notebooks] (Torino, Italy: Giulio Einaudi Editore, 1975).

27. Peter L. Lorentzen, *Regularizing Rioting: Permitting Public Protest in an Authoritarian Regime*, June 9, 2010, available at http://ssrn.com/abstract=995330 or http://dx.doi.org/10.2139/ssrn.995330; Xi Chen, *Social Protest and Contentious Authoritarianism in China* (Cambridge: Cambridge University Press, 2012).

28. Xi Chen, *Social Protest*, 13.

29. Lisa Hoffman, "Autonomous Choices and Patriotic Professionalism: On Governmentality in Late-Socialist China," *Economy and Society* 35, no. 4 (2006): 550–70, and Lisa Hoffman, *Patriotic Professionalism in Urban China: Fostering Talent* (Philadelphia: Temple University Press, 2010).

30. Mayer N. Zald, "Culture, Ideology, and Strategic Framing," in *Comparative Perspectives on Social Movements*, ed. McAdam, McCarthy, and Zald, 261–74.

31. As Lorentzen notes, limited and localized social conflicts not only do not threaten regime stability but also increase the ability for the state to deal with local weaknesses in the administration and to tackle corruption and inefficiencies. Lorentzen, *Regularizing Rioting*.

32. Nikolas Rose, *Powers of Freedom: Reframing Political Thought* (Cambridge: Cambridge University Press, 1999). See also the discussion of "governing through community" in Cho, *Specter of "The People,"* 97–100.

33. Bray, "Designing to Govern."

34. Aihwa Ong, *Neoliberalism as Exception: Variations in Citizenship and Sovereignty* (Durham, NC: Duke University Press, 2006), 78.

35. From an interview with Michel Foucault entitled "Truth and Power," published in Michel Foucault, *Power*, ed. James D. Faubion (New York: New Press, 2000), 120.

36. Mitchell Dean, "Liberal Government and Authoritarianism," *Economy and Society* 31 (February 2002): 39.

37. The idea is discussed in Nikolas Rose's work but has been taken up, for example, in Li Zhang and Aihwa Ong, eds., *Privatizing China: Socialism from Afar* (Ithaca, NY: Cornell University Press, 2008). See, for example, Yan Hairong, *New Masters, New Servants: Migration, Development, and Women Workers in China* (Durham, NC: Duke University Press, 2008); Susan Greenhalgh and Edwin Winckler, *Governing China's Population: From Leninist to Neoliberal Biopolitics* (Stanford: Stanford University Press, 2005); Ong, *Neoliberalism as Exception*.

38. Ong, *Neoliberalism as Exception*, 16.

39. In a more recent work, Ong adopted a different position that places much greater emphasis on the role that states play in Asia in the production of "urban assemblages" of local and global characteristics and criticizing both neo-Marxist theorists (placing emphasis only on the role of global capital) and postcolonial theorists (placing emphasis on the postcolonial struggle of subaltern subjects) for fostering a one-size-fits-all explanation. Ananya Roy and Aihwa Ong "Introduction: Worlding Cities, or the Art of Being Global," *Worlding Cities: Asian Experiments and the Art of Being Global* (Chichester, U.K.: Blackwell, 2011), 1–25.

40. Cho, *Spectre of "The People,"* 99.

41. Wright, *Accepting Authoritarianism*.

42. Martin King Whyte, *The Myth of the Social Volcano: Perceptions of Inequality and Distributive Injustice in Contemporary China* (Stanford: Stanford University Press, 2010).

43. Pastoral refers here to one of Foucault's modalities of power, where the ruler performs a function of service of the ruled, but in a relation of dependency, as in the relationship between a pastor and its flock.

1. Social Clustering

1. Edward J. Blakely and Mary Gail Snyder, *Fortress America: Gated Communities in the United States* (Washington, DC: Brookings Institution, 1997), 1.

2. Teresa Caldeira, *City of Walls: Crime, Segregation, and Citizenship in São Paulo* (Berkeley: University of California Press, 2000).

3. Jing Wang, "Bourgeois Bohemians in China? Neo-Tribes and the Urban Imaginary," *China Quarterly* 183 (2005): 532–48.

4. Carolyn Hsu, *Creating Market Socialism: How Ordinary People Are Shaping Class and Status in China* (Durham, NC: Duke University Press, 2007). On the discourse of stratification, see Ann Anagnost, "From Class to Social Strata: Grasping the Social Totality in Reform-Era China," *Third World Quarterly* 29, no. 3 (2008): 497–519.

5. Anagnost, "From Class to Social Strata," 501.

6. Hsing, *China's Great Urban Transformation*.

7. Xinhua News Press, "Chinese 4.2 Million Security Guards to Wear New Uniforms," available at www.chinadaily.com.cn/china/2011-07/06/content_12844755.htm, accessed October 26, 2013.

8. Gu Lei, "Xiaoqu: fengbi haishi kaifang" [Residential areas: Closed or open?], *Shequ* [Community] 2 (2006): 6–9.

9. Wang Dongliang, "Zhongguo minsheng fazhan baogao: Zhongguo renjun zhufang mianji 36 pingfangmi [Report on people's livelihood in China: The average per capita living space has reached 36 square meters], *Beijing Ribao*, August 6, 2012; Wang Yanli, "Life Measures improving in China," *Shanghai Daily*, December 2, 2011.

10. I deal with the details of these policies in chapter 4. See also Li Bin, "Zhongguo zhufang gaige zhidu de fenge xing" [The unequal nature of China's housing reform], *Shehuixue yanjiu* [Research in the social sciences] 2 (2002): 80–87, and Gu Haibing, "Gongzheng yunzuo haishi qianjiu jide liyi: Zhongguo zhufang tizhi gaige zhengce de fansi" [A fair process or the adjustment of vested interests: Considerations on the policies of housing reform in China], *Dangdai zhongguo yanjiu* [Research in contemporary china] 63 (1998).

11. Pu Miao, "Deserted Streets in a Jammed Town: The Gated Community in Chinese Cities and Its Solution," *Journal of Urban Design* 8, no. 1 (2003): 45–66.

12. Li Zhang, "Contesting Spatial Modernity in Late Socialist China," *Current Anthropology* 37, no. 3 (2006): 461–84.

13. *Qingdao ribao* [Qingdao daily], December 12, 2007, http://news.idoican.com.cn/qdrb/html/2007-12/12/content_1906190.htm. Interviews with private managers revealed that, under

mounting pressure from owners and local authorities to split the two functions, this situation is changing in the direction of a more professional service.

14. Human Rights Watch, "Demolished: Forced Evictions and the Tenants' Rights Movement in China," Human Rights Watch Report, 2004, available at www.hrw.org/reports/2004/china0304/china0304.pdf, accessed October 26, 2013.

15. Both You-Tien Hsing and Li Zhang call these land-endowed organizations "socialist land masters." See Hsing, *Great Urban Transformation*; Li Zhang, *In Search of Paradise:Middle Class Living in a Chinese Metropolis* (Ithaca: Cornell University Press, 2010).

16. Tomba and Tang, "Forest City."

17. The term *xiaoqu*, micro-district, originates as the translation of the Russian *mikrorayon*, the Soviet residential compound that inspired China's early socialist residential areas in the 1950s. See Bray, *Social Space and Governance*; and Duanfang Lu, *Remaking China's Urban Form: Modernity, Scarcity, and Space, 1949–2005* (London: Routledge, 2010).

18. See also Li, "Zhongguo zhufang gaige zhidu de fenge xing."

19. Anthony G. O. Yeh, "Dual Land Market and Internal Spatial Structure of Chinese Cities," in *Restructuring the Chinese City: Changing Society, Economy, and Spaces*, ed. Laurence J. C. Ma and Fulong Wu (London and New York: Routledge, 2005), 59–79.

20. Donggen Wang and Siming Li, "Housing Preferences in a Transitional Housing System: The Case of Beijing, China," *Centre for Urban and Regional Studies Occasional Paper* (Hong Kong: Hong Kong Baptist University, 2002).

21. "Beijing shi guotu fangguanju, Beijing shi gong'an ju, Beijing shi mingzhengju guanyu jiaqiang juzhu xiaoqu anquan fangfan guanli gongzuo de tongzhi" [Communiqué of the Beijing Land Bureau, Police Bureau, and Civil Affairs Bureau on strengthening security management in residential areas], Beijing, November 5, 2001.

22. Wu Qinghua, Dong Xiangwei, and Wang Guofeng, "Jianyi chengshi shequ jiecenghua qushi dui shequ jianshe de yingxiang" [The impact of urban community stratification on community building], *Zhongyang shehuizhuyi xueyuan bao* [Journal of the central institute of socialism] 3 (2009).

23. See "Beijing Daxing 'fengcun'" (A large scale "gated village" in Beijing) in Renmin wang (People.com.cn), May 19, 2010, available at http://scitech.people.com.cn/GB/11635201.html. Accessed December 27, 2013.

24. Ibid.

25. Hsing, *Great Urban Transformation*.

26. Ong, *Neoliberalism as Exception*, 78.

27. A critique of Ong's approach in this direction can be found in Neil Brenner, Jamie Peck, and Nik Theodore, "Variegated Neoliberalization: Geographies, Modalities, Pathways," *Global Networks* 10, no. 2 (2010): 182–222, esp. 199–205.

28. Ma Jiantang, "Press Release on Major Figures of the 2010 Population Census," April 28, 2011, available at www.stats.gov.cn/english/newsandcomingevents/t20110428_402722237.htm, accessed October 26, 2013.

29. One of the characteristics of China's postsocialist cities is the reemergence of a functional subdivision of the urban territory. While the work-unit system required that areas shared functions (for example residence and production within the same compound), the new planning culture of the 1990s has increasingly recovered functional specialization (commercial, residential, industrial areas). See Victor F. S. Sit, *Beijing: The Nature and Planning of a Chinese Capital City* (Chichester, U.K.: Wiley, 1999).

30. On the social and political role played by the work units, see Lü Xiaobo and Elizabeth Perry, eds., *Danwei: The Changing Chinese Workplace in Historical and Comparative Perspective* (Armonk, NY: M.E. Sharpe, 1997); Bray, *Social Space and Governance*.

31. Walder, "Organized Dependence."

32. See, for example, Nan and Bian, "Getting Ahead in Urban China."

33. Li, "Zhongguo zhufang gaige zhidu de fenge xing."

34. There is a growing literature on the *suzhi* discourse in China. See, for example, Ann Anagnost, "The Corporeal Politics of Quality (*Suzhi*)," *Public Culture* 16 (2004): 189–208; Tamara Jacka, *Rural Women in Urban China* (Armonk, NY: M.E. Sharpe, 2006); Yan Hairong, "Neoliberal Governmentality and Neohumanism: Organizing *Suzhi*/Value Flow through Labor Recruitment Networks," *Cultural Anthropology* 18, no. 4 (2003): 493–523; Andrew Kipnis, "*Suzhi*: A Keyword Approach," *China Quarterly* 186 (2006): 295–313; and a 2009 special issue of the journal *Positions: East Asia Cultures Critiques* 17, no. 3, edited by Tamara Jacka.

35. For an initial evaluation of these types of residential communities, see Tomba and Tang, "Forest City."

36. See Lee, *Against the Law*.

37. The three provinces of the Chinese Northeast have suffered the most from the long-lasting restructuring of the state industrial system, with over a quarter of the nationwide 28 million layoffs between 1999 and 2004.

38. Schurmann, *Ideology and Organization*; Read, *Roots of the State*; Benjamin Read, "Revitalizing China's Urban Nerve Tips," *China Quarterly* 163 (September 2000): 806–20; Luigi Tomba, "Residential Space and Collective Interest Formation."

39. The works already cited by Heberer and Göbel and by Read are the most comprehensive analysis of these institutions. Also see Read, "Democratizing the Neighborhood?" and my "Creating a Chinese Middle Class: Social Engineering in Beijing," *China Journal* 51 (July 2004): 1–29.

40. The Street Offices (*jiedao banshichu*) are the lowest level of urban government. Cities, below the municipality are formally organized in "two levels of government and one level of administration," administration being the community-neighborhood and government being the district and the sub-district (street) level. With the progressive expansion of the role of communities, discussion is unfolding on the hollowing-out of street offices and on their possible future demise as an intermediate level of governance.

41. Although no one is willing to admit it, the political clout of community directors is a marker of better access to municipal or district-level funding for renovations and special activities. Communities also compete with one another for scarce public resources.

42. Shenyang shi minzhengju [Shenyang Civil Affairs Department], "Guanyu tigao shequ gongzuozhe daiyu de tongzhi" [Communiqué on raising the salaries of community workers], available at www.symzj.gov.cn/zwgkw/show.jsp?id=349.

43. *Beijing ribao* [Beijing daily], January 30, 2010, available at www.bjrd.gov.cn/xwzx/xwbt/201001/t20100130_54938.html, accessed October 27, 2013.

44. Household registration is the responsibility of the local police office but is often performed by guards hired with funds from the labor bureau and working on the premises of the community committees. In general communities have been given increasing responsibility to control the movement, behavior, and registration of long-term migrants who might rent apartments in the community on a regular basis. Falungong is a *qigong* practice that in 1999 was banned by the government and labeled an "evil cult." Since then the eradication and alleged prosecution of Falungong practitioners has continued and has been one of the social control tasks assigned to the *shequ*. On Falungong, see Benjamin Penny, *The Religion of Falungong* (Chicago: University of Chicago Press, 2012).

45. On the *dibao*, see also Dorothy Solinger, "The *Dibao* Recipients: Mollified Anti-Emblem of Urban Modernization," in *China Perspectives* 4 (2008): 36–46; Cho, *Spectre of the People*.

46. See Chen Jiandong and Armando Barrientos, *Extending Social Assistance in China: Lessons from the Minimum Living Standard Scheme*, Chronic Poverty Research Centre, Working paper 67 (November 2006); World Bank, Poverty Reduction and Economic Management Unit East Asia and Pacific Region, *China: Revitalizing the Northeast: Towards a Development Strategy* (Washington, DC: World Bank, 2006).

47. Ministry of Civil Affairs, *China Civil Affairs Statistical Yearbook, 2011* (Beijing: Zhongguo Tongji Chubanshe, 2012).

48. "Self-management," "self-education," and "self-service" are heralded as the core of this concept.

49. Typically, a community of this kind would have a Consultative Committee (*xieshanghui*) and an Owner committee, but communities also often nominate a "building representative" and establish recreational associations that generally are registered with the community.

50. Eva P. W. Hung and Stephen K. W. Chiu, "The Lost Generation: Life Course Dynamics and Xiagang in China," *Modern China* 29, no. 2 (April 2003): 204–36.

51. Xinhua News Agency, "Gaodang xiaoqu chengle "chaosheng bifeng gang" (High end residential communities have become "safe heavens for excess births") June 15, 2003 available at http://news.xinhuanet.com/newscenter/2003-06/15/content_919944.htm accessed 27 December 2013. On the one-child policy, see Greenhalgh and Winckler, *Governing China's Population*.

52. *Qiju: Wanke de fangzi* [Poetic dwelling: Vanke's house] (Wuhan, China: Huazhong Keji Daxue Chubanshe, 2007).

53. Hung and Chiu, "Lost Generation."

54. World Bank, *China: Revitalizing the Northeast*, 108.

55. Hoffman, *Patriotic Professionalism in Urban China*, and Hoffman, "Autonomous Choices and Patriotic Professionalism."

56. Bei Ye, *Guanyu jianshe meihao shenghuo de sikao* [On building a beautiful life] (Beijing: Self-published pamphlet, 2003).

57. Title and author withheld. Document in possession of the author. Beijing 2003.

2. Micro-Governing the Urban Crisis

1. Michel Foucault, *Discipline and Punish: The Birth of a Prison* (London: Penguin, 1991).

2. Cho, *Specter of "The People,"* 157.

3. See in particular a special issue on "Chinese governmentalities" in *Economy and Society* 35, no. 4 (2006), and the volume edited by Elaine Jeffreys, *China's Governmentalities: Governing Change, Changing Government* (Milton Park, U.K., and New York: Routledge, 2009); Ong, *Neoliberalism as Exception*; Rose, *Powers of Freedom*; Mitchell Dean, "Liberal Government and Authoritarianism," *Economy and Society* 31, no. 1 (2002): 37–61; Zhang and Ong, eds., *Privatizing China*.

4. The survey was made possible by the contacts I established during a lecture I gave at the Tiexi Party School in 2008, where all community directors of the district were invited. Besides returning the questionnaire, many of the directors also became part of my interview sample.

5. The Northeastern Rustbelt has been the focus of several recent works on the Chinese working class and social change. See Lee, *Against the Law*; Hurst, *Chinese Worker after Socialism*; and Cho, *Specter of "The People."*

6. James Derleth and Daniel Koldyk, "The *Shequ* Experiment: Grassroots Political Reform in Urban China," *Journal of Contemporary China* 13, no. 41 (November 2004): 747–77.

7. Dorothy Solinger, "*Dibao* Recipients."

8. Heberer and Göbel, *Politics of Community Building*.

9. He Zengke, Thomas Heberer, and Gunther Schubert, *Chengxiang gongmin canyu he zhengzhi hefaxing* [Citizen participation in rural and urban areas and political legitimacy] (Beijing: Zhongyang Bianyi Chubanshe, 2007).

10. *Shangmian you zhengce, xiamian zanmen gaichuo*. The expression is a variation on the traditional "above are the policies, below are the countermeasures."

11. This point is made most clearly in Cho, *Specter of "The People."*

12. Ibid., 170.

3. Housing and Social Engineering

1. For a discussion of how the term *shehui gongcheng* has been central to the discussion of social policies, see Børge Bakken, *The Exemplary Society: Human Improvement, Social Control, and the Dangers of Modernity in China* (Oxford: Oxford University Press, 2000), esp. ch. 2.

2. Hopetown is a fictitious translation of the name of the neighborhood where fieldwork for this chapter and the next was undertaken. All information concerning the area, unless otherwise indicated, is taken from participatory observation, materials published by residents of Hopetown and a set of fifty open-ended interviews that I carried out with residents and officials in spring 2002 and again in summer 2003, while I was living in the neighborhood. I went back to the neighborhood on several occasions after that, until 2010. In order to protect the interviewees' identity, I use pseudonyms and avoid mentioning personal details. Unless otherwise indicated, information and quotations in this chapter are from interviews with local residents.

3. Many magazines and websites are available to pet (*chongwu*) lovers, including http://www.chinapet.net/ and http://www.chinapet.com/.

4. Pet ownership is believed to have passed the 900,000 figure in Beijing, but it is unclear how many unregistered dogs roam the neighborhoods. Michael Wines, "Once Banned, Dogs Reflect China's Rise," *New York Times*, October 25, 2010, available at www.nytimes.com/2010/10/25/world/asia/25dogs.html, accessed October 26, 2013.

5. The organization's website is available at: http://www.capn.ngo.cn/.

6. The developer in question had in 2004 a total asset capitalization in excess of US$1.5 billion and was already responsible for the construction of 11 million square meters of housing in the capital, or around 180,000 residential units (an estimated 660,000 Beijing residents were living in houses built by this company).

7. *China Daily*, January 31, 1999.

8. There also are price differences within "economy" buildings (depending on *feng shui*, views, floor space, and so on).

9. Jin Biao and Chuan Shan, "[name deleted] Yezhu: wo de siyou caichang zai nali?" [(name deleted) homeowners: Where are my private property rights?], *Sanlian shenghuo zhoukan* [Sanlian life week], March 20, 2002.

10. According to Li Shouen, the concept of *xiaokang* comes from the definition of an ideal society in the Confucian *Book of Rites* (*Li ji*). Its first appearance in the Communist era is attributed to a reference Deng made to a foreign guest in 1978, when he argued that China's reform target was to reach a per capita GDP of US$1,000 by the end of the century. Li Shouen, "Lun quanmian jianshe xiaokang shehui" [On building a well-off society in an all-around way"], *Shishi qiushi* [Seek truth from facts] 1 (2003): 13–16. Its more recent revival is related to Jiang Zemin's use of the expression in his report to the 16th Party Congress in 2002.

11. The two most recent volumes on the broad topic of the Chinese middle class are Cheng Li, ed., *China's Emerging Middle Class: Beyond Economic Transformation* (Washington, DC: Brookings Institution, 2010); Goodman, ed., *New Rich in China*. See also He Li, "Emergence of the Chinese Middle Class and Its Implications," *Asian Affairs* 33, no. 2 (2006): 67–83; David S. G. Goodman, "The People's Republic of China: The Party State, Capitalist Revolution, and New Entrepreneurs," in *The New Rich in Asia: Mobile Phones, McDonald's, and Middle-class Revolution*, ed. Richard Robison and David S. G. Goodman (London: Routledge, 1996), 225–42; Christopher Buckley, "How a Revolution Becomes a Dinner Party: Stratification, Mobility and the New Riches in Urban China," in *Culture and Privilege in Capitalist Asia*, ed. Michael Pinches (London: Routledge, 1999), 208–29; David S. G. Goodman, "The New Middle Class," in *The Paradox of China's Post-Mao Reforms*, ed. Merle Goldman and Roderick MacFarquhar (Cambridge, MA: Harvard University Press, 1999), 241–61; Xiuhong Hu and David H. Kaplan, "The Emergence

of Affluence in Beijing: Residential Social Stratification in China's Capital City," *Urban Geography* 22, no. 1 (2001): 54–77.

12. Goodman, "People's Republic of China," 229; Bruce Dickson, *Red Capitalists in China: The Party, Private Entrepreneurs, and Prospects for Political Change* (Cambridge: Cambridge University Press, 2002).

13. See Yan Zhimin, ed., *Zhongguo xian jieduan jieji jieceng yanjiu* [Research on the classes and strata in China during the initial phase] (Beijing: Zhonggong Zhongyang Dangxiao Chubanshe, 2002), 238.

14. I borrow this term from Ezra Vogel's study of the Japanese salaried middle class in the 1950s, despite the obvious differences. Ezra Vogel, *Japan's New Middle Class: The Salary Man and His Family in a Tokyo Suburb* (Berkeley: University of California Press, 1963).

15. See also Tomba, *Paradoxes of Labour Reform*.

16. Wu Fulong, "Sociospatial Differentiation in Urban China: Evidence from Shanghai's Real Estate Markets," *Environment and Planning A* 34 (2002): 1591. A similar point has been made by Li Jian and Niu Xiaohan, who define this group as a "middle class within the system" (*tizhinei zhongchan jieji*) in "New Middle Class(es)." I prefer the definition of "salary-earning middle class," since this today covers not only state employees but also people who have managed to maintain a certain level of administrative status while moving more recently to the private or foreign-invested sector.

17. Pun Ngai, "Subsumption or Consumption? The Phantom of Consumer Revolution in 'Globalizing' China," *Cultural Anthropology* 18, no. 4 (November 2003): 472.

18. "Quanmian jianshe xiaokang shehui," Jiang Zemin's Report at the 16th Party Congress.

19. See Yi Shijie, "Tigao xiaofeilü ladong jingji cengzhang" [Increase the consumption rate, stimulate economic growth], *Jingjixue dongtai* [Trends in economics] 10 (2002): 14–17.

20. "Consumption and Urbanization to Drive China's Economy," *People's Daily Online*, December 14, 2009, available at http://english.peopledaily.com.cn/90001/90778/90862/6841622.html, accessed October 26, 2013.

21. "Two Twists in the Dragon's Tail," *The Economist*, January 21, 2012; Lin Yuying, "Woguo jumin xiaofei zhan GDP bizhong guodi zhi daliang channeng guocheng [The reduction in consumption to GDP ratio in China points to a discrepancy in production capacity], *Zhongguo xinwen wang* [China news network], December 18, 2012.

22. This quotation is from a study commissioned by the State Development and Planning Commission. See Zhou Changcheng, ed., *Shehui fazhan yu shenghuo zhiliang* [Social development and the quality of life] (Beijing: Shehui Kexue Wenxian Chubanshe, 2001), 2. Others have stressed the same point. See, for example, Li Qiang, *Shehui fenceng yu pinfu chabie* [Social stratification and inequality] (Xiamen, China: Lujiang Chubanshe, 2001), 91. The link between political and social stability on the one side and the need to improve living conditions and reduce poverty on the other is also one of the favorite topics of political scientist Kang Xiaoguang's work. See, for example, "Weilai 3–5 nian Zhongguo dalu zhengzhi wending xing fenxi" [Analysis of mainland China's political stability in the next 3–5 years], *Zhanlue yu guanli* [Strategy and management] 3 (2002). 1–15.

23. Lu Xueyi, ed., *Dangdai Zhongguo shehui jieceng yanjiu baogao* [Research report on contemporary China's social stratification] (Beijing: Shehui Kexue Wenxian Chubanshe, 2002). Lu Xueyi was, at the time, the head of the Sociology Department of CASS. The book was criticized by conservative elements in the Party for suggesting a much more complex stratification in China than the traditional "two classes and one stratum" and for pointing at bureaucrats and Party officials as an independent upper class, with workers and peasants at the bottom.

24. This is indeed a rather vague definition, and one that allow for variations in the assessment of who belongs to the middle classes. Lu Xueyi's report suggests that, at the time of the research, an income of 25,000 to 30,000 yuan (US$3,300 to US$4,000) per person per year is the average in

the "initial phase of socialism," even though average incomes are much lower, even in the most affluent urban areas. See Lu Xueyi, ed., *Dangdai Zhongguo shehui jieceng yanjiu baogao*, 252–53.

25. Advanced and civilized forces are, incidentally, central to Jiang Zemin's Theory of the "Three Represents" (*sange daibiao*), which refers to the Party's role in representing the development trend of China's advanced productive forces, the orientation of China's advanced culture, and the fundamental interests of the overwhelming majority of the Chinese people.

26. Lu Xueyi, ed., *Dangdai Zhongguo shehui jieceng yanjiu baogao*, 252. The topic of the middle strata and consumption has attracted many scholarly works in China. Li Qiang's study of stratification, which was published in 2000, contained warnings about the risks for stability and economic development of a declining consumption capacity among the "traditional white collar middle strata." See Li Qiang, *Shehui fengceng yu pinfu chabie*, 91.

27. All of the many new works on "community building" (*shequ jianshe*) use this slogan-like definition of the ongoing social transformation of urban society. The "official" inspiration for the slogan is the document "Minzhengbu guanyu zai quanguo tuijin chengshi sheque jianshe de yijian" [Ministry of Civil Affairs' opinion on speeding up urban community building across the country], *Zhongguo minzheng* [China civil affairs] 1 (2001): 4–6.

28. *Beijing Tongji nianjian* [Beijing statistical yearbook], 1996 and 2001. The Chinese Academy of Sciences, for example, spent about 600 million yuan (US$80 million) to recruit three hundred talented young researchers. See Cao Cong, "Strengthening China through Science and Education: China Development Strategy toward the 21st Century," *Issues and Studies* 38, no. 3 (September 2002): 122–49.

29. Government Work Report to the 10th NPC, March 5, 2003, available at http://app1.china daily.com.cn/highlights/nbc/news/319zhufull.htm accessed 28 December 2013.

30. See Beibei Tang, *The Making of Housing Status Groups in Post Reform Urban China: Social Mobility and Status Attainment of Gated Community Residents in Shenyang*, PhD dissertation, Australian National University, Canberra, 2009.

31. Unger and Chan, "Internal Politics." See also Tang, *Making of Housing Status Groups*; and Luigi Tomba and Beibei Tang, "The Great Divide: Institutionalized Inequality in China's Market Socialism," in *Unequal China: The Political Economy and Cultural Politics of Inequality*, ed. Guo Yingjie and Sun Wanning (London: Routledge, 2012), 91–110.

32. Beibei Tang, Luigi Tomba, and Werner Breitung, "The Work-Unit Is Dead. Long Live the Work-Unit! Spatial Segregation and Privilege in a Work-Unit Housing Compound in Guangzhou," *Geographische Zeitschrift* 1 (2011): 36–49.

33. *Zhongguo tongji nianjian* [China statistical yearbook] (Beijing: Zhongguo Tongji Chubanshe, 2008).

34. Zhonghong jiaoyu (Macro education), 2012 guojia gongwuyuan kaoshi baoming zongrenshu da 123wan (1.23 million register for the National civil service exam in 2012), available at www.ncgwy.com/columns/news/20111026/n523920111027.html, accessed October 27, 2013.

35. On the rationale for this policy, a hot topic in Chinese academic journals during the first years of last decade, see, for example, Xie Ming, "Lun 'Gaoxin yanglian'" [On "High salaries to foster honesty"], *Beijing xingzheng xueyuan xuebao* [Journal of the Beijing institute of public administration] 3 (2002): 14–19.

36. Pan Jianfeng, "Gaoxin zhi: shenpan gongzhen, lianjie he faguan gao suzhi de jiben baozhang" [High salaries system: The basic guarantee of fair trials and honest and high-quality judges], *Zhengfa luntan* [Legal forum] 6 (2001): 15–21.

37. See, for example, Huang Yongyan, "Guanyu woguo guowuyuan 'gaoxin yanglian' de sikao [Thoughts on "High salaries to foster honesty" for public servants], *Zhongguo shangjie* [Business China] (March 2009): 171–72.

38. *China Labour and Security Statistical Yearbook*, 1996 and 2001.

39. The last decade was the golden era for university enrollments. Despite a reported recent drop in enrollments, the 2010 population census reported that 8,930 Chinese per 100,000 have a university degree, a dramatic increase over the 2000 figure of 3,611. See "Decreased enrollment has Chinese universities scrambling," *People's Daily Online English*, June 7, 2011, available at http://english.people.com.cn/90001/90782/7401909.html, accessed October 27, 2011; Ma Jiantang, "Press Release on Major Figures of the 2010 Population Census, April 28, 2011," available at www.stats.gov.cn/english/newsandcomingevents/t20110428_402722237.htm, accessed October 27, 2013.

40. State Council Decision No. 146, "Guowuyuan guanyu zhigong gongzuo shijian de guiding" [State Council decision on the work-time of staff and workers], February 3, 1994, later modified by Decision No. 174, March 25, 1995. On the desire to stimulate consumption as the impetus for this decision, see Zhu Jialiu, "Shuanxiuzhi gei shangye yingxiao celüe dailai de sikao" [The implications of a short working week for the strategies of commercial marketing], *Shanghai shangye* [Shanghai commerce] 2 (1995).

41. Wang Yalin, *Chengshi xiuxian: Shanghai, Tianjin, Haerbin chengshi jumin shijian fenpei de kaocha* [Report on the distribution of time among urban residents in Shanghai, Tianjin, and Harbin] (Beijing: Shehui Kexue Wenxian Chubanshe, 2003).

42. Ibid., 159–61.

43. *Beijing Statistical Yearbook*, 2001. Also see Wang Ya Ping, "Housing Reform and Its Impact on the Urban Poor," *Housing Studies* 15, no. 6 (2000): 845–64.

44. *Beijing Statistical Yearbook*, 2001.

45. Friedrich Engels, *The Condition of the Working Class in England in 1844* (London: Allen and Unwin, 1936 [1892]). For accounts of the anti-city attitude in Chinese socialism, see Lewis and Cohen, eds., *City in Communist China*; Janet Salaff, "Urban Communes and Anti-City Experiments in Communist China," *China Quarterly* 29 (January 1967): 82–109.

46. Robert Park, *Human Communities: The City and Human Ecology* (Glencoe, IL: Free Press, 1952). The classic work of the Chicago School is Robert E. Park, Ernest W. Burgess, and Roderick McKenzie, *The City* (Chicago: University of Chicago Press, 1967 [1926]).

47. For an overview of the literature and of the different research traditions, see A. Sule Ozuekren and Ronald Van Kempen, "Ethnic Segregation in Cities: New Forms and Explanation in a Dynamic World," *Urban Studies* 35, no. 10 (1998): 1631–56.

48. John Rex and Robert Moore, *Race, Community, and Conflict: A Study of Sparkbrook* (London and New York: Oxford University Press, 1967).

49. Ozuekren and Van Kempen, "Ethnic Segregation in Cities," 1642. See also Ronald Van Kempen, "The Academic Formulations: Explanations for a Partitioned City," in *Of States and Cities: The Partitioning of Urban Space*, ed. Peter Marcuse and Ronald Van Kempen (Oxford: Oxford University Press, 2002), 35–58.

50. Anthony Giddens, *The Class Structure of the Advanced Societies* (London: Hutchinson, 1973). Giddens's formulation is that the "structuration of classes is facilitated to the degree to which mobility closure exists in relation to any specified form of market capacity," 107. Quite significantly for this book, Giddens sees the formation of "working class neighborhoods" separated from "middle class" neighborhoods as the possible outcome of differential access to home loans. The facilitation of housing consumption would therefore be a distinctive factor in class formation, 109–10. On this topic, see also Manuel Castells, *City, Class, and Power* (London: Macmillan, 1978).

51. Ibid., 109.

52. Sit, *Beijing*, esp. ch. 11, which provides a review of the earlier literature on spatial transformation in China.

53. The relationship between spatial organization and social segregation has been the focus of a number of studies on contemporary urban China. Geographers should be praised for pointing out the relevance of the housing reform in reshaping postsocialist Chinese metropolises.

Their studies have especially concentrated on Shanghai and Guangzhou, but several tackle the transformation and residential mobility of the capital city. See Laurence J. C. Ma, "Urban Transformation in China, 1949–2000: A Review and Research Agenda," *Environment and Planning A* 34 (2002): 1545–69; Fulong, "Sociospatial Differentiation in Urban China"; Anthony G. O. Yeh et al., "The Social Space of Guangzhou City, China," *Urban Geography* 16 (1995): 595–621; Piper Gaubatz, "Changing Beijing," *Geographical Review* 85, no. 1 (January 1995): 74–96; Ya Ping Wang and Alan Murie, "Commercial Housing Development in Urban China," *Urban Studies* 36, no. 9 (August 1999): 1475–94; Fulong Wu, "The New Structure of Building Provision and the Transformation of the Urban Landscape in Metropolitan Guangzhou," *Urban Studies* 35, no. 2 (February 1998): 277–83; Hu and Kaplan, "Emergence of Affluence in Beijing"; Siming Li and Doris K. W. Fung, "Housing Tenure and Residential Mobility in Urban China: Analysis of Survey Data," *Occasional Papers Series* (Hong Kong: Hong Kong Baptist University, Centre for China Urban and Regional Studies, July 2001); Siming Li, "Housing Consumption in Urban China: A Comparative Study of Beijing and Guangzhou," *Environment and Planning A* 32, no. 6 (2000): 1115–34.

54. To give one example of the pace of this process, one should consider that by 2001, about 15 percent of all the floor space in Beijing's residential buildings higher than nine floors had been built in one single year, 2000. Beijing Statistical Yearbook, Beijing: Beijing Statistical Bureau, 2001.

55. Hu and Kaplan, "Emergence of Affluence in Beijing."

56. Ibid., 70.

57. See, for example, Wang Lina, "Urban Housing Welfare and Income Distribution," in *China's Retreat from Inequality: Income Distribution and Economic Transition*, ed. Carl Riskin, Zhao Renwei, and Li Shi (Armonk, NY: M.E. Sharpe, 2001), 167–83. In 2001, central and local work units still built around 33 percent of all newly built residential floor space in Beijing, while developers built the remaining two-thirds. *Beijing Statistical Yearbook*, 2002, p. 143.

58. Both Beijing University and People's University purchased entire buildings within newly constructed compounds for the purpose of being resold to their employees. Despite the private nature of these transactions, on some occasions the universities maintained some level of administrative control over the management of these sections of the compound and acted as a go-between when conflicts arose with the developer. I am grateful to Zhang Jing for bringing this situation to my attention.

59. "Beijingers Concerned over House Prices," *China Daily*, January 4, 2002 available at http://www.chinadaily.com.cn/en/home/2002-01/04/content 100559.htm, accessed 28 December 2013.

60. *Beijing Statistical Yearbook, 2002*. The average price per square meter in Beijing in 2001 was 4,517 yuan (US$600), the highest rate in China and well above the national average, which is 2,227 yuan (US$300). This would place the average price of a "raw" (without internal decoration and appliances) apartment of 70 square meters at about 320,000 yuan (US$38,000). If we consider that work-unit housing is generally located in what are now Beijing's central suburbs—compensating for the lower construction quality of such housing—such a heavily subsidized sale means the apartments have in fact been allocated at a two-thirds discount.

61. *Beijing Statistical Yearbook*, different years, 2005–2012.

62. Li and Niu present a number of examples of the comparative monetary advantages generated by such purchases. Li and Niu, "New Middle Class(es) in Peking."

63. Li, "Zhongguo zhufang gaige zhidu de fenge xing."

64. Ibid., 81.

65. A waiting time of five years imposed between the purchase of a public apartment and its possible sale was dropped in 2002. The secondary market in 2001 was only about 85 percent of the new housing market. Ministry of Construction, *Guanyu Beijing zhufang er san ji shichang wenti diaocha baogao* [Research report on Beijing secondary and tertiary housing market], October 2002.

66. Tang, *Making of Housing Status Groups*, 102.

67. Provident funds pool resources from employers and employees and are aimed at providing monetary incentives for the purchase of apartments by employees. For an analysis, see Wang Ya Ping, "Urban Housing Reform and Finance in China: A Case Study of Beijing," *Urban Affairs Review* 36, no. 5 (May 2001): 620–45; Mathias Burrell, "China's Housing Provident Fund: Its Success and Limitations," *Housing Finance International*, March 1, 2006.

68. Li, "Zhongguo zhufang gaige zhidu de fenge xing."

69. Ibid.

70. Burrell, "China's Housing Provident Fund," 9.

71. The price of economy housing is therefore not standard (as also is generally the case for the sale of public housing) but is linked to the quality and prices of the commercial housing in the vicinity. See Xing Quan Zhang, "Governing Housing in China: State, Market, and Work Units," *Journal of Housing and the Built Environment* 17, no. 1 (2002); 7–20.

72. "Time to put Economy Housing in Order" *China Daily* June 23 2005, available at http://www.china.org.cn/english/BAT/132926.htm accessed 28 December 2013. Also, limits were imposed in a second phase of the policy initiative. At the beginning, the only requirement was a Beijing *hukou* (household registration).

73. Lan Deng, Qingyun Shen, and Lin Wang, "Housing Policy and Finance in China: A Literature Review," unpublished paper prepared for the U.S. Department of Housing and Urban Development, November 2009. In recent years the Beijing government also restarted the construction of low-rent public housing. 2.7 million square meters of this type of housing were under construction in 2011. See *Beijing Statistical Yearbook*, 2012.

74. China's official media also highlighted the anomaly. See Lan Xinzhen, "Housing Policy Falls Short," *Beijing Review*, May 8, 2003, pp. 24–25.

75. Economy apartments should, according to the regulations, not exceed 80 square meters in size, but many are much larger. In Hopetown 2, small economy apartments remain the exception, and I visited apartments that are more than double the maximum size. In 2003 the Ministry of Construction even launched an investigation on the violations of sales regulations by developers. *China Economic Information*, April 1, 2003.

76. Deng, Shen, and Wang, "Housing Policy and Finance," 34.

77. Ibid., 9.

78. Li, "Zhongguo zhufang gaige zhidu de fenge xing," 85–86.

79. See People's Bank of China, *Monetary Policy Report 2002*, January 2003.

80. Economist Intelligence Unit, *Country Profile: China and Mongolia*, 2009.

81. The Beijing Statistical Bureau's yearly sample survey of 1,000 urban household signals a steep decline in public home occupancy after the 1998 reform (from 76.6 percent in 1998 to 53.2 percent in 2000). *Beijing Statistical Yearbook*, 2001.

82. *Beijing Statistical Yearbook*, 2010.

83. *Beijing Review*, May 8, 2003.

84. At the rates offered by the Construction Bank of China at the time of my fieldwork, a repayment of 3,000 yuan (US$400) a month was enough to pay back 350,000 yuan (US$45,000) over fifteen years. Provident funds that in Beijing were managed through CBC can provide better conditions but generally involve a more thorough check of the employees' entitlements.

85. It is not uncommon for people who work in positions that involve money and responsibility to join the Party, at the request of their employer, as a condition for a promotion. This was the case for this young lady.

86. He Yingchuan and Liang Yi, "Toushi: Beijing xiaofeixin bianhua" [A perspective: New changes in Beijing consumption], *Hongguan jingji guanli* [Macroeconomic management] 2 (2002): 9–17. The upward trend has continued, with China recently becoming the largest market for automobiles in the world.

87. Tang and Tomba, "Great Divide."

88. Jonathan Unger, "China's Conservative Middle Class," *Far Eastern Economic Review* (April 2006): 27–31.

4. Contained Contention

1. *Zhongguo falü nianjian* [China law yearbook] (Beijing: Zhongguo Falü Nianjian Chubanshe, 1998 and 2001).

2. "Xiaoxie tishi: goufang bu gai tashang 'shangxin zhilü'" [Consumers' association points out: Buying a house should not become a heart-breaking journey], *Beijing Chenbao* [Beijing morning news], March 8, 2002.

3. Shen Yan, "Yezhu weiquan you duo nan" [How hard it is for homeowners to protect their rights], *Renmin Wang*, June 26, 2006; *Zuigao renmin fayuan gongzuo baogao* [Work report of the Supreme People's Court], 2010, available at http://www.npc.gov.cn/huiyi/dbdh/11_3/2010-03/18/content_1564762.htm. Accessed 29 December 2013.

4. Wang et al. attempted a classification of such conflicts in Shanghai. See Feng Wang, Haitao Yin, and Zhiren Zhou, "The Adoption of Bottom Up Governance in China's Homeowner Associations," *Management and Organization Review* 8, no. 3 (2012): 559–83.

5. Rui Xiao, "Jiannan de wuye guanli qiye weiquan zhilu" [Management companies' difficult road to protecting (owners') interests], *Chengshi Kaifa* [Urban development] 9 (2004): 12–13.

6. Lee Ching-kwan, "Rights Activism in China," *Contexts* 7, no. 3 (2008): 14–19.

7. See Jae Ho Chung, Hongyi Lai, and Ming Xia, "Mounting Challenges to Governance in China: Surveying Collective Protestors, Religious Sects, and Criminal Organizations," *China Journal* 56 (July 2006): 1–31.

8. Zhang, *In Search of Paradise*.

9. Ira Katznelson, *City Trenches: Urban Politics and the Patterning of Class in the United States* (New York: Pantheon Books, 1981), 19.

10. Clarence Y. H. Lo, "Communities of Challengers in Social Movement Theory," in *Frontiers in Social Movement Theory*, ed. Aldon D. Morris and Carol McClurg Mueller (New Haven, CT: Yale University Press, 1992).

11. Among the numerous book-length studies on this subject, see Deng Minjie, *Chuangxin shequ* [Renewing communities] (Beijing: Zhongguo Shehui Chubanshe, 2002); Wang Bangzuo, *Juweihui yu shequ zhili*; Yu Yongyang, *Shequ fazhan lun* [On community development] (Shanghai: Huadong Ligong Daxue Chubanshe, 2000). "Framing processes" are the "conscious strategic efforts by groups of people to fashion shared understandings of the world and of themselves that legitimate and motivate collective action." See McAdam, McCarthy, and Zald, "Introduction," 6.

12. David Harvey, *The Urbanization of Capital: Studies in the History and Theory of Capitalist Urbanization* (Baltimore: Johns Hopkins University Press, 1985). See also David Harvey, "Labor, Capital, and Class Struggle around the Built Environment in Advanced Capitalist Society," in *Urbanization and Conflict in Market Societies*, ed. Kevin Cox (London: Methuen, 1978), 9–37. David Harvey's formulation is a "class struggle that has its origin in the work process but that ramifies and reverberates throughout all aspects of the system of relations that capitalism establishes," Harvey, "Labor, Capital, and Class Struggle," 27.

13. Davies, *Contested Ground*, 27.

14. Ibid., 26.

15. Rex and Moore, *Race, Community, and Conflict*, 273.

16. Peter Saunders, "Domestic Property and Social Class," *International Journal of Urban and Regional Research* 2 (1978): 233–51. See also Saunders, *Social Theory and the Urban Question* (New York: Holmes and Meier, 1981).

17. Davies, *Contested Ground*, 44–61. For a later spatial interpretation of neighborhood conflict, see Mark Purcell, "Neighborhood Activism among Homeowners as a Politics of Space," *Professional Geographer* 53, no. 2 (2001): 178–94.

18. Davies, *Contested Ground*, 6.

19. David Morris and Karl Hess, *Neighborhood Power: The New Localism* (Boston: Beacon Press, 1975), 1.

20. Li Zhang, *Strangers in the City: Reconfiguration of Space, Power, and Social Networks within China's Floating Population* (Stanford, CA: Stanford University Press, 2001); Dorothy Solinger, *Contesting Citizenship in Urban China: Peasant Migrants, the State, and the Logic of the Market* (Berkeley: University of California Press, 1999).

21. *Beijing Statistical Yearbook*, 2011

22. Lü and Perry, eds., *Danwei*.

23. As an unwritten rule well known to residents, the local *paichusuo* (police station) never authorizes public gatherings. Experience, however, also taught owners that the police would not prevent demonstrations as long as they remained within the boundaries of the neighborhood.

24. This specific incident was reported by both local and international press. See "Yezhu: yike zhadan" [Homeowners: A bomb], *Xinwen zhoukan* [News weekly], March 26, 2002, and were covered by all Beijing newspapers. Among others, see "Zhuizong [Redacted] qu gaibian guihua shijian" [Reconstructing the "plan change" accident at (Redacted) neighborhood], *Beijing qingnian bao* [Beijing youth], March 7, 2002; *Zhongguo qingnian bao*, March 20, 2002. International media also covered the story as well. See, among others, Peter Harmsen, "Demonstrating Beijing Residents Scuffle with Police," Agence France Press, March 3, 2002; Andreas Lorenz, "Protest der Reichen" [Protest of the rich], *Der Spiegel*, March 4, 2002.

25. The title of the letter was "Appeal on the Problem of the Construction of Hopetown's Garden and Other Issues," March 18, 2002.

26. Information provided by the representative of the management company during a public meeting with the owners, March 17, 2002.

27. Interview, May 7, 2002.

28. "Zhongyang zai jing yi gou gongfang keyi shangshi le" [Former central public houses allowed to get on the market], *Beijing wanbao*, September 16, 2003. Former municipal housing has been available on the market since 2000.

29. Wang and Li, "Housing Preferences."

30. Caldeira, *City of Walls*, 1.

31. The video was posted on the neighborhood's website.

32. From a posting on the neighborhood Internet forum, March 28, 2002.

33. On homeowner committees, see Read, "Democratizing the Neighborhood?"

34. Wang, Yin, and Zhou, "Adoption of Bottom Up Governance."

35. Interview, September 17, 2003.

36. Zhou Hongyun, "Zhengfu yu gongmin shehui de huoban guanxi" [The partnership between government and civil society], in *Zhongguo shequ fazhan baogao 2008–2009* [China's community development report, 2008–2009], ed. Yu Yanyan (Beijing: Shehui Kexue Wenxian Chubanshe, 2009), 81–104.

37. There was no mention of such a norm in the original regulation that established management committees. Also, the *xiaoquban* is required to approve the elected committees within ten days of the application. *Guanyu kaizhang zujian juzhu xiaoqu wuye guanli weiyuanhui shidian gongzuo de tongzhi* [Communiqué on the experimental work to establish neighborhood management committees], Beijing Land and Housing Administration Ordinance no. 485, 1997.

38. "Wuye guanli tiaoli" [Regulations on realty management], approved by the State Council on June 8, 2003, effective as of September 1, 2003.

39. The document is dated February 24.
40. Record of owners meeting, September 20, 2003.
41. Interview, May 18, 2002.

5. A Contagious Civilization

1. For a contemporary study of China's civilizing mission, see Geremie R. Barmé, ed., *Civilizing China: The China Story Yearbook, 2013* (Canberra: Australian Centre on China in the World, 2013).

2. Bakken, *Exemplary Society*, 54.

3. For example, Chen Jie, *Popular Political Support in Urban China* (Stanford, CA: Stanford University Press, 2004); Tang Wenfang, *Public Opinion and Political Change in China* (Stanford, CA: Stanford University Press, 2005).

4. Paul E. Festa, "Mahjong Politics in Contemporary China: Civility, Chineseness, and Mass Culture," *Positions: East Asia Cultures Critique* 14, no. 1 (Spring 2006): 7–36.

5. Ibid.

6. On the origins of the Chinese "self-improvement" ideology, see Andrew Kipnis, "Audit Cultures: Neoliberal Governmentality, Socialist Legacy, or Technologies of Governing?" *American Ethnologist* 35, no. 2 (2008): 275–89.

7. These questions, as we have seen, have been central to recent academic concerns on the Chinese middle class. See the most recent collections in Cheng Li, ed., *China's Emerging Middle Class*; Goodman, ed., *New Rich in China*.

8. Luigi Tomba, "Creating an Urban Middle Class: Social Engineering in Beijing," *China Journal* 51 (January 2004): 1–29; Tomba and Tang, "Forest City."

9. Mitchell Dean and Barry Hindess, *Governing Australia: Studies in Contemporary Rationalities of Government, Reshaping Australian Institutions* (Cambridge and New York: Cambridge University Press, 1998), 6.

10. Dean, "Liberal Government and Authoritarianism," 42.

11. Yuen Yuen Ang, "Counting Cadres: A Comparative View of the Size of China's Public Employment," *China Quarterly* 211 (2012): 676–96.

12. References to democracy must be understood in the traditional sense of strengthening "socialist democracy." Hu Jintao, *Zai sheng buji zhuyao lingdao ganbu tigao goujian shehui zhuyi hexie shehui nengli zhuanti yantaoban shang de jianghua* [Speech at the special meeting of provincial cadres to discuss the construction of a socialist harmonious society] (Beijing: Renmin Chubanshe, 2005).

13. The speech initiated an ongoing public discussion about what, beyond the slogan, a harmonious society is supposed to mean. As it happens, the expression "harmonious society" (*hexie shehui*) now appears in the title of a discouraging preponderance of scholarly essays in the social sciences and in almost every official speech by Party officials. With the help of new technology, the surge in the use of the expression can be calculated. A title query in the Chinese Academic Journals full text database reveals that the term *hexie shehui* appears only twice in the 1994–2002 period, but 88 times in 2004 and 155 times in the first six months of 2005.

14. Tao Xidong, "Jiakuai chengshi hexie shequ jianshe jizhi de chongjian yu zaizao" [Accelerate the reconstruction of the mechanisms for the edification of harmonious communities in the cities], *Renmin ribao* [People's daily], June 21, 2005.

15. Ibid.

16. Ibid.

17. Qiao Farong, "Chengyan: goujian hexie shehui de daode jichu" [Truth: The moral foundation of a harmonious society], *Renmin ribao* [People's daily], July 19, 2005.

18. Ibid.

19. Zhao Beihai, "Goujian hexie shehui er san yan" [A few words on harmonious society], *Renmin ribao* [People's daily], July 14, 2005.

20. Feng Shuquan, "Goujian hexie shehui bixu jiejue ruoshi qunti wenti" [The construction of a harmonious society must solve the problem of the disadvantaged groups], *Renmin ribao* [People's daily], July 21, 2005.

21. Ibid.

22. Ibid.

23. Tomba, "Residential Space and Collective Interest Formation."

24. Shu and Bei have become very popular through the Beijing media and the internet for organizing social activities in their own gated communities and for their strong stance on issues of civic coexistence. They both run popular websites and have become consultants for other communities on best practices in self-management.

25. The reference here is to Mao's August 1937 speech "On Contradictions," in which he highlighted the rationale for continuing class struggle in a socialist society. The claim being made is that the contradictions between interests today are no longer "antagonistic."

26. Residential proprietary communities have in recent years been characterized by frequent disputes involving management companies, developers, and residents. In a number of cases, these have turned into open protest and occasional skirmishes and have received attention in the press.

27. From documents collected in 2004, originals in possession of the author.

28. Cheng Li presents the most complete summary of the Chinese debates about the idea and character of the middle class. Cheng Li, ed., *China's Emerging Middle Class*.

29. Zhu Yaoqun, *Zhongchan jieceng yu hexie shehui* [Middle strata and harmonious society] (Beijing: Zhongguo Renmin Gong'an Daxue Chubanshe, 2005), 148.

30. Shanghai shi qingshi wenmin jianshe weiyuanhui bangongshi [Office of the Shanghai Municipal Committee for the edification of spiritual civilization], *Zuo ke'ai de Shanghai ren: Shanghai shimin shouce* [How to be a lovely Shanghainese: Instructions for Shanghai citizens] (Shanghai: Shanghai Cishu Chubanshe, 2005).

31. Sun Wanning, "*Suzhi* on the Move: Body, Place, and Power," *Positions: East Asia Cultures Critique* 17, no. 3 (2009): 617–42. The attempt to "produce human beings," for the sake of the country's development, out of uncivilized peasants by encouraging them to migrate to the cities and civilize has been, according to Yan Hairong, an effect of the discourses framing *suzhi* as a "value articulation of human subjectivity." Yan, "Neoliberal Governmentality and Neohumanism"; Nicole Newendorp, "Teaching Responsibility: Social Workers' Efforts to Turn Chinese Citizens into Ideal Hong Kong Citizens," in *Chinese Citizenship: Views from the Margin*, ed. Vanessa Fong and Rachel Murphy (London: Routledge, 2005), 123–50.

32. Zou Lihong, "Dajian wenming de pingtai" [Build the platforms of civilization], *Zhongguancun* 104 (January 2012): 78.

33. Chengdu residents often portray their lifestyle as leisurely, and the city is often called *yucheng*, city of desire.

34. Housing Provident Funds are available only to employees in large, mainly state-owned enterprises. After the end of housing allocation in 1998, the funds helped to facilitate access to housing property for employees and professionals in this section of the labor market.

35. Li Yang, "Zhongchan yu 'Chengdong' de miyue" [The honeymoon between the "middle class" and the "Eastern Districts"], *Ju zhoukan* [Housing weekly], August 19, 2005, p. 11.

36. Lisa Hoffman, "Urban Modeling and Contemporary Technologies of City Building in China: The Production of Regimes of Green Urbanisms," in *Worlding Cities*, ed. Roy and Ong, 66.

37. Chen was later promoted to Governor of Liaoning province. Chen Zhenggao, "Jianshe senlin chengshi jiasu tuijin Shenyang laogongye diqu quanmian zhenxing" [Build a forest city, speed up the transformation of Shenyang's industrial base], *Zhongguo chengshi linye* [Chinese journal of urban forestry] 3–4 (2005): 7.

38. Pow Choon-piew, *Gated Communities in China: Class Privilege and the Moral Politics of the Good Life* (London: Routledge, 2009).

39. Beijing documentarist Wang Bing's nine-hour film *Tiexiqu* ("West of the tracks"), shot between 1999 and 2001, is possibly the only remaining document of the industrial aspect of the district and of the struggle of the workers and residents to retain some of the traditional entitlements and lifestyles that had characterized the harsh life of industrial workers.

40. *Shenyang Nianjian 2006* [Shenyang Yearbook, 2006] (Beijing: Zhongguo Tongji Chubanshe, 2007).

41. Neil Smith, *The New Urban Frontier: Gentrification and the Revanchist City* (London and New York: Routledge, 1996); Rowland Atkinson and Gary Bridge, eds., *Gentrification in a Global Context: The New Urban Colonialism* (London and New York: Routledge, 2005); Huang Yi, *Chengshi shehui fenceng yu juzhu geli* [Urban social stratification and residential segregation] (Shanghai: Shanghai Tongji Chubanshe, 2006).

42. Smith, *New Urban Frontier*, 70.

43. Lee, *Against the Law*.

44. Samer Bagaeen and Ola Uduku, eds., *Gated Communities: Social Sustainability in Contemporary and Historical Gated Developments* (London: Earthscan, 2010); Caldeira, *City of Walls*.

45. Ziauddin Sardar, "Opening the Gates: An East-West Transmodern Discourse?" in *Gated Communities*, ed. Bagaeen and Uduku, Kindle locations 617–790.

46. Karina Landman, "Gated Minds, Gated Places: The Impact and Meaning of Hard Boundaries in South Africa," in *Gated Communities*, ed. Bagaeen and Uduku, Kindle locations 1913–2379.

47. Caldeira, *City of Walls*.

Conclusion

1. Read, *Roots of the State*, 272.

2. Sebastian Heilmann and Elizabeth J. Perry, "Embracing Uncertainty: Guerrilla Policy-Style and Adaptive Governance in China," in *Mao's Invisible Hand: the Political Foundation of Adaptive Governance in China*, ed. Sebastian Heilmann and Elizabeth J. Perry (Cambridge, MA: Harvard University Press, 2011), 4.

3. Kevin J. O'Brien and Lianjiang Li, *Rightful Resistance in Rural China* (New York and Cambridge: Cambridge University Press, 2006); Wright, *Accepting Authoritarianism*.

4. Lianjiang Li and Kevin O'Brien, "Villagers and Popular Resistance in Contemporary China," *Modern China* 22, no. 1 (January 1996): 41; Elizabeth J. Perry, "A New Rights Consciousness?" *Journal of Democracy* 20, no. 3 (July 2009): 17–20. On this debate, see also Lianjiang Li, "Rights Consciousness and Rules Consciousness in Contemporary China," *China Journal* 64 (July 2010): 47–68.

5. Baogang He and Mark Warren coined the term *authoritarian deliberation* to encapsulate the way that deliberative methods are used in China. He and Warren, "Authoritarian Deliberation: The Deliberative Turn in Chinese Political Development," *Perspectives on Politics* 9, no. 2 (2011): 269–89.

6. He Baogang, "Tightening Control," *Boston Review* (June/July 2011), available at http://bostonreview.net/BR36.4/ndf_baogang_he_china.php.

7. Xi Chen, *Social Protest*, 5.

8. Read, *Roots of the State*, 272.

9. Notable was the example of the protest against the Maglev train in Shanghai in 2008, although the international media greatly exaggerated its significance. Howard F. French, "Plan to Extend Shanghai Rail Line Stirs Middle Class to Protest," *New York Times*, January 27, 2008, available at www.nytimes.com/2008/01/27/world/asia/27shanghai.html, accessed October 26, 2013.

10. Wang Shu, "1979 yilai defang zhengfu zhuyao kao maidi huanzhai" [Since 1979 local governments have mostly relied on land sales to repay their debt], *Xin Jingbao*, July 30, 2013.

11. The "lost generation" is a term generally associated with the generation of urban dwellers who suffered doubly, first when the Cultural Revolution (1966–76) deprived them of the opportunity to study and then during the restructuring of the public sector when they found themselves the weakest group of employees "within the system," losing their security of employment in State Owned Enterprises as a consequence. See, for example, Hung and Chiu, "Lost Generation."

12. Ong, *Neoliberalism as Exception*.

13. Neil Brenner and Nik Theodore, "Cities and the Geography of 'Actually Existing Neoliberalism,'" *Antipodes* 34, no. 3 (2002): 349.

14. Rose, *Powers of Freedom*; Ong and Roy, "Introduction"; Heilmann and Perry, "Embracing Uncertainty."

15. An Chen, "Capitalist Development, Entrepreneurial Class, and Democratization in China," *Political Science Quarterly* 117, no. 3 (2002): 401–22; Gilley, *China's Democratic Future*; R. M. Glassman, *China in Transition*; Goodman, "People's Republic of China"; Goodman, ed. *New Rich in China*; Cheng Li, ed., *China's Emerging Middle Class*; Li and Niu, "New Middle Class(es)"; Tomba, "Creating an Urban Middle Class."

16. Yongshun Cai, "China's Moderate Middle Class," *Asian Survey* 45, no. 5 (2005): 777–99; Unger, "China's Conservative Middle Class."

17. Nathan, "Authoritarian Resilience."

18. Xi Chen, *Social Protest*.

19. Ibid., 10.

20. Ibid., 11.

21. William Hurst, "Mass Frames"; Lee, "Rights Activism in China."

22. Zhang, *In Search of Paradise*.

BIBLIOGRAPHY

Anagnost, Ann. "From Class to Social Strata: Grasping the Social Totality in Reform-Era China." *Third World Quarterly* 29, no. 3 (2008): 497–519.

——. "The Corporeal Politics of Quality (*Suzhi*)." *Public Culture* 16 (2004): 189–208.

——, ed. *National Past-Times: Narrative, Representation, and Power in Modern China.* Durham, NC: Duke University Press, 1997.

Ang, Yuen Yuen. "Counting Cadres: A Comparative View of the Size of China's Public Employment." *China Quarterly* 211 (2012): 676–96.

Atkinson, Rowland, and Sarah Blandy, eds. *Gated Communities.* London and New York: Routledge, 2006.

Atkinson, Rowland, and Gary Bridge, eds. *Gentrification in a Global Context: The New Urban Colonialism.* London and New York: Routledge, 2005.

Bagaeen, Samer, and Ola Uduku, eds. *Gated Communities: Social Sustainability in Contemporary and Historical Gated Developments.* London: Earthscan, 2010.

Bakken, Børge. *The Exemplary Society: Human Improvement, Social Control, and the Dangers of Modernity in China.* Oxford: Oxford University Press, 2000.

Barmé, Geremie R., ed. *Civilizing China: The China Story Yearbook, 2013.* Canberra: Australian Centre on China in the World, 2013.

Bei Ye. *Guanyu jianshe meihao shenghuo de sikao* [On building a beautiful life]. Beijing: Self-published pamphlet, 2003.

Beijing shi guotu fangguanju, Beijing shi gong'an ju, Beijing shi mingzhengju guanyu jia-qiang juzhu xiaoqu anquan fangfan guanli gongzuo de tongzhi [Communiqué of the Beijing Land Bureau, Police Bureau, and Civil Affairs Bureau on strengthening security management in residential areas]. Beijing, November 5, 2001.

"Beijingers Concerned over House Prices," *China Daily*, January 4, 2002 available at http://www.chinadaily.com.cn/en/home/2002-01/04/content100559.htm, accessed 28 December 2013

Benewick, Robert, and Akio Takahara. "Eight Grannies and Nine Teeth between Them: Community Construction in China." *Journal of Chinese Political Science* 7, no. 1–2 (2002): 1–18.

Benewick, Robert, Irene Tong, and Jude Howell. "Self-Governance and Community: A Preliminary Comparison between Villagers' Committees and Urban Community Councils." *China Information* 18, no. 1 (2004): 11–28.

Bian, Yanjie, and John R. Logan. "Market Transition and the Persistence of Power: The Changing Stratification System in Urban China." *American Sociological Review* 61, no. 5 (1996): 739–58.

Blakely, Edward J., and Mary Gail Snyder. *Fortress America: Gated Communities in the United States.* Washington, DC: Brookings Institution, 1997.

Blecher, Marc, and Vivienne Shue. *Tethered Deer: Government and Economy in a Chinese County.* Stanford, CA: Stanford University Press, 1999.

Bourdieu, Pierre. *Distinction: A Social Critique of the Judgment of Taste*. Trans. Richard Nice. London: Routledge and Kegan Paul, 1989.

———. *The Logic of Practice.* Stanford, CA: Stanford University Press, 1977.

Bray, David. "Building 'Community': New Strategies of Governance in Urban China." *Economy and Society* 35, no. 4 (2006): 530–49.

———. "Designing to Govern: Space and Power in Two Wuhan Communities." *Built Environment* 34, no. 4 (2008): 392–407.

———. *Social Space and Governance in Urban China: The Danwei System from Origins to Reform.* Stanford, CA: Stanford University Press, 2005.

Brenner, Neil, Jamie Peck, and Nik Theodore. "Variegated Neoliberalization: Geographies, Modalities, Pathways." *Global Networks* 10, no. 2 (2010): 182–222.

Brenner, Neil, and Nik Theodore, "Cities and the Geography of 'Actually Existing Neoliberalism,'" *Antipodes* 34, no. 3 (2002): 349.

Brown, Jeremy. *City versus Countryside in Mao's China: Negotiating the Divide.* Cambridge: Cambridge University Press, 2012.

Buckley, Christopher. "How a Revolution Becomes a Dinner Party: Stratification, Mobility and the New Rich in Urban China." In *Culture and Privilege in Capitalist Asia*, ed. Michael Pinches, 208–29. London and New York, Routledge, 1999.

Burrell, Mathias. "China's Housing Provident Fund: Its Success and Limitations." *Housing Finance International*, March 1, 2006.

Cai, Yongshun. "China's Moderate Middle Class." *Asian Survey* 45, no. 5 (2005): 777–99.

Caldeira, Teresa. *City of Walls: Crime, Segregation, and Citizenship in São Paulo.* Berkeley: University of California Press, 2000.

Castells, Manuel. *City, Class, and Power.* London: Macmillan, 1978.

Chang, Gordon. *The Coming Collapse of China.* New York: Random House, 2001.

Chen, An. "Capitalist Development, Entrepreneurial Class, and Democratization in China." *Political Science Quarterly* 117, no. 3 (2002): 401–22.

Chen, Jiandong, and Armando Barrientos. *Extending Social Assistance in China: Lessons from the Minimum Living Standard Scheme.* Chronic Poverty Research Centre, Working Paper 67 (November 2006).

Chen, Jie. *Popular Political Support in Urban China.* Stanford, CA: Stanford University Press, 2004.

Chen, Xi. *Social Protest and Contentious Authoritarianism in China.* Cambridge: Cambridge University Press, 2012.

Chen Zhenggao. "Jianshe senlin chengshi jiasu tuijin Shenyang laogongye diqu quanmian zhenxing" [Build a forest city, speed up the transformation of Shenyang's industrial base]. *Zhongguo chengshi linye* [Journal of Chinese urban forestry] 3–4 (2005): 7–10.

Cho, Mun Young. *The Specter of "The People": Urban Poverty in Northeast China.* Ithaca, NY: Cornell University Press, 2013.

Chung, Jae Ho, Hongyi Lai, and Ming Xia. "Mounting Challenges to Governance in China: Surveying Collective Protestors, Religious Sects, and Criminal Organizations." *China Journal* 56 (July 2006): 1–31.

Cong, Cao. "Strengthening China through Science and Education: China Development Strategy toward the 21st Century." *Issues and Studies* 38, no. 3 (September 2002): 122–49.

"Consumption and Urbanization to Drive China's Economy." *People's Daily Online*, December 14, 2009. Available at http://english.peopledaily.com.cn/90001/90778/90862/6841622.html, accessed October 26, 2013.

Cox, Kevin, ed. *Urbanization and Conflict in Market Societies.* London: Methuen, 1978.

Davies, John Emmeus. *Contested Ground: Collective Action and the Urban Neighborhood.* Ithaca, NY: Cornell University Press, 1991.

Davis, Deborah S., ed. *The Consumer Revolution in Urban China.* Berkeley: University of California Press, 2000.

———. "Social Class Transformation in Urban China: Training, Hiring, and Promoting Urban Professionals and Managers after 1949." *Modern China* 26, no. 3 (2000): 251–75.

Davis, Deborah S., Richard Kraus, Barry Naughton, and Elizabeth J. Perry. *Urban Spaces in Contemporary China: The Potential for Autonomy and Community in Post-Mao China.* Cambridge: Cambridge University Press, 1995.

Davis, Deborah, and Ezra F. Vogel, eds. *Chinese Society on the Eve of Tiananmen.* Cambridge, MA: Harvard University Press, 1990.

Dean, Mitchell. "Liberal Government and Authoritarianism." *Economy and Society* 31 (February 2002): 37–61.

Dean, Mitchell, and Barry Hindess. *Governing Australia: Studies in Contemporary Rationalities of Government, Reshaping Australian Institutions.* Cambridge and New York: Cambridge University Press, 1998.

Deng Lan, Qingyun Shen, and Lin Wang. "Housing Policy and Finance in China: A Literature Review." Unpublished paper prepared for the U.S. Department of Housing and Urban Development, November 2009.

Deng Minjie. *Chuangxin shequ* [Renewing communities]. Beijing: Zhongguo Shehui Chubanshe, 2002.

Derleth, James, and Daniel Koldyk. "The *Shequ* Experiment: Grassroots Political Reform in Urban China." *Journal of Contemporary China* 13, no. 41 (November 2004): 747–77.

Dickson, Bruce. *Red Capitalists in China: The Party, Private Entrepreneurs, and Prospects for Political Change.* Cambridge: Cambridge University Press, 2002.

Duckett, Jane. *The Entrepreneurial State in China.* London: Routledge, 1998.

Dutton, Michael Robert. *Policing and Punishment in China: From Patriarchy to "The People."* Cambridge and Melbourne: Cambridge University Press, 1992.

———. *Streetlife China.* Cambridge: Cambridge University Press, 1998.

Engels, Friedrich. *The Condition of the Working Class in England in 1844.* London: Allen and Unwin, 1936 (1892).

Feng Shuquan. "Goujian hexie shehui bixu jiejue ruoshi qunti wenti" [The construction of a harmonious society must solve the problem of the disadvantaged groups]. *Renmin ribao* [People's daily], July 21, 2005.

Festa, Paul E. "Mahjong Politics in Contemporary China: Civility, Chineseness, and Mass Culture." *Positions: East Asia Cultures Critique* 14, no. 1 (Spring 2006): 7–36.

Fleischer, Friederike. *Suburban Beijing: Housing and Consumption in Contemporary China.* Minneapolis: University of Minnesota Press, 2010.

Fong, Vanessa, and Rachel Murphy, eds. *Chinese Citizenship: Views from the Margin.* London: Routledge, 2005.

Foucault, Michel, *Discipline and Punish: The Birth of a Prison.* London: Penguin, 1991.

———. "Truth and Power." In *Power: The Essential Works of Foucault, 1954–1984,* vol. 3, ed. James D. Faubion, 111–33. New York: New Press, 2000.

French, Howard F. "Plan to Extend Shanghai Rail Line Stirs Middle Class to Protest." *New York Times,* January 27, 2008. Available at www.nytimes.com/2008/01/27/world/asia/27shanghai.html, accessed October 26, 2013.

Gaubatz, Piper. "Changing Beijing." *Geographical Review* 85, no. 1 (January 1995): 74–96.

———. "Urban Transformation in Post-Mao China: Impacts of the Reform Era on China's Urban Form." In *Urban Spaces in Contemporary China: The Potential for Autonomy and Community in Post-Mao China,* ed. Deborah Davis, Richard Kraus, Barry Naughton, and Elizabeth J. Perry, 28–61. Cambridge: Cambridge University Press, 1995.

Giddens, Anthony. *The Class Structure of the Advanced Societies.* London: Hutchinson, 1973.

Gilley, Bruce. *China's Democratic Future: How It Will Happen and Where It Will Lead.* New York: Columbia University Press, 2004.

Giroir, Guillaume. "The Purple Jade Villas (Beijing)." In *Private Cities: Global and Local Perspectives,* ed. George Glasze, Chris Webster, and Klaus Frantz, 139–50. London: Routledge, 2006.

Glassman, Ronald. M. *China in Transition: Communism, Capitalism, and Democracy.* New York: Praeger, 1991.

Glasze, George, Chris Webster, and Klaus Frantz, eds. *Private Cities: Global and Local Perspective.* London: Routledge, 2006.

Goodman, David S. G. "The New Middle Class." In *The Paradox of China's Post-Mao Reforms*, ed. Merle Goldman and Roderick MacFarquhar, 241–61. Cambridge, MA: Harvard University Press, 1999.

———, ed. *The New Rich in China: Future Rulers, Present Lives.* London: Routledge, 2008.

———. "The People's Republic of China: the Party State, Capitalist Revolution and New Entrepreneurs." In *The New Rich in Asia: Mobile Phones, McDonald's, and Middle-class Revolution,* ed. Richard Robison and David S. G. Goodman, 225–42. London: Routledge, 1996.

Government Work Report to the 10th NPC, March 5, 2003, available at http://app1.china daily.com.cn/highlights/nbc/news/319zhufull.htm accessed 28 December 2013.

Gramsci, Antonio. *Quaderni del Carcere* [Prison notebooks]. Torino, Italy: Giulio Einaudi Editore, 1975.

Greenhalgh, Susan, and Edwin Winckler. *Governing China's Population: From Leninist to Neoliberal Biopolitics.* Stanford, CA: Stanford University Press, 2005.

Gu Haibing. "Gongzheng yunzuo haishi qianjiu jide liyi: Zhongguo zhufang tizhi gaige zhengce de fansi" [A fair process or the adjustment of vested interests: Considerations on the policies of housing reform in China]. *Dangdai zhongguo yanjiu* [Research in contemporary China] 63 (1998).

Gu Lei. "Xiaoqu: fengbi haishi kaifang" [Residential areas: Closed or open?]. *Shequ* [Community] 2 (2006): 6–9.

Guanyu kaizhang zujian juzhu xiaoqu wuye guanli weiyuanhui shidian gongzuo de tongzhi [Communiqué on the experimental work to establish neighborhood management committees]. Beijing Land and Housing Administration Ordinance No. 485 (1997).

Guo, Yingjie, and Sun Wanning, eds. *Unequal China: The Political Economy and Cultural Politics of Inequality.* London: Routledge, 2012.

Harmsen, Peter. "Demonstrating Beijing Residents Scuffle with Police." Agence France Press, March 3, 2002.

Harvey, David. *A Brief History of Neoliberalism.* Oxford: Oxford University Press, 2006.

———. "Labor, Capital, and Class Struggle around the Built Environment in Advanced Capitalist Society." in *Urbanization and Conflict in Market Societies,* ed. Kevin Cox, 9–37. Chicago: Maaroufa Press, 1978.

———. *The Urbanization of Capital: Studies in the History and Theory of Capitalist Urbanization.* Baltimore: Johns Hopkins University Press, 1985.

He, Baogang. "Tightening Control." *Boston Review* (June/July 2011). Available at http://www.bostonreview.net/he-tightening control.

He, Baogang, and Mark Warren. "Authoritarian Deliberation: The Deliberative Turn in Chinese Political Development." *Perspectives on Politics* 9, no. 2 (2011): 269–89.

He, Shenjing, Zhigang Li, and Fulong Wu. "Transformation of the Chinese City, 1995–2005: Geographical Perspectives and Geographers' Contributions." *China Information*, no. 20 (2006): 429–56.

He Yingchuan and Liang Yi. "Toushi: Beijing xiaofeixin bianhua" [A perspective: New changes in Beijing consumption]. *Hongguan jingji guanli* [Macroeconomic management] 2 (2002): 9–17.

He Zengke, Thomas Heberer, and Gunther Schubert. "Citizen Participation in Rural and Urban Areas and Political Legitimacy" [Chengxiang gongmin canyu he zhengzhi hefaxing]. Beijing: Zhongyang Bianyi Chubanshe, 2007.

Heberer, Thomas, and Christian Göbel. *The Politics of Community Building in Urban China.* London: Routledge, 2011.

Heberer, Thomas, and Gunther Schubert. "Political Reform and Regime Legitimacy in Contemporary China." *Asien* 99 (2006): 9–28.

Heilmann, Sebastian, and Elizabeth J. Perry. "Embracing Uncertainty: Guerrilla Policy-Style and Adaptive Governance in China." In *Mao's Invisible Hand: The Political Foundations of Adaptive Governance in China*, ed. Sebastian Heilmann and Elizabeth J. Perry, 1–29. Cambridge, MA: Harvard University Asia Center, 2011.

——, eds. *Mao's Invisible Hand: The Political Foundation of Adaptive Governance in China.* Cambridge, MA: Harvard University Press, 2011.

Hoffman, Lisa. "Autonomous Choices and Patriotic Professionalism: On Governmentality in Late-Socialist China." *Economy and Society* 35, no. 4 (November 2006): 550–70.

——. *Patriotic Professionalism in Urban China: Fostering Talent.* Philadelphia: Temple University Press, 2010.

——. "Urban Modeling and Contemporary Technologies of City Building in China: The Production of Regimes of Green Urbanisms." In *Worlding Cities: Asian Experiments and the Art of Being Global*, ed. Ananya Roy and Aihwa Ong, 55–76. Chichester, U.K.: Blackwell, 2011.

Hsing, You-tien. *The Great Urban Transformation: Politics of Land and Property in China.* Oxford: Oxford University Press, 2010.

Hsing, You-tien, and Ching Kwan Lee. *Reclaiming Chinese Society: The New Social Activism.* London and New York: Routledge, 2010.

Hsu, Carolyn. *Creating Market Socialism: How Ordinary People Are Shaping Class and Status in China.* Durham, NC: Duke University Press, 2007.

Hu Jintao. *Zai sheng buji zhuyao lingdao ganbu tigao goujian shehui zhuyi hexie shehui nengli zhuanti yantaoban shang de jianghua* [Speech at the special meeting of provincial cadres to discuss the construction of a socialist harmonious society]. Beijing: Renmin Chubanshe, 2005.

Hu, Xiuhong, and David H. Kaplan. "The Emergence of Affluence in Beijing: Residential Social Stratification in China's Capital City." *Urban Geography* 22, no. 1 (2001): 54–77.

Huang Yi. *Chengshi shehui fencing yu juzhu geli* [Urban social stratification and residential segregation]. Shanghai: Shanghai Tongji Chubanshe, 2006.

Huang Yongyan. "Guanyu woguo guowuyuan 'gaoxin yanglian' de sikao" [Thoughts on "High salaries to foster honesty" for public servants]. *Zhongguo shangjie* [Business China] (March 2009): 171–72.

Human Rights Watch. "Demolished: Forced Evictions and the Tenants' Rights Movement in China." Human Rights Watch Report, 2004. Available at www.hrw.org/reports/2004/china0304/china0304.pdf, accessed October 26, 2013.

Hung, Eva P. W., and Stephen K. W. Chiu. "The Lost Generation: Life Course Dynamics and *Xiagang* in China." *Modern China* 29, no. 2 (April 2003): 204–36.

Hurst, William. *The Chinese Worker after Socialism.* Cambridge: Cambridge University Press, 2009.

———. "The City as the Focus: The Analysis of Contemporary Chinese Urban Politics." *China Information* 20 (2006): 457–79.

———. "Mass Frames and Worker Protest." In *Popular Protest in China*, ed. Kevin J. O'Brien, 71–87. Cambridge, MA: Harvard University Press 2008.

Jacka, Tamara, ed. "Cultivating Citizens. *Suzhi* (Quality) Discourse in the PRC." Special issue, *Positions: East Asia Cultures Critiques* 17, no. 3 (2009).

———. *Rural Women in Urban China*. Armonk, NY: M.E. Sharpe, 2006.

Jeffreys, Elaine. *China's Governmentalities: Governing Change, Changing Government*. Milton Park, U.K., and New York: Routledge, 2009.

Jin Biao and Chuan Shan. "XX Yezhu: wo de siyou caichang zai nali?" [XX homeowners: Where are my private property rights?] *Sanlian shenghuo zhoukan* [Sanlian life week], March 20, 2002.

Kang Xiaoguang. "Weilai 3–5 nian Zhongguo dalu zhengzhi wending xing fenxi" [Analysis of mainland China's political stability in the next 3–5 years]. *Zhanlüe yu guanli* [Strategy and management] 3 (2002): 1–15.

Katznelson, Ira. *City Trenches: Urban Politics and the Patterning of Class in the United States*. New York: Pantheon Books, 1981.

Kipnis, Andrew. "Audit Cultures: Neoliberal Governmentality, Socialist Legacy, or Technologies of Governing?" *American Ethnologist* 35, no. 2 (May 2008): 275–89.

———. "Neoliberalism Reified: Suzhi Discourse and Tropes of Neoliberalism in the People's Republic of China." *Journal of the Royal Anthropological Institute* 13, no. 2 (2007): 383–400.

———. "*Suzhi*: A Keyword Approach." *China Quarterly* 186 (June 2006): 295–313.

Lan, Xinzhen. "Housing Policy Falls Short." *Beijing Review*, May 8, 2003, pp. 24–25.

Landman, Karina. "Gated Minds, Gated Places: The Impact and Meaning of Hard Boundaries in South Africa." In *Gated Communities: Social Sustainability in Contemporary and Historical Gated Developments*, ed. Samer Bagaeen and Ola Uduku, 49–62. London: Earthscan, 2010.

Lee, Ching-Kwan. *Against the Law: Labor Protests in China's Rustbelt and Sunbelt*. Berkeley: University of California Press, 2007.

———. "From Organized Dependency to Disorganized Despotism: Changing Labour Regimes in Chinese Factories." *China Quarterly* 157 (March 1999): 44–71.

———. "The Revenge of History: Collective Memories and Labour Protests in North-Eastern China." *Ethnography* 1, no. 2 (2000): 217–37.

———. "Rights Activism in China." *Contexts* 7, no. 3 (July 2008): 14–19.

Lei, Guang. "Rural Taste, Urban Fashions: The Cultural Politics of Rural/Urban Difference in Contemporary China." *Positions: East Asia Cultures Critique* 11, no. 3 (2003): 613–46.

Lewis, John Wilson, and Jerome Alan Cohen, eds. *The City in Communist China*. Stanford, CA: Stanford University Press, 1971.

Li Bin. "Zhongguo zhufang gaige zhidu de fenge xing" [The unequal nature of China's housing reform]. *Shehuixue yanjiu* [Research in the social sciences] 2 (2002): 80–87.

Li, Cheng, ed. *China's Emerging Middle Class: Beyond Economic Transformation*. Washington, DC: Brookings Institution, 2010.

Li, He. "Emergence of the Chinese Middle Class and Its Implications." *Asian Affairs* 33, no. 2 (2006): 67–83.

Li, Jian, and Xiaohan Niu. "The New Middle Class(es) in Peking: A Case Study." *China Perspectives* 45 (January 2003): 4–20.

Li, Lianjiang. "Rights Consciousness and Rules Consciousness in Contemporary China." *China Journal* 64 (July 2010): 47–68.

Li, Lianjiang, and Kevin O'Brien. "Villagers and Popular Resistance in Contemporary China." *Modern China* 22, no. 1 (January 1996): 41.

Li Peilin. *Zhongguo shehui fenceng* [Social stratification in China today]. Beijing: Shehui Kexue Xueshu Chubanshe, 2004.

Li Qiang. *Shehui fenceng yu pinfu chabie* [Social stratification and inequality]. Xiamen, China: Lujiang Chubanshe, 2000.

Li Ruiyang. *Chengshi renmin gongshe yundong yanjiu* [Research on the urban people's communes movement]. Changsha, China: Hunan Renmin Chubanshe, 2006.

Li Shouen. "Lun quanmian jianshe xiaokang shehui" [On building a well-off society in an all-around way]. *Shishi qiushi* [Seek truth from facts] 1 (2003): 13–16.

Li, Siming. "Housing Consumption in Urban China: A Comparative Study of Beijing and Guangzhou." *Environment and Planning A* 32, no. 6 (2000): 1115–34.

Li, Siming, and Doris K. W. Fung. "Housing Tenure and Residential Mobility in Urban China: Analysis of Survey Data." *Occasional Papers Series*. Hong Kong: Hong Kong Baptist University, Centre for China Urban and Regional Studies, July 2001.

Li Yang, "Zhongchan yu 'chengdong' de miyue" [The honeymoon between the "middle class" and the "Eastern District"]. *Ju zhoukan* [Housing weekly], August 19, 2005.

Li, Zhigang, and Fulong Wu. "Socio-Spatial Differentiation and Residential Inequalities in Shanghai: A Case Study of Three Neighborhoods." *Housing Studies* 21, no. 5 (2006): 695–717.

Lin, George C. S. *Developing China: Land Politics and Social Conditions*. London and New York: Routledge, 2009.

Lin, Nan, and Yanjie Bian. "Getting Ahead in Urban China." *American Journal of Sociology* 97, no. 3 (November 1991): 657–88.

Lin Yuying. "Woguo jumin xiaofei zhan GDP bizhong guodi zhi daliang channeng guocheng" [The reduction in consumption to GDP ratio in China points to a discrepancy in production capacity]. *Zhongguo xinwen wang* [China news network], December 18, 2012.

Lo, Clarence Y. H. "Communities of Challengers in Social Movement Theory." In *Frontiers in Social Movement Theory*, ed. Aldon D. Morris and Carol McClurg Mueller, 224–48. New Haven, CT: Yale University Press, 1992.

Logan, John R., ed. *The New Chinese City: Globalization and Market Reform*. Oxford: Blackwell Publishers, 2002.

Lorentzen, Peter L. *Regularizing Rioting: Permitting Public Protest in an Authoritarian Regime*, June 9, 2010. Available at SSRN: http://ssrn.com/abstract=995330.

Lorenz, Andreas. "Protest der Reichen" [Protest of the rich]. *Der Spiegel*, March 4, 2002.

Low, Setha. *Behind the Gates: Life, Security, and the Pursuit of Happiness in Fortress America*. New York: Routledge, 2003.

Lu, Duanfang. *Remaking China's Urban Form: Modernity, Scarcity, and Space, 1949–2005*. London: Routledge, 2010.

Lü, Xiaobo, and Elizabeth Perry, eds. *Danwei: The Changing Chinese Workplace in Historical and Comparative Perspective.* Armonk, NY: M.E. Sharpe, 1997.

Lu Xueyi, ed. *Dangdai Zhongguo shehui jieceng yanjiu baogao* [Research report on contemporary China's social stratification]. Beijing: Shehui Kexue Wenxian Chubanshe, 2002.

Ma Jiantang. "Press Release on Major Figures of the 2010 Population Census, April 28, 2011." Available at www.stats.gov.cn/english/newsandcomingevents/t20110428_40 2722237.htm, accessed October 26, 2013.

Ma, Laurence J. C. "Urban Transformation in China, 1949–2000: A Review and Research Agenda." *Environment and Planning A* 34 (2002): 1545–69.

Ma, Laurence J. C., and Fulong Wu, eds. *Restructuring the Chinese City: Changing Society, Economy, and Spaces.* London and New York: Routledge, 2005.

Marcuse, Peter, and Ronald Van Kempen, eds. *Of States and Cities: The Partitioning of Urban Space.* Oxford: Oxford University Press, 2002.

McAdam, Doug, John D. McCarthy, and Mayer N. Zald, eds. *Comparative Perspective on Social Movements: Political Opportunities, Mobilizing Structures, and Cultural Framings.* New York: Cambridge University Press, 1996.

Miao, Pu. "Deserted Streets in a Jammed Town: The Gated Community in Chinese Cities and Its Solution." *Journal of Urban Design* 8, no. 1 (2003): 45–66.

Ministry of Civil Affairs [Minzhengbu]. *China Civil Affairs Statistical Yearbook, 2011.* Beijing: Zhongguo Tongji Chubanshe, 2012.

———. "Minzhengbu guanyu zai quanguo tuijin chengshi sheque jianshe de yijian" [Ministry of Civil Affairs' opinion on speeding up urban community building across the country]. *Zhongguo minzheng* [China civil affairs] 1 (2001): 4–6.

Ministry of Construction [Jianshebu]. *Guanyu Beijing zhufang er san ji shichang wenti diaocha baogao* [Research report on Beijing secondary and tertiary housing market]. October 2002.

Morris, Aldon D., and Carol McClurg Mueller, eds. *Frontiers in Social Movement Theory.* New Haven, CT: Yale University Press, 1992.

Morris, David, and Karl Hess. *Neighborhood Power: The New Localism.* Boston: Beacon Press, 1975.

Nathan, Andrew. "Authoritarian Resilience." *Journal of Democracy* 14, no. 1 (January 2003): 6–17.

Nee, Victor. "The Emergence of a Market Society." *American Journal of Sociology* 101, no. 4 (1996): 908–49.

———. "A Theory of Market Transition: From Redistribution to Markets in State Socialism." *American Sociological Review* 54, no. 5 (1989): 663–81.

Newendorp, Nicole. "Teaching Responsibility: Social Workers Efforts to Turn Chinese Citizens into Ideal Hong Kong Citizens." In *Chinese Citizenship: Views from the Margins,* ed. Vanessa Fong and Rachel Murphy, 123–50. Oxon, U.K.: Routledge, 2006.

O'Brien, Kevin J., ed. *Popular Protest in China.* Cambridge, MA: Harvard University Press, 2008.

O'Brien, Kevin J., and Lianjiang Li. *Rightful Resistance in Rural China.* New York and Cambridge: Cambridge University Press, 2006.

Ong, Aihwa. *Flexible Citizenship: The Cultural Logics of Transnationality*. Durham, NC: Duke University Press, 1999.

———. "Introduction: Worlding Cities, or the Art of Being Global." In *Worlding Cities: Asian Experiments and the Art of Being Global*, ed. Ananya Roy and Aihwa Ong, 1–26. Chichester, U.K.: Blackwell, 2011.

———. *Neoliberalism as Exception: Mutations in Citizenship and Sovereignty*. Durham, NC: Duke University Press, 2006.

Ozuekren, A. Sule, and Ronald Van Kempen. "Ethnic Segregation in Cities: New Forms and Explanation in a Dynamic World." *Urban Studies* 35, no. 10 (1998): 1631–56.

Pan Jianfeng. "Gaoxin zhi: shenpan gongzhen, lianjie he faguan gao suzhi de jiben baozhang" [High salaries system: The basic guarantee of fair trials and honest and high-quality judges]. *Zhengfa luntan* [Legal forum] 6 (2001): 15–21.

Park, Robert. *Human Communities: The City and Human Ecology*. Glencoe, IL: Free Press, 1952.

Park, Robert E., Ernest W. Burgess, and Roderick McKenzie. *The City*. Chicago: University of Chicago Press, 1967 (1926).

Pei, Minxin. *Trapped Transition: The Limits of Developmental Autocracy*. Cambridge, MA: Harvard University Press, 2006.

Penny, Benjamin. *The Religion of Falungong*. Chicago: University of Chicago Press, 2012.

People's Bank of China. *Monetary Policy Report 2002*, January 2003.

Perry, Elizabeth J. "Chinese Conceptions Of 'Rights': From Mencius to Mao—and Now." *Perspectives on Politics* 6, no. 1 (2008): 37–50.

———. "A New Rights Consciousness?" *Journal of Democracy* 20, no. 3 (July 2009): 17–20.

Perry, Elizabeth J., and Merle Goldman, eds. *Grassroots Political Reform in Contemporary China*. Cambridge, MA: Harvard University Press, 2007.

Perry, Elizabeth J., and Mark Selden, eds. *Chinese Society: Change, Conflict, and Resistance*. London: Routledge Curzon, 2003.

Pinches, Michael, ed. *Culture and Privilege in Capitalist Asia*. London: Routledge, 1999.

Polanyi, Karl. *The Great Transformation*. Boston: Beacon Press, 1957.

Pow, Choon-piew. *Gated Communities in China: Class Privilege and the Moral Politics of the Good Life*. London: Routledge, 2009.

Pun Ngai. "Subsumption or Consumption? The Phantom of Consumer Revolution in 'Globalizing' China." *Cultural Anthropology* 18, no. 4 (November 2003): 469–92.

Purcell, Mark. "Neighborhood Activism among Homeowners as a Politics of Space." *Professional Geographer* 53, no. 2 (2001): 178–94.

Qiao Farong. "Chengyan: goujian hexie shehui de daode jichu" [Truth: The moral foundation of a harmonious society]. *Renmin ribao* [People's daily], July 19, 2005.

Qiju: Wanke de fangzi [Poetic dwelling: Vanke's house]. Wuhan, China: Huazhong Keji Daxue Chubanshe, 2007.

Read, Benjamin. "Democratizing the Neighborhood? New Private Housing and Home-Owner Self-Organization in Urban China." *China Journal* 49 (January 2003): 31–60.

———. "Revitalizing China's Urban 'Nerve Tips.'" *China Quarterly* 163 (September 2000): 806–20.

———. *Roots of the State: Neighborhood Organizations and Social Networks in Beijing and Taipei*. Stanford, CA: Stanford University Press, 2012.

Rex, John, and Robert Moore. *Race, Community, and Conflict: A Study of Sparkbrook.* London and New York: Oxford University Press, 1967.

Riskin, Carl, Zhao Renwei, and Li Shi, eds. *China's Retreat from Inequality: Income Distribution and Economic Transition.* Armonk, NY: M.E. Sharpe, 2001.

Robison, Richard, and David S. G. Goodman, eds. *The New Rich in Asia: Mobile Phones, McDonald's, and Middle-Class Revolution.* London: Routledge, 1996.

Rose, Nikolas. *Powers of Freedom: Reframing Political Thought.* Cambridge: Cambridge University Press, 1999.

Roy, Ananya, and Aihwa Ong, eds. *Worlding Cities: Asian Experiments and the Art of Being Global* (Chichester, U.K.: Blackwell, 2011).

Rui Xiao. "Jiannan de wuye guanli qiye weiquan zhilu" [Management companies' difficult road to protecting (owners') interests]. *Chengshi Kaifa* [Urban development] 9 (2004): 12–13.

Saich, Tony. "Negotiating the State: The Development of Social Organizations in China." *China Quarterly* 161 (March 2000): 124–41.

Salaff, Janet. "Urban Communes and Anti-City Experiment in Communist China." *China Quarterly* 29 (January 1967): 82–110.

Sardar, Ziauddin. "Opening the Gates: An East-West Transmodern Discourse?" In *Gated Communities: Social Sustainability in Contemporary and Historical Gated Developments,* ed. Samer Bagaeen and Ola Uduku, 9–14. London: Earthscan, 2010.

Sassen, Saskia. *The Global City.* 2nd ed. Princeton, NJ: Princeton University Press, 2001.

Saunders, Peter. "Domestic Property and Social Class." *International Journal of Urban and Regional Research* 2 (1978): 233–51.

———. *Social Theory and the Urban Question.* New York: Holmes and Meier, 1981.

Schurmann, Franz. *Ideology and Organization in Communist China.* Berkeley: University of California Press, 1968.

Selden, Mark, and Elizabeth J. Perry, eds. *Chinese Society: Change, Conflict, and Resistance.* 2nd ed. New York: RoutledgeCurzon, 2003.

Shambaugh, David. *The Chinese Communist Party: Atrophy and Adaptation.* Washington, DC: Woodrow Wilson Center Press, 2008.

Shanghai shi qingshi wenmin jianshe weiyuanhui bangongshi [Office of the Shanghai municipal committee for the edification of spiritual civilization]. *Zuo ke'ai de Shanghai ren: Shanghai shimin shouce* [How to be a lovely Shanghainese: Instructions for Shanghai citizens]. Shanghai: Shanghai Cishu Chubanshe, 2005.

Shen Yan. "Yezhu weiquan you duo nan" [How hard it is for homeowners to protect their rights]. *Renmin Wang,* June 26, 2006.

Shenyang Civil Affairs Department [Shenyang shi minzhengju]. "Guanyu tigao shequ gongzuozhe daiyu de tongzhi" [Communiqué on raising the salaries of community workers], 2010. Document in author's possession.

Sigley, Gary. "Liberal Despotism: Population Planning, Subjectivity, and Government in Contemporary China." *Alternatives: Global, Local, Political* 29, no. 5 (2004): 557–75.

Sit, Victor F. S. *Beijing: The Nature and Planning of a Chinese Capital City.* Chichester, U.K.: Wiley, 1999.

Smith, Neil. *The New Urban Frontier: Gentrification and the Revanchist City.* London and New York: Routledge, 1996.

Solinger, Dorothy. *Contesting Citizenship in Urban China: Peasant Migrants, the State, and the Logic of the Market*. Berkeley: University of California Press, 1999.

———. "The *Dibao* Recipients: Mollified Anti-Emblem of Urban Modernization." *China Perspectives* 4 (2008): 36–46.

Sun Wanning. "*Suzhi* on the Move: Body, Place and Power." *Positions: East Asia Cultures Critique* 17, no. 3 (2009): 617–42.

Tang, Beibei. *The Making of Housing Status Groups in Post Reform Urban China: Social Mobility and Status Attainment of Gated Community Residents in Shenyang*. PhD dissertation. Australian National University, Canberra, 2009.

Tang, Beibei, Luigi Tomba, and Werner Breitung. "The Work-Unit Is Dead. Long Live the Work-Unit! Spatial Segregation and Privilege in a Work-Unit Housing Compound in Guangzhou." *Geographische Zeitschrift* 1 (2011): 36–49.

Tang, Wenfang. *Public Opinion and Political Change in China*. Stanford, CA: Stanford University Press, 2005.

Tao Xidong. "Jiakuai chengshi hexie shequ jianshe jizhi de chongjian yu zaizao" [Accelerate the reconstruction of the mechanisms for the edification of harmonious communities in the cities]. *Renmin ribao* [People's daily], June 21, 2005.

"Time to put Economy Housing in Order" *China Daily* June 23 2005, available at http://www.china.org.cn/english/BAT/132926.htm accessed 28 December 2013

Tomba, Luigi. "Creating an Urban Middle Class: Social Engineering in Beijing." *China Journal* 51 (January 2004): 1–29.

———. "Gating Urban Spaces: Inclusion, Exclusion, and Government." In *Gated Communities: Social Sustainability in Contemporary and Historical Gated Developments*, ed. Samer Bagaeen and Ola Uduku, 27–38. London: Earthscan, 2010.

———. "Making Neighborhoods: The Government of Social Change in China's Cities." *China Perspective* 4 (2008): 48–61.

———. *Paradoxes of Labour Reform: Chinese Labour Theory and Practice from Socialism to Market*. Honolulu: University of Hawai'i Press, 2002.

———. "Of Quality, Harmony, and Community: Civilization and the Middle Class in Urban China." *Positions: East Asia Cultures Critique* 17, no. 3 (2009): 591–616.

———. "Residential Space and Collective Interest Formation in Beijing's Housing Disputes." *China Quarterly* 184 (December 2005): 934–51.

Tomba, Luigi, and Beibei Tang. "The Forest City: Homeownership and New Wealth in Shenyang." In *The New Rich in China: Future Rulers, Present Lives*, ed. David S. G. Goodman, 171–86. London: Routledge, 2008.

———. "The Great Divide: Institutionalized Inequality in China's Market Socialism." In *Unequal China: The Political Economy and Cultural Politics of Inequality*, ed. Guo Yingjie and Sun Wanning, 91–110. London: Routledge, 2012.

"Two Twists in the Dragon's Tail." *The Economist*, January 21, 2012.

Unger, Jonathan. "China's Conservative Middle Class." *Far Eastern Economic Review* (April 2006): 27–31.

Unger, Jonathan, and Anita Chan. "The Internal Politics of an Urban Chinese Work Community: A Case Study of Employee Influence on Decision-Making at a State Owned Factory." *China Journal* 52 (July 2004): 1–26.

Van Kempen, Ronald. "The Academic Formulations: Explanations for a Partitioned City." In *Of States and Cities: The Partitioning of Urban Space*, ed. Peter Marcuse and Ronald Van Kempen, 35–58. Oxford: Oxford University Press, 2002.

Vogel, Ezra. *Japan's New Middle Class: The Salary Man and His Family in a Tokyo Suburb*. Berkeley: University of California Press, 1963.

Walder, Andrew G. "Organized Dependence and Cultures of Authority in Chinese Industry." *Journal of Asian Studies* 43, no. 1 (1983): 51–76.

Wang Bangzuo. *Juweihui yu shequ zhili* [Resident committees and community governance]. Shanghai: Shanghai Renmin Chubanshe, 2003.

Wang Dongliang, "Zhongguo minsheng fazhan baogao: Zhongguo renjun zhufang mianji 36 pingfangmi" [Report on people's livelihood in China: The average per capita living space has reached 36 square meters], *Beijing Ribao*, August 6, 2012.

Wang, Donggen, and Siming Li. "Housing Preferences in a Transitional Housing System: The Case of Beijing, China." *Centre for Urban and Regional Studies Occasional Paper* no. 28. Hong Kong: Hong Kong Baptist University, December 2002.

Wang, Feng, Haitao Yin, and Zhiren Zhou. "The Adoption of Bottom Up Governance in China's Homeowner Associations." *Management and Organization Review* 8, no. 3 (2012): 559–83.

Wang, Jing. "Bourgeois Bohemians in China? Neo-Tribes and the Urban Imaginary." *China Quarterly* 183 (September 2005): 532–48.

Wang, Lina. "Urban Housing Welfare and Income Distribution." In *China's Retreat from Inequality: Income Distribution and Economic Transition*, ed. Carl Riskin, Zhao Renwei, and Li Shi, 167–83. Armonk, NY: M.E. Sharpe, 2001.

Wang Shu. "1979 yilai defang zhengfu zhuyao kao maidi huanzhai" [Since 1979 local governments have mostly relied on land sales to repay their debt]. *Xin Jingbao*, July 30, 2013.

Wang, Ya Ping. "Housing Reform and Its Impact on the Urban Poor." *Housing Studies* 15, no. 6 (2000): 845–64.

———. "Urban Housing Reform and Finance in China: A Case Study of Beijing." *Urban Affairs Review* 36, no. 5 (May 2001): 620–45.

Wang, Ya Ping, and Alan Murie. "Commercial Housing Development in Urban China." *Urban Studies* 36, no. 9 (August 1999): 1475–94.

Wang Yalin. *Chengshi xiuxian: Shanghai, Tianjin, Haerbin chengshi jumin shijian fenpei de kaocha* [Report on the distribution of time among urban residents in Shanghai, Tianjin, and Harbin]. Beijing: Shehui Kexue Wenxian Chubanshe, 2003.

Wang Yanli. "Life Measures Improving in China." *Shanghai Daily*, December 2, 2011.

Whyte, Martin King. *The Myth of the Social Volcano: Perceptions of Inequality and Distributive Injustice in Contemporary China*. Stanford, CA: Stanford University Press, 2010.

Wines, Michael. "Once Banned, Dogs Reflect China's Rise." *New York Times*, October 25, 2010. Available at www.nytimes.com/2010/10/25/world/asia/25dogs.html, accessed October 26, 2013.

World Bank, Poverty Reduction and Economic Management Unit East Asia and Pacific Region. *China: Revitalizing the Northeast: Towards a Development Strategy*. Washington, DC: World Bank, 2006.

Wright, Teresa. *Accepting Authoritarianism: State-Society Relations in China's Reform Era*. Stanford, CA: Stanford University Press, 2010.

Wu Fulong. "The New Structure of Building Provision and the Transformation of the Urban Landscape in Metropolitan Guangzhou." *Urban Studies* 35, no. 2 (February 1998): 277–83.

———. "Sociospatial Differentiation in Urban China: Evidence from Shanghai's Real Estate Markets." *Environment and Planning A* 34 (2002): 1591–1615.

Wu Qinghua, Dong Xiangwei, and Wang Guofeng. "Jianyi chengshi shequ jiecenghua qushi dui shequ jianshe de yingxiang" [The impact of urban community stratification on community building]. *Zhongyang shehuizhuyi xueyuan bao* [Journal of the central institute of socialism] 3 (2009).

"Wuye guanli tiaolie" [Regulations on realty management]. Approved by the State Council on June 8, 2003, effective September 1, 2003.

"Xiaoxie tishi: goufang bu gai tashang 'shangxin zhilü'" [Consumers' association points out: Buying a house should not become a heart-breaking journey]. *Beijing Chenbao* [Beijing morning news], March 8, 2002.

Xie Ming. "Lun 'Gaoxin yanglian'" [On "High salaries to foster honesty"]. *Beijing xingzheng xueyuan xuebao* [Journal of the Beijing institute of public administration] 3 (2002): 14–19.

Xinhua News Press. "Chinese 4.2 Million Security Guards to Wear New Uniforms," 2011. Available at www.chinadaily.com.cn/china/2011-07/06/content_12844755.htm, accessed October 25, 2013.

Xinwen zhoukan [News weekly]. March 26, 2002.

Yan Hairong. "Neoliberal Governmentality and Neohumanism: Organizing *Suzhi/*Value Flow Through Labor Recruitment Networks." *Cultural Anthropology* 18, no. 4 (2003): 493–523.

———. *New Masters, New Servants: Migration, Development, and Women Workers in China*. Durham, NC: Duke University Press, 2008.

Yan Zhimin, ed. *Zhongguo xian jieduan jieji jieceng yanjiu* [Research on the classes and strata in China during the initial phase]. Beijing: Zhonggong Zhongyang Dangxiao Chubanshe, 2002.

Yeh, Anthony G. O. "Dual Land Market and Internal Spatial Structure of Chinese Cities." In *Restructuring the Chinese City: Changing Society, Economy, and Space*, ed. Laurence J. C. Ma and Fulong Wu, 59–79. London and New York: Routledge, 2005.

Yeh, Anthony G. O., Xueqiang Xu, and Huaying Hu. "The Social Space of Guangzhou City, China." *Urban Geography* 16 (1995): 595–621.

"Yezhu: yike zhadan" [Homeowners: A bomb]. *Xinwen zhoukan* [News weekly], March 26, 2002.

Yi Shijie. "Tigao xiaofeilü ladong jingji cengzhang" [Increase the consumption rate, stimulate economic growth]. *Jingjixue dongtai* [Trends in economics] 10 (2002): 14–17.

Yu Yanyan, ed. *Zhongguo shequ fazhan baogao 2008–2009* [China's community development report, 2008–2009]. Beijing: Shehui Kexue Wenxian Chubanshe, 2009.

Yu Yongyang. *Shequ fazhan lun* [On community development]. Shanghai: Huadong Ligong Daxue Chubanshe, 2000.

Zald, Mayer N. "Culture, Ideology, and Strategic Framing." In *Comparative Perspective on Social Movements: Political Opportunities, Mobilizing Structures, and Cultural Framings*, ed. Doug McAdam, John D. McCarthy, and Mayer N. Zald, 261–74. New York: Cambridge University Press, 1996.

Zhang, Li. "Contesting Spatial Modernity in Late Socialist China." *Current Anthropology* 37, no. 3 (2006): 461–84.

———. *Strangers in the City: Reconfiguration of Space, Power, and Social Networks within China's Floating Population*. Stanford, CA: Stanford University Press, 2001.

Zhang, Li and Aihwa Ong, eds. *Privatizing China: Socialism from Afar*. Ithaca, NY: Cornell University Press, 2008.

Zhang, Xing Quan. "Governing Housing in China: State, Market, and Work Units." *Journal of Housing and the Built Environment* 17, No. 1 (2002): 7–20.

Zhao Beihai. "Goujian hexie shehui er san yan" [A few words on harmonious society]. *Renmin ribao* [People's daily], July 14, 2005.

Zhou Changcheng, ed. *Shehui fazhan yu shenghuo zhiliang* [Social development and the quality of life]. Beijing: Shehui Kexue Wenxian Chubanshe, 2001.

Zhou Hongyun. "Zhengfu yu gongmin shehui de huoban guanxi" [The partnership between government and civil society]. In *Zhongguo shequ fazhan baogao 2008–2009* [China's community development report 2008–2009], ed. Yu Yanyan, 81–104. Beijing: Shehui Kexue Wenxian Chubanshe, 2009.

Zhu Jialiu. "Shuanxiuzhi gei shangye yingxiao celüe dailai de sikao" [The implications of a short working week for the strategies of commercial marketing]. *Shanghai shangye* [Shanghai commerce] 2 (1995).

Zhu Yaoqun. *Zhongchan jieceng yu hexie shehui* [Middle strata and harmonious society]. Beijing: Zhongguo Renmin Gong'an Daxue Chubanshe, 2005.

Zou Lihong, "Dajian wenming de pingtai" [Build the platforms of civilization]. *Zhongguancun* 104 (January 2012).

Zuigao renmin fayuan gongzuo baogao [Work report of the Supreme People's Court]. 2010. Available at http://www.npc.gov.cn/huiyi/dbdh/11_3/2010-03/18/content_1564762.htm. Accessed 29 December 2013.

INDEX

Page references in italics indicate images; 'n' refers to a note.